THE ART OF POLITICS

AS PRACTICED BY
THREE GREAT AMERICANS:
FRANKLIN DELANO ROOSEVELT,
LUIS MUÑOZ MARÍN,
AND
FIORELLO H. LA GUARDIA

By the Same Author

THE TREND OF ECONOMICS
(*with others*)

AMERICAN ECONOMIC LIFE AND THE MEANS OF ITS IMPROVEMENT
(*with others*)

REDIRECTING EDUCATION
(*with others*)

SOVIET RUSSIA IN THE SECOND DECADE
(*with others*)

INDUSTRY'S COMING OF AGE

THE INDUSTRIAL DISCIPLINE AND THE GOVERNMENTAL ARTS

THE BATTLE FOR DEMOCRACY

PUERTO RICAN PUBLIC PAPERS

THE STRICKEN LAND

THE PLACE OF PLANNING IN SOCIETY

A CHRONICLE OF JEOPARDY

THE DEMOCRATIC ROOSEVELT

THE ART OF POLITICS

The Art of
POLITICS

AS PRACTICED BY
THREE GREAT AMERICANS:
FRANKLIN DELANO ROOSEVELT,
LUIS MUÑOZ MARÍN,
AND
FIORELLO H. LA GUARDIA

Rexford G. Tugwell

1958
DOUBLEDAY & COMPANY, INC.
GARDEN CITY, NEW YORK

LIBRARY OF CONGRESS CATALOG CARD NUMBER 58–12056

COPYRIGHT © 1958 BY REXFORD G. TUGWELL

ALL RIGHTS RESERVED

PRINTED IN THE UNITED STATES OF AMERICA

FIRST EDITION

To the memory of

LEONARD DUFEE WHITE

friend and colleague

It is the agglomeration of physical power, social power, economic power and propagandistic power, as the potentially single prize for which artists in political power contend, that most alarms the community of scholars. For politics is an art of the immediate, and statesmanship, which rests on longer, deeper views, is rare. . . .

J. B. Brebner:

"The Common Ground in Humility." University Oration at the Columbia bicentennial convocation, 1954.

Introduction

It has been my fortune to have been closely associated, in one or another way, with three of the most successful political leaders of my generation and so to have had exceptional opportunity for observing them both in repose and in action; I was with them for a time as their decisions were reflected upon and as their policies were shaped. My association with President Roosevelt began in 1932 and ran until 1936; after that it was intermittent, but I was not exiled from his confidence. My connection with Fiorello La Guardia began in 1938 and lasted until 1941, although I could have been classified as friend and ally both before and after. With Luis Muñoz Marín my alliance began abruptly in 1941 and ended as abruptly in 1946.

All three of these leaders would have to be classified as eminent, I believe, in the sense of having made significant differences in the environment in which they moved and in having affected the lives of many of their contemporaries. Each had objectives in view beyond the enlargement of his own career; and each was proved by the test of election and re-election to be a successful politician. Franklin D. Roosevelt was elected governor of New York twice and to the presidency four times; Fiorello H. La Guardia was elected to the Congress seven times, to the aldermanic presidency in New York City once, and to the mayoralty three times; and Muñoz Marín, as this is written, is serving his third term as the first elected Governor of Puerto Rico after having been the founder of a party and twice its winning candidate for the presidency of the Senate.

Roosevelt met and struggled valiantly with the problems of the Great Depression and captained the nation through World War II; La Guardia was an ardent Progressive in Washington and finally became the acknowledged leader of a formidable congressional bloc, after which he rescued New York City (at least temporarily) from the clutches of gangsters, racketeers, and a corrupt officialdom, identifying himself with the City Charter of 1936 (which would be the most advanced municipal ordinance for two decades); and Muñoz

Marín led a movement and created a party which consolidated the latent power of the stricken Puerto Rican masses and used it to force into being a disciplined program for rejuvenation. This effort had a significance beyond itself. It soon became the wonder of a world looking for the means to lift backward peoples from the stew of poverty and demagogism which had become so characteristic of all the old colonial areas. He was the creator, as much as one man could be, of a new status for a whole people and a new relationship among political entities. The Commonwealth of Puerto Rico was a brilliant invention and its bringing into being a remarkable achievement.

It would be strange if my association with three such notable figures had not resulted in some comparison and some generalizing about leadership. And, of course, I have had such thoughts. The more I have considered them, however, the less systematic they have seemed. Nothing I would say about any—or all—of them is the kind of thing that could be proved. Perhaps none of it is of any use as guidance, either; yet because of professional interest on my own part, I set down my conclusions, claiming nothing except that they are mine.

I am indebted to Henry Wells, now of the University of Pennsylvania, formerly of the University of Puerto Rico, for a critical reading and helpful suggestions; also to Thomas P. Hayes, Librarian of the University of Puerto Rico, for discussing these matters with me. And to other friends and fellow workers of many years I owe the debt of one who has always found conversation about politics entertaining and sometimes useful.

There follows an outline of the careers I have used as my examples —Roosevelt's, La Guardia's, and Muñoz Marín's. Most of my essay is a commentary on their various adventures in the political world.

FRANKLIN DELANO ROOSEVELT
1882–1945

Son of wealthy parents who lived on an estate in Dutchess County, New York. He reversed the rule that an origin in poverty is necessary to political success and rose as a regular political officeholder to be the thirty-second President of the United States. He was educated by tutors and at the Groton School and Harvard University. He

studied law at Columbia University. He was elected to the New York
State Senate in 1910 and almost at once gained the attention of a wide
audience by opposing Tammany. He escaped punishment by joining his fortunes with those of Woodrow Wilson, and when Wilson
became President was appointed Assistant Secretary of the Navy,
where he served throughout the war. He was nominated for the
Vice-Presidency in 1920, was defeated, and retired to business in
New York. In 1921 was stricken by polio and was left without the use
of his legs. He spent the next few years struggling to overcome this
handicap, meanwhile cultivating his political acquaintance. He was
drafted to run for the governorship of New York when Smith was
the Presidential candidate, and surprisingly was elected. He was
re-elected in 1930 and was at once marked for the Democratic
presidential nomination in 1932. He defeated a coalition of conservative Democrats and won the nomination, afterward defeating
Hoover in the election. He was re-elected three more times, being
the first to break the third-term prohibition. At the end of his life,
after successfully acting as Commander in Chief through another
war and being instrumental in establishing a new organization for
peace, he was engaged in maneuvering for a political realignment
which would bring together the liberal progressives of both of the
older parties.

LUIS MUÑOZ MARÍN
1898–

Son of a professional politician in Puerto Rico who had much to
do with the transition of that island from Spanish to American rule
and who afterward served as Resident Commissioner in Washington.
The boy grew up in a political atmosphere and was familiar with
affairs both in the United States and Puerto Rico. Long residence
in Washington and New York and life as a littérateur left him dissatisfied and restless. The political parties in Puerto Rico were, he
felt, preoccupied with unreal issues; and meanwhile the people of
the island were drifting into a more and more hopeless state of
poverty and virtual peonage. He was elected to the Senate of Puerto
Rico as a follower of one of the political leaders in 1932, but served
only one term. For several years following this he schemed in a
desultory way to create a situation which would allow him to

become the dominant insular politician, as his father had been. Out of nothing he created a new party. He had at first only a small group of devotees, but he had an enormous appeal for the poverty-stricken masses and he was soon a formidable contender for leadership. His party came to the top by 1940. He was made President of the insular Senate. He was able to gain most of the credit with the voters for the improvement in their condition under the New Deal. Agitation for a new status, which had gone on for many years, finally resulted in the agreement of the Congress to an elective governorship to which he succeeded in 1950. Following this he contended for and finally secured Congressional agreement to a considerably enlarged self-government for the island which took the form of a Congressional Act and ratification by the Puerto Rican electorate. This he called a "Constitution" and was the first Governor to be elected under its terms.

FIORELLO HENRY LA GUARDIA
1882–1947

Son of an immigrant Italian who was a professional bandsman in the American army. He went to school in Prescott, Arizona, where his father was stationed. When the Spanish-American War began, he followed his father to Tampa as a newspaper correspondent and was infuriated by the conditions of the soldiers. His father was one of those who died from the effects of bad food furnished to the Army by corrupt contractors. Following this he went with his mother back to Hungary, but presently was employed by the American consular service. He served in Budapest, Trieste, and Fiume, then resigned to return to New York. He worked as an interpreter for the Immigration service while going to night school and studying law. He was from the first interested in politics and his first legal work was as a Deputy Attorney General in New York. He soon managed to persuade the Republican machine to allow him the nomination for hopeless Congressional districts. On the second try he won and served in the Sixty-fifth and Sixty-sixth Congresses, a service interrupted by the war. He took leave to join the Air Service and rose to command the American flyers in Italy as a major. He afterward represented the 20th District in New York (Harlem) from 1923 to 1933. He was defeated in the Democratic sweep of 1932, but the next year ran for Mayor and won. This began an extraordinary career as an independent who sometimes had Republican backing but was always fought by Tammany. He continued to be Mayor until 1945. Meanwhile he hoped to return to Washington as a Cabinet member or as a general. Roosevelt made him first head of Civil Defense, which was a disappointment, then head of the Joint Defense Board of Canada and the United States. After his retirement as Mayor he was for a time the Director General of the United Nations Relief and Rehabilitation Administration. But he died a disappointed man because he had not become President.

THE ART OF POLITICS

AS PRACTICED BY
THREE GREAT AMERICANS:
FRANKLIN DELANO ROOSEVELT,
LUIS MUÑOZ MARÍN,

AND

FIORELLO H. LA GUARDIA

I

My three exemplars were very much alike, as I recall them, not necessarily in externals, though there are some striking likenesses even at first glance, but in attitudes, in sensitivity or lack of it, in manner, and in conception of self. All three were (I speak in the past tense, although Muñoz Marín is still very much alive, because my official contacts with him have long since ended) spectacular personalities, unordinary, having flair, but not so much that it passed over into the bizarre. They were easily caricatured because they were so aggressive and positive, but they were not easily made ridiculous to their publics.

All three approached the supreme test of election, however often it came, with intense concentration, with tireless devotion to detail, and with a willingness to make superhuman efforts to catch and ensnare the voters. They were first of all politicians. It was their métier; through it the satisfactions they most yearned for were attained; and they savored electoral approval as others might the winning of a game, the attainment of great wealth, or a prize for poetry or sculpture or scientific discovery. The deep draught of victory at the polls was for each a life-renewing medicine and all the reward he asked for the labors and sacrifices of his exhausting years.

These three were certainly superior examples; yet their genius was essentially for the strategic rather than the tactical. At times, indeed, their tactics were so weak or mistaken as to verge on childishness. But their faults of this sort were so often buried by successive avalanches of votes that their mistakes seem unimportant. They were not above making virtue of their obvious errors and faults. And, because of this, in explaining themselves they not infrequently created confusion. They tended to do this the more, also, because they hoped ardently to attain a high place in the regard of posterity.

This was a very important matter to all of them and ought never to be forgotten.

The two who are gone, at least, could not be trusted to respect historical accuracy concerning themselves. The thing of most importance always seemed the painting of the picture as conceived by the artist. What matter if false strokes had from time to time to be painted out and done over? It was their picture and they were the artists.

If investigators had been able to assemble in one company the half dozen closest working intimates of each and pressed for a concensus, certain common impressions would gradually have emerged. The comparing of exasperations, griefs, and irritations would have yielded to a kind of wry and grudging admission that, in spite of having repeatedly taken erroneous decisions, each had nevertheless been right in his large political conceptions. He would seem to have arrived at them by the most mysterious means; he would have touched them tentatively and fearfully at first, trying their suitability, but then would have grasped them hard and harder until they seemed his own. Presently their enlargement and elaboration would seem unrealistic and even fantastic. But they would turn out in the end to have been what was generally approved, even if the consenting voters had not known at the outset, any more than the leader had for certain, that they were to yield consent.

This ability to sound and to exploit the reservoir of unconscious political approvals latent in the electorate was, I should say, the supremely useful common ability shared by all three, perhaps that which could account for the difference between these majors and the numerous contemporaneous minors in their profession. The talk going round would certainly instance, for example, President Roosevelt's advancing of a generalized Social Security, La Guardia's long campaign against the obsolete boss system in New York City, and Muñoz Marín's winning of "Commonwealth" status for Puerto Rico. The mincing approach, the embrace, the final public proclaiming of commitment were so precisely similar in each of these cases as to form a pattern. But at no time did any of these leaders seem to say to himself, "This is the way others have done; there are precedents to follow." Far from it.

Each coup was a creative act, called out by need and by particular circumstances, having little if any reference to precedent. Nor would it even be possible, I think, to discover that any experience was a precise forerunner of others of a similar sort. Not only do supreme political strategists seem not to learn very much from others, they seem to learn nothing much from themselves. President Roosevelt's Supreme Court reorganization scheme in 1937 was so inadequately prepared that he lost the battle for it. It was a major issue that he had not taken to the people and aroused them about as he had done in other instances. All his finesse seemed to have deserted him. And much as he apparently wanted to leave the nation with a nationalized power industry, he fumbled with the issue over and over like any amateur, and left it not too much forwarded from where he had found it.

(La Guardia, after having established himself securely in the affections of New Yorkers as the embodiment of energetic civic virtue, allowed his heart to be drawn so strongly Washington-ward that finally his mayoral functions were mostly mechanical. All he had learned as a politician seemed to have taught him nothing about the appearance of constancy. And Muñoz Marín's political intelligence seemed to fail entirely when he considered a possible defeat for the Democrats in a national election, although it was to them that he owed his rise. [1] This weakness led to a series of mistakes in judgment as to the likely defeat of President Roosevelt in 1944 and of President Truman in 1948, and of anticipated congressional overturns in 1942 and 1946. He always thought the Republicans were going to win and that the success of his Puerto Rican venture depended on adjustment to more conservative standards. [2])

The mythical expert analysts working with my three would have plenty of experiences to relate. The listener would presumably begin to see how much alike the experiences had been; he might begin to

[1] Washington was a little far away and unknown and he tended to shy at any suggestion of disapproval there. Yet at times he acted with such precise correctness in emergencies that he seemed to know congressmen's hearts better than they knew their own.

[2] It could be said, of course, that he was wrong only in timing; but timing is an essential political aptitude. To think that what did happen in 1952 was likely to happen in 1944 was a major error. It was made far more serious because the Puerto Rican program had, as an important element, the public ownership of utilities and of the land. The modifications made in anticipation of Republican accession were major ones. In effect it required the giving up of state socialism as a gesture of appeasement.

enumerate and to classify. But before he had gone very far his categories would begin to overlap and intermingle. And at the end I am afraid he might have no more reliable generalizations than that a genius had been at work in favoring circumstances—a fallible genius, in not-too-reliable circumstances! It would emerge that there had been embarrassing forgotten failures to set against the more emphatically enumerated successes and that much more might have been accomplished than was. But there would have been instances also, many of them, when everything had been superbly conceived and had been carried through with an élan and precision which would seem inspired. These last instances might, to the honest expert, have seemed to have about them a good deal of the accidental. It could not be denied, however, that they had happened. They had even happened repeatedly. And although the earnest analyzer could not tell quite why, or if the concurrence still seemed to him puzzling and even unlikely, still there it was! It had to be accepted. The inference was inescapable. It could not all be luck.

2

It is quite noticeable that the genuine experts in the operations of politics—those who have run, or helped to run, campaigns, who have coddled machines, kept workers up to the mark, restrained and guided candidates—have very few words of wisdom to offer. Not infrequently, especially in more recent years, they have been represented in the publication lists; but there is no very earnest attempt to conceal the "assistance" they have had in the writing. I do not know of many such books that have not resulted from publishers' enterprise and ghost writers' skill. [1] They are not very useful, therefore, in plumbing the political depths. Sometimes their wholly artistic nature is ludicrously obvious—as, for instance, in the two volumes whose ostensible author was James A. Farley. They did appear ten years apart, and Mr. Farley undoubtedly had a change of heart about President Roosevelt and the New Deal in the interval, but the difference between the two productions is much greater than can be accounted for by any such change. [2]

To believe that Jim Farley wrote both books, it would be necessary to believe that he was two persons. But we know that what happened was simply that he was persuaded to allow ghost writers with different instructions to pose him before the American audience at different times. Mention of this is not intended as a criticism of either genial Jim Farley or of a system that allows this kind of representa-

[1] An exception to this is Charles Michelson's *The Ghost Talks* (New York: Putnam, 1944), perhaps the least informative of all. Mr. Michelson wrote with such restraint that he said almost nothing. In an earlier day Thurlow Weed, Roscoe Conkling, and other professionals appeared as authors; but what they told of their experiences was always a severely edited version.

[2] The first of these was *Behind the Ballots* (New York: Harcourt, Brace, 1939), and second was *Jim Farley's Story* (New York: McGraw-Hill, 1948).

tion to be made. That would be another matter. My point is that if there are pretensions to generalizations or to wisdom in such writings they are clearly unjustified. They are more the thoughts of a journalist or of his principal than of the political practitioner.

Edward J. Flynn, who is represented in this field of literature by *You're the Boss,* [3] may be taken as another example. Ed did not have two books written for him, because he never changed affiliations, as Jim Farley did, or allowed anyone to persuade him that he had emerged from being a boss and had become a statesman; but the one book that represents him can be read with searching care without discovering any genuine guidance to successful action. It is an amusing book, enriched here and there by observations about life in the political jungle. There can be found in it some things that seem probable and some that are doubtful. One that is generally reliable is that loyalty is a virtue highly regarded among professionals—which, incidentally, is a severe criticism of Farley; one that is doubtful is that being a boss is merely an administrative job like any other, complex and requiring special skills, but neither mysterious nor shady. After reading Flynn the student will do well to go back to that classic of reporting, Lincoln Steffens' *Autobiography.* Either Flynn is having fun with us or Steffens was writing imaginary tales.

And in any case, as I have been saying here, if anything is to be learned from Farley or Flynn, it is the frustration of the professional who struggles to convey anything of any account to outsiders—and especially through the medium of a ghost writer with instructions. I have an idea that if either or both had been backed into a corner and convinced that there was reason for trying to expose the realities he would have said, "You can't really tell it; you can only live it. You don't learn how to do things; you feel your way through, and it is beyond all putting into words." [4]

---

[3] New York: Viking, 1947.

[4] But I do not mean to convey the impression that Ed Flynn was not a discerning and preceptive person, or even that he was taciturn. He was open and charming; and in a final chapter of his book he told something of the system of rewards and punishments he used in his Bronx machine. But the subtler relationships, the personal pressures, the maneuvers and deals are far from fairly described. He did make it clear, however, that the boss operates with support from the officeholders above him, transmitting to his host of small workers the favors of public life. It is interesting that Ed testified to the com-

I have been speaking of Farley and Flynn, two of the Roosevelt "managers." But if methodology is discussed, their principle is no more revealing. I can recall innumerable occasions when important matters were in suspense and those to be consulted were in attendance, and when the Governor or the President was mysteriously "engaged." "Who is it?" we would inquire, impatient and ridden by the pressure of necessity for decision. We would be put off if it could be done, but finally we would learn. He was closeted with one or two or half a dozen professionals. They might be from anywhere, but if they were from New York we knew it would be a long time. The old master was playing with the chessmen in the most absorbing of games. Jim Farley might be there or he might be hanging nervously about outside, wondering what was going on, exactly like a senator when a governor from his state goes to the White House. When the President's interest was engaged he was quite likely to forget all about chains of command. He wanted the plain, firsthand account. He would do his own sifting, or filtering, or whatever took place as he processed the raw material in his mind.

And sometimes, speaking to Moley on the campaign trains from the Brains Trust headquarters in the Hotel Roosevelt in 1932, we would ask about progress and he would tell us of his despair. There was a speech to be made in a matter of hours and the candidate could not be separated from the locals who were boarding the train in ever-increasing numbers. They went through the Roosevelt machinery like so much sea water through a big fish's gills. From them he got the political plankton that nourished victory. Finally Moley

plete amenability of Roosevelt. Beginning at once after 1928, he allowed Ed —and of course Farley—to dictate appointments. It was to this, Ed said, that Roosevelt owed his electoral invulnerability. "Because he paid attention to his leaders and made the party appointments they recommended (always after previously investigating the candidates' abilities), Roosevelt built up the greatest vote-getting machine, both state and federal, that has ever been known." This allows, it will be seen, very little scope for strategy, for adopting policies with appeal to voters, and for leadership. It is, indeed, the partial view of the practical boss. I doubt whether Ed believed, himself, that patronage was all that important; also, he must have been aware of the many occasions on which this system produced extremely embarrassing results. It was this, in fact, which was responsible for the conditions uncovered by the Kefauver investigations of 1951–52. But, as I have said, he could not say all he knew or felt. The air of frankness which informs his book—and Farley's too—is deceptive.

invented the routine that saved the situation; he got the politicians to sit over the writing of forthcoming speeches, thus combining Roosevelt's pleasures and duties. There were some weird productions. But they were politically perfect.

3

One favorite device of all my subjects here was a paradoxical one that I may as well mention at once. It illustrates the rule that in politics all rules are often disregarded! Each on occasion carried out an elaborate pretense of abandoning political considerations and turning pure. At such times he was not above the public defiling of his profession, so taking, as I always felt, a rather mean advantage of the general prejudice against professionals; and so, also, making complete chaos of all attempts to shape a pattern of behavior.

This drawing of a sharp distinction between themselves in office and themselves as bosses (which all of them were) could not seriously be sustained; it never fooled even the most innocent of their constituents; yet I was compelled to conclude that it was an effective device. This must have been because their public was amused by the trick, felt itself party to it, and enjoyed the embarrassment of the professionals who were by inference repudiated. The electorate must savor the sense of sophistication that comes from seeing through subterfuges.

It was because of this kind of thing that neither Roosevelt nor La Guardia nor Muñoz Marín commanded a continuing affection among the permanent workers in their entourages, only that which was yielded them because they were winners. Real bonhomie existed in the entourage of Farley; it was so abundant finally that he mistook it for a demand that he himself should become a candidate and displace Roosevelt in 1940. In the instances of my other two, they never allowed such a competing loyalty to develop. No rival head for La Guardia's Fusion movements could ever be discerned, and Muñoz

Marín, searching for years for a political captain, managed never to find one who was more than tentatively favored. [1]

In this connection, of course, Roosevelt pretty clearly allowed Farley, when the time came, to hang himself. Some good straight talk could have won Jim back to sense and to loyalty any time in the spring of 1940 when Garner and Hull were showing him how opposition to a third term could be at once patriotic and convenient. But the heart-to-heart talk never occurred. Jim's time had run out; he was due for exile.

I had an exceptional opportunity to observe—and even to be part of—one of President Roosevelt's most elaborate non-political charades. It was in 1936, in summer, and Alf Landon had been nominated by the Republicans to run against the President. He was, of course, the Governor of Kansas. That was a season of drought. Although 1934 had been a bad year on the Great Plains, 1936 was disastrous. Since spring my Resettlement Administration had been laboring to mitigate the misfortune. All rural relief had been turned over to us and we had done our very best. I myself had traveled by plane and car into every administrative center of our vast organization, seeing to it that everything possible was done. [2]

It did not rain. For hundreds of miles in each direction from the

---

[1] Those who were close to him in this way were Sola Morales and Roberto Sanchez Villela, but they never presumed on their intimacy, were both hardly used, and were never potential rivals. Both illustrate one of the curious facts of political life—that such journeyman workers will go on serving beyond all reasonable limits. Their motivation can perhaps be compared to that of the army man who will work and if need be die for his outfit without asking that his officers be ones he can admire and without understanding why he is commanded to fight.

[2] Accounts of the President's drought trip will be found in daily newspapers of the time. The dates to look for center in September 3 when Roosevelt and Landon met in Des Moines. On September 5 there was a similar governors' conference in Indianapolis. The President arrived in Bismarck, N.D., on August 27. Secretary Dern's death made it necessary to detour from Rapid City to Salt Lake City for the funeral, so that the Des Moines conference was postponed for two days from the original intention. Especially recommended are the accounts in the Des Moines *Register and Tribune* and the New York *Times*. My own earlier travels in the drought country were rather fully reported by Felix Belair of the New York *Times*, who for some time traveled with me in the almost unbearable heat. The historian will also find that Ernie Pyle of the Scripps-Howard papers crossed the devastated area that summer and wrote about it. Felix Belair and I met him in the midst of it and exchanged greetings. His columns were used in many newspapers.

center of North and South Dakota, Colorado, Oklahoma, and Texas, reaching west to the mountains and east almost to the Mississippi, the land was as bare as desert. The cattle and sheep had even dug up and consumed the roots of the dead grasses. We had bought and shipped out the animals by hundreds of thousands, we had brought in feed for others, and we had put on relief something like three quarters of all the farm families in the area. Many of them were moving out, mostly westward to the coast, and these we were helping, too, as we could.

All this effort, even though it was sometimes inefficient, as improvised relief always is, was not unappreciated. Even in their misery the stricken folk had some credit to yield for a valiant endeavor. I could see this appreciation growing and thought it might develop into something important. Morale might be re-established if confidence was restored; and confidence might come from a promise that the help now being given would be sustained into reconstruction. The President saw the opportunity.

Besides, the drought—as such occurrences do—finally became a *cause célèbre*. It reached the headlines of the metropolitan press. Special reporters and photographers were assigned, and gradually there was a genuine focus of interest in the Great Plains. [3] It was not at all impolitic for the President to show an interest. Pity and sympathy for people in distress, even when they were genuine, might as well be capitalized on. The government—the New Deal—was going to the rescue. If this sounds cynical, it is not meant to be. I would put it this way: Roosevelt had a feeling for the land and for the people who worked it. He shared their victories and defeats. But he could do something for them only when he moved at the head of a widespread generous impulse among those who were far

[3] Captain Patterson himself, then owner-editor of the New York *Daily News*, flew out to the drought area in a private plane. He was wavering at that time in his earlier New Deal enthusiasm, and the President asked me to show him the work we were doing. As everyone knows, he, like most other publishers, soon turned against Roosevelt and all his policies. One of the hardest lessons the President had to learn was that these defections served to convince people that he must be right, otherwise the tycoons of the press would not bother to attack him. In fact he never really accepted the reality. He was always bothered by the carping. I have thought since, however, that he may have been concerned mostly about the picture of him he could imagine to be shaping in people's minds—something I shall speak of again.

from the particular scene. The dramatization of drought might put Roosevelt in a favorable light, but also it might bring adequate relief to the drought-stricken farmers.

My suggestion to the President was almost coincident with another from Morris Cooke that a Great Plains Drought Committee be set up to recommend a permanent policy for the short-grass country. About two weeks before the President was expected in Bismarck, North Dakota, this committee began a detailed examination of the damage already done and consultations with people in the area as to what kind of rehabilitation measures ought to be taken. We were ready with a preliminary report when we met the presidential party. On that day our report was released by the President. Our recommendations were serious ones and some of them were far-reaching. They showed that a real attempt was being made to discover remedies. [4]

On the morning of the President's arrival it was raining. It had not rained before, they said, in seven months. It was a miracle! The politicians on the platform nearly cried with joy. Even the reserved and scientific-minded Henry Wallace, Secretary of Agriculture, beamed with satisfaction.

Presently, however, the President made something clear. It was a "non-political" trip. Americans in a wide area of the land were in trouble. Their President had come to see what more could be done for them than was already being done, and to assure them that their government would stand by. I cannot here tell the whole story as it deserves to be told for its own interest. I want only to emphasize the use of the "non-political" technique. That train was taken through the drought country over tracks on which passenger trains had not run in years. Often it ran at eight or ten miles an hour while the President looked at the devastation, spoke words of cheer from the platform, and now and again left his car to make an automobile circuit away from the railroad.

---

[4] As I was writing these words and reading our old advice again, in 1956, the press was reporting conditions in that same country not very different from those we encountered in 1936. Our remedial measures were never taken very seriously. When a cycle of increased moisture began, farming returned to the old pattern with some modifications induced by the Soil Conservation Service. These were not sufficient to avert a new crisis whenever the rains failed. It looked as though they never would be.

In the drought-stricken counties, for the next week, we went about, trailed by sweating reporters, driving into farmyards, and halting in little towns, talking to people, shaking hands, promising help. There was no newspaper in the nation, even the most disaffected, that could resist the drama of a President in a farmyard. None did. It was the most effective political trip I ever knew or heard of. The campaign of '36 might well have been called off right there.

To emphasize its non-political nature, Jim Farley and all his henchmen were left worrying in the East while the President entertained in his car squads of local officials, Republican and Democratic alike. He was flanked not by political aides, but by Harry Hopkins and myself, his relief chiefs, and of course Henry Wallace and Robert Fechner (head of the Civilian Conservation Corps). None of us ranked as politicians of any grade whatever.

Those midwestern states were not as a rule Democratic. They were much oftener Republican. Farley was engaged in building a Democratic machine, an enterprise that seemed to him more important than winning any one election. The President was obviously impressed by the bit of wisdom Henry Wallace and I had picked up from M. L. Wilson and passed on to him. It referred to midwestern farmers. "You can't make Democrats of them," said M.L. "But they will vote for Roosevelt." I must say it seemed to do a local Republican chieftain just as much good as a Democratic one to have sat for a few moments across the table from the President of the United States, in his private car. He invariably went out from his visit with his chest out and absorbed with pleasure the admiring glances of his neighbors in the crowd outside. And when sometimes the President, in a back-platform speech, mentioned a Republican Mayor or Sheriff or Congressman by name, that designee was a made man.

This technique infuriated the local Democrats, and presently Farley's Washington people were protesting stridently. But this only emphasized the President's master stroke—one of the most amusing incidents I can recall from my political years—the so-called "non-political" drought conference in Des Moines, attended by all the midwestern Governors. And Alf Landon, who had already been nominated by the Republicans for the presidency, was one of them. Was he going to help Alf Landon be elected? we asked him. He laughed and laughed. "He won't come," we said. "You'll see," he answered. "He'll have to come." And he did.

I think Landon was the most embarrassed candidate I ever saw. He came to Des Moines, of course, as Governor of a state needing help from the federal establishment. But there was never an instant when the hordes of watchers present could forget that he was the candidate suggested by the Republicans as a substitute for the confident and majestic Roosevelt. It was absurd and pathetic. The reporters saw him as "Little Alf," and a whole nation was looking over the reporters' shoulders. Anyone had to be blind not to see the effect. That night on the train—while Landon was dining with the President in his special car, along with Herring of Iowa and a couple of other Governors—I offered a series of bets to all comers. My best—and the one I still pride myself on most—was one with Carl Hatch, senator from New Mexico. He had to buy me a Stetson when that fall the President easily carried Kansas, Landon's own state. He came through in good humor. I wore the hat for years.

No one who lived in New York during La Guardia's mayoralty could escape the shrill castigations of the politicians that rose like effluvia from City Hall. Indeed La Guardia made little distinction between them and the "punks, tinhorns, and cheap crooks" who were his favorite targets. It was true in his case that he had leaned most heavily on "Fusion," which meant that minority Republicans were joined with other than organization Democrats and independents of all sorts to support a movement to beat Tammany. But in the course of two terrific campaigns, and by controlling the city government from top to bottom, La Guardia himself created something indistinguishable from a machine. And if he and his co-workers were not politicians, there must be something wrong with the definition. What he meant to convey to his loyal electorate, of course, in his passionate diatribes, was that *his* politicians did not have the attributes of *ordinary* politicians. It was, therefore, unfair to call them by the same name.

This was in a sense true. City machines, as they had developed in America, had bosses; but the bosses were not Mayors. The Mayors, in fact, were classically puppets, and the real business of dispensing jobs and favors in return for cash or other payment went on behind a respectable front furnished by some more or less well-known figurehead. The city was run for the benefit of the insiders; "the interests" were let alone; gambling and rackets throve; municipal services were provided at high expense and at minimum levels.

In New York this system had three active headquarters, one in the Bronx, one in Brooklyn, and one in Manhattan. The machines controlled from these centers were old and tradition-bound. They had been challenged and defeated before—for instance, by Low in 1901 and by Mitchel in 1913—but these reform movements had never found the formula for perpetuation. They tended to crumble when enthusiasm died away and the evils they had set out to combat were no longer embodied in obvious dragons to be slain.

La Guardia found the answer to this problem of impermanence. He kept his dragons alive and attacked them every day. His riposte lay essentially in the paradox of a machine that was anti-machine, that depended not on graft and corruption to hold together a working nucleus, but on strident and brassy leadership forever warning that the devil had not been driven farther away than just across the river into New Jersey or out into Nassau County on Long Island. He lurked there, hiding in the political clubhouse, ready to resume control if vigilance should for an instant be relaxed. Just for luck he trumpeted a challenge periodically and found imaginary engagements when no real ones turned up.

La Guardia's techniques might have been borrowed from Theodore Roosevelt. They were very similar. But I never heard him mention Roosevelt in this connection or, indeed, any of his reformist or Progressive Republican predecessors. I think they simply found the same solution for the same problem. Theodore Roosevelt, when he was a police commissioner decades before La Guardia's time, went about New York at night in disguise, poking into odd corners, catching patrolmen off their beats, and noting various misdemeanors. His comments on what he found had exactly the same value as La Guardia's later ones. They were violent, dramatic, quotable, and intended to attract attention. Newspapermen who regarded both of them as ridiculous, or even as "phonies," were compelled to assist in creating the din and hassle that were essential to their way of maintaining power. [5]

[5] It is as impossible to believe that Theodore Roosevelt was not having a wonderful time as to believe that La Guardia was not. Turn, for instance, to his letters (selected and edited by Elting E. Morison, Harvard University Press, 1951, Vol. 1). Writing to his sister Anna in May 1895, when he was just getting started, he said: *I have never worked harder than during the last two weeks; I am down town at nine, and leave the office at six—once at eight. The*

This political method may be an essential of our kind of representative democracy, which tends easily to escape representativeness and to become captive to special interests. The safety of the system of quiet corruption, of alliances that trade support in elections for legislative favors, consists in keeping the whole conspiracy under cover. This is true even when there is nothing sinister about it: that is, when it does not operate against the general interest. A demagogue can operate almost as effectively against a benevolent as against an exploitative conspiracy. It is the process of exposing secrecy that makes popular heroes. It can be done in the Huey Long style or in the Franklin D. Roosevelt style. Huey ranted; Roosevelt was praised, again and again, for being "well bred." [6] These are the extremes; La Guardia was somewhere in between. He had Huey's eruptions of indignation, which nobody thought (as many did of Huey's) were simulated or invoked against phantoms; and he had a device similar to Roosevelt's "fireside chat," adapted to his own personality. For months and years he talked regularly to his New York audience from the municipal radio station, WNYC, building up a confidence and rapport that can hardly ever have been equaled. On occasion he read comics to the children; he told housewives how to cook; he feuded with judges who behaved in ways he disliked; he denounced small sins (such as race-track gambling) that broke up

actual work is hard; but far harder is the intense strain. I have the most important, and the most corrupt, department in New York on my hands. I shall speedily assail some of the ablest, shrewdest men in this city, who will be fighting for their lives, and I know well how hard the task ahead of me is. Yet, in spite of the nervous strain and worry, I am glad I undertook it; for it is a man's work.

Some weeks later he was writing as follows: *I am immensely amused and interested in my work. It keeps me so busy I can hardly think. . . . Twice this week I had to spend the night in town . . . After dinner I got my patrolman and spent three or four hours investigating the conduct of the police in a couple of precincts where I considered the captains to be shady. I make some rather startling discoveries at times. These midnight rambles are great fun. . . .*

La Guardia could never have read these or TR's other letters. He undoubtedly heard a good deal about him, but he never mentioned it that we know of. Nevertheless, he was TR all over again.

[6] A good instance of this was the reception given his speech at the Houston convention in 1928. This was the second "Happy Warrior" speech putting Al Smith into nomination. The New York *Times* actually called it "A High-Bred Speech" and went on to comment:

homes; he thundered against unwarranted high prices for food or against extortionate landlords, and so endeared himself to women; then, on occasion, he spoke in a calm and earnest voice in the larger cause of civic morals. But recurrently the villains were "politicians." The aim was to persuade his constituents that if it was against La Guardia it was politics; if it was for him it was something else.

There were those who noticed, and said, that the methods of La Guardia and his machine were the same as those of other professionals and their machines. They were. He gave jobs to friends and supporters and he favored certain interests that favored him, but no one ever said that he was corrupt or that he had anything to gain except the good of his city—that is, beyond the possession of power. It was hinted that he sometimes seemed to identify his own fortunes with those of the public. This is said of every leader, and it is inevitably the fact. But democracy cannot have everything. It must glorify its leaders and allow them their effulgences or it must be resigned to back-room government and the humiliation of corruptions.

Muñoz Marín illustrates the same facility with Democratic methodology—but of course with characteristic variations. Taken in the terms used here, he has to be judged the most successful of my three. The ultimate measure of that success was that, after more than a decade of active leadership, his monopoly was so impregnable that it was found expedient to create an artificial opposition in the constitution of the new Commonwealth. [7]

There was nothing strained or fantastic or extravagant in what he said. It was the address of a fair minded and cultivated man, avoiding the usual perils of national convention oratory and discussing in an intelligent way the qualifications which should be sought for in the President of the United States. . . .

Those were the years when Roosevelt was a "detached" elder-statesman Democrat. The appearance of sanity, good judgment, and selfless interest was important. His performance matched exactly his intention—and not only at Houston. All his appearances during that time showed the same style; it ran through all his letters. It was a masterly construction. At the end of it he was no "politician" in the public estimation; he was a statesman.

[7] The constitutional device that provided for a Puerto Rican opposition was indeed unique. A formula was devised to increase the representation of minority parties whenever, in a general election, a single party gained as many as two thirds of the seats in either house.

By this formula each minority party was permitted to add to its representa-

There were times during the Roosevelt era when publicists of the John T. Flynn-Mark Sullivan-David Lawrence-Westbrook Pegler-John Donnelly-Frank Kent type professed to believe that the presidency was about to be turned into a dictatorship. There was a remarkable lack of popular interest in this particular bogey; that lack sometimes seemed proportional to the effort spent on it. The man so often seen and heard going about democracy's business was not even, in most people's opinion, *enough* of a dictator. He was, if anything, too reluctant to discipline recalcitrant legislators and members of his official family, and he never gave his enemies hell enough to satisfy his supporters. How far this tolerance went has since become evident in such disgraceful disclosures of disloyalty as Jesse Jones's story of his relations with his superior [8] as well as Farley's admissions of apostasy. Even Harold Ickes had his wavering moments and ought obviously to have had a periodic spanking. [9]

To pretend that one's own political group is not a party, to join in the disparagement of politics and politicians—meaning anyone who disagrees—is a device so often used by the most successful politicians that it can be set down, perhaps, as one of the more reliable generalizations concerning the art. At least it is a useful

tion as many additional members as would bring its percentage of the total up to a figure roughly equal to the percentage of votes cast for its gubernatorial candidate in the same election. (Article III, Sec. 7, Commonwealth Charter.) This matter is more complicated than it seems worth while to explain here beyond what has been said.

[8] In *Fifty Billion Dollars* (New York: Macmillan, 1951).

[9] The Ickes story stands pretty well revealed in the *Diary* allowed to be published after his death. The published volumes contained only part of his written notes, and what was not published could be more revealing than what did appear. But there was quite enough to show the traditional competition among the Cabinet members and between them and the President. In Ickes' case his feeling sorry for himself was almost a phobia. The isolation of the President with such associates is a rather terrible thing to contemplate. Fortunately there were a few in Franklin Roosevelt's case whose personal affection and loyalty, however tried, never wavered. These few never felt themselves more important than he; what is more, they never allowed the policies within their jurisdiction to become in their eyes the fulcrum about which national policy ought to turn. Among these were Frances Perkins and Homer Cummings. Henry Wallace was another of the same sort. He was undoubtedly driven by ambition, but he stayed within the bounds allowable to a subordinate both as a counselor and as the executive of a department.

resort, even if to the outsider it seems at first a paradoxical, even an unnatural, almost cannibalistic one. [10]

[10] This device of the candidate-bosses nauseates the real back-room professionals, although they admit the effectiveness of the device. I quote a passage from Ed Flynn (*You're the Boss*, pp. 138–40) to that effect, which at the same time pays a tribute to La Guardia:

Possibly outside of President Roosevelt and Governor Smith, La Guardia is the smartest politician I have ever met in my political career. His stock-in-trade was abuse and name-calling . . . the phrase "spoils system" was made to order for him. It has an ominous sound. It seems to imply wrongdoing, if not outright dishonesty. La Guardia tried to make it appear that all the evils of government could be traced to it. He emphatically stated his opposition. With one breath proclaiming his freedom from the dictates of political leaders and "club-house loafers," in the next he appointed, with a scratch of the pen, some man who had been active in the Republican party, or in some "Fusion" group that had supported him—in other words, "club-house loafers" who could be distinguished from the Tammany ilk only by a difference in party labels.

I am not disapproving these appointments. I am, however, rebuking the chief critic of the "spoils system" for using it at the same time that he denounced it . . . La Guardia's appointments were as partisan to him as any appointment a Tammany Hall Mayor ever made was partisan to Tammany.

4

In three diverse but important areas, over significant stretches of time, party politics was shaped by my three giants into something unrecognizable from the conceptions of the textbooks. In La Guardia's case there was no party of any account when he was gone; he had neither created one of his own nor strengthened the Republicans who had more or less accepted him. In the case of Muñoz there was an entirely new one spread out in his lengthening shadow; and in the case of Roosevelt the New Deal adherents supplemented the party and interpenetrated it so that it was impossible to tell, except at the extremes, which was which. On the one side urban radicalism and western progressivism were not Democratic; but, on the other, neither the South nor the city machines were New Dealish. The Roosevelt vote was never any measure of purely party strength. This was true even in the hold-over election of 1948 when Truman was the nominal candidate but when a revived New Deal was the issue. [1]

It is arguable that Roosevelt damaged the party; but this is to suggest a party structure and position which have, if I am right, never really existed and never will exist. Roosevelt won after being nominated by the Democrats; but, as perhaps half the Democrats of 1932 would have described themselves, he was not a Democrat. They did not know it, naturally, although some of them would soon find it out. Needless to say, he never became one; he became less one as time went on. But then, at the end, it was difficult to say what was Democratic and what was Rooseveltian. And when he had formally abandoned the New Deal in favor of anti-totalitarianism, the confusion was worse.

[1] Called by the Trumanites the "Fair Deal."

It is true of all my three that they had to have a place from which to begin—that is, a nomination which gave them a license to campaign. Only Roosevelt had a strictly orthodox beginning of this sort. He was nominated by a real and existing party, not one composed for his convenience. There was a genuine fight at Chicago in 1932 for the right to represent the Democracy. The diversity among the candidates who might have been nominated shows how flexible were the party principles involved. Suppose Al Smith of New York, Newton D. Baker of Ohio, Governor Ritchie of Maryland, or Speaker Garner of Texas had been nominated. Any of them could probably have defeated Hoover. At least the shrewdest observers of the time thought so. And Roosevelt was nominated not only because he was most likely to win but because of a complex of other reasons as well. [2] So it was not really very much a matter of principle.

The truth about this is that Franklin Roosevelt intended to gain that nomination and to become President by way of it, not to win for his party, but to win for the policies he had in the back of his mind—and, it must be said, for himself. As I look at this sentence it seems exact, and yet it does not get at the truth, and I must make some further explanation. This again will be one I cannot document but yet is, I am convinced, correct. It is, moreover, one entry to an understanding of several decades of American political history; and, specifically, it goes toward an explanation of the peculiar role of parties in our system.

To suggest that Franklin Roosevelt might have been nominated by a Republican convention is to suggest something recognizably bizarre in the light of later developments. Even in 1932 he was plainly not a Republican, and he had become identified in various ways with the Democrats—in election to the New York State Senate,

---

[2] These included his long pre-convention campaign for pledged or favoring delegates, in which he had the devoted assistance of Jim Farley and Louis Howe. But more important even than this was the putting together of the West-South coalition, not needed for election in that year of disaffection from Hoover, but indispensable to the nomination. It was symbolized by the acceptance of Garner for the vice-presidential nomination, and later by the composition of the Cabinet.

As to the Republicans at their convention and their nomination of Hoover, an old story out of the big book of American humor was passed around. It was the account of the unhappy farmer who, passing his neighbor's house on a bright morning, was asked where he was going. "Goin'?" he said. "Goin' to town to get drunk! And gosh, how I dread it!"

in being the vice-presidential candidate in 1920, in participating prominently in several conventions, and in being a two-term Democratic Governor. But he ordinarily spoke of himself as a *Progressive* Democrat; and a *Progressive* Democrat was not clearly distinguishable from a Progressive Republican. What this meant was that he disassociated himself from the reactionary racism, the intolerant Protestantism, the extreme laissez faire, and the feudalistic ideology of the South as well as from the graft, corruption, and racketeering with which the big-city machines were identified. But these differences were not emphasized in the pre-convention campaign. He did not disapprove of anything or anybody—except Hoover, of course, and his associates; he sought and found a mildly positive, if very general, statement of objectives. And the first to denounce his attitude was no Republican; it was Al Smith, the then Mr. Democrat. Al said Roosevelt was fomenting class war by talking about the "forgotten man." And when at Oglethorpe University Roosevelt talked eloquently of the necessity of planning, he spoke for the abandonment of the discredited system which had resulted in the debacle of 1929 and for a new conception of visualized goals co-operatively achieved. This last was an attempt to redefine and rejuvenate progressivism and to amalgamate it with Democracy.

These Roosevelt aims were not traditional Democratic ones. They were not ones in which either the southern or the big-city politicians had any interest. One was not even orthodox progressivism—that, if it was anything, was atomistic rather than holistic. So, at Chicago, plain, even if not emphasized, evidence was available that Roosevelt wore no factional dress. And indeed the Chicago result was achieved mostly because the candidate did not seem to belong to any faction— that and evidence that he had no bizarre beliefs of one or another sort.

The convention delivered the party to Franklin Roosevelt and he never gave it back. It was his from then on, although he had to struggle and compromise to keep it. And if it is pointed out that he began by saying that he accepted the platform "one hundred per cent" and later on in the campaign gave other similar assurances, I reply that he did this good-naturedly because Louis Howe insisted and because he himself did not much care. What exemption events give to campaign pledges, he knew well enough. And if afterward for some time he liked to claim fidelity, it was because he still felt it important to maintain the fiction that he was a party man.

The coalition that came into being in 1932 between West and South would, in time, dissolve, and another would form; the South would draw aside except for election purposes, but its place would be taken by a new and more powerful aggregation. The big-city machines were against Roosevelt in 1932. But they never would be against him again. And they would be reinforced by the mighty power of labor in the years to come. The Southerners would become sulky partners, strategically seated in the Congress and vindictively effective in preventing legislation from passing, but not completely so. And every four years they would come around. They did not "take a walk" with the Liberty Leaguers.

It was the Roosevelt idea that he was what the country needed. That was also La Guardia's idea about New York City, as it was Muñoz's about Puerto Rico. They were not reluctant candidates. The job did not seek them. They worked, maneuvered, traded, and intrigued to establish themselves. In all the cases here, the notion of being needed was correct. All of them were therapeutic and reconstructive agents. So it seems to me not very relevant to sneer at them —as has very often been done—because they were active seekers for preferment rather than coy and retiring citizens drafted into service.

5

The good, non-professional man of substance, chosen in spite of himself and preferably by surprise, is, from the point of view of the boss, the ideal candidate. It was always considered irresponsible of Tammany and the Brooklyn machine to have selected Hylan, O'Brien, and Walker. They were amenable to discipline, which was good, but they were vulnerable, which was bad. They were certain, sooner or later, to be discredited in matters having nothing to do with the machine's operations. They were, therefore, not effective as protective façades. The selection showed, perhaps, how great the decline was from the sachemship of Murphy to that of Curry. Murphy would have known better.

There are always exceptions to any rule in politics, and one exception to the deduction that a "front" is necessary is furnished by the case of Al Smith, who, in spite of having come up the Tammany escalator, was counted as one of New York's best Governors. But the reference is nevertheless fairly trustworthy. It is often better, from the point of view of the boss, to compromise with a stuffed-shirt candidate—that is, to promise him, openly or tacitly, as seems necessary, not to risk outright scandal—rather than to fill the top job with a subservient retainer who is notoriously known to take orders from party headquarters. And this is true even if he is personally impeccable. It is safer and, in the long run, more profitable to have a stuffed shirt even if it costs a good deal. But the temptation to use a Walker seems somehow hard to resist, and there are many examples of surrender to it.

It is difficult to follow the reasoning which led to the judgments of that group of bosses who ran New York City's government in the decade before La Guardia, after Charles F. Murphy died—Curry,

Olvany, McCooey, et al. It has to be concluded, I think, that for bossism there are no recognized principles either. Certainly every canon of caution and compromise was violated; and eventually a situation evolved which first Roosevelt in his presidential candidacy and then La Guardia in his bid for the mayoralty could exploit with telling effect. It is very impressive to read the newspapers and weekly journals of the spring and summer of 1932 and to learn what a production was made of Walker's cornering by Roosevelt. The suspense was considerable, Roosevelt's good faith and courage were questioned; and he was given a chance to slay a dragon with vast, nationwide publicity. [1] It was purely because of Tammany's stupidity that this opportunity was so fortunately presented to him. Of course he handled it with consummate skill, allowing all the pundits —including Walter Lippmann—to embarrass themselves by pointing out prematurely what he would not dare to do, then doing it and demonstrating with what ease a genuine political expert could gain an important advance.

At the time I wondered whether, knowing the local *genus politicus*, as by then he did, he had not deliberately laid the trap that sprang so perfectly when it was of maximum advantage as a spectacle. But I was assured by all those who were otherwise involved in the proceedings that the whole affair was "played by ear" and that, when the newspapers were taunting him for his hesitation and generalizing about his fears and weaknesses, the hesitations and misgivings were actual. The overture played itself out in finished fashion, but apparently it was improvised from start nearly to finish. No one in the Roosevelt camp—including, I was told, the Governor himself (which I found it hard to believe)—approached the affair with anything but dread and loathing or hoped to get through it without a serious loss of prestige.

If these assurances are accepted—and I myself accept them now—it follows that neither the bosses, who allowed Jimmy Walker to get into his jam and then supported him to the end, nor Roosevelt and his advisers, who took such deft advantage of the situation, were following any plan or acting on any generalization from previous

[1] This was the second such affair. There had been one a few months earlier, involving Sheriff Farley and a certain mysterious box, which had allowed the Governor to proclaim resoundingly that "a public office is a public trust."

experience. If there had been a rule for boss-controlled Mayors, it must have been one that Tammany ignored; but if there had been a rule for disciplining them, it would have been precisely that followed by Roosevelt. I conclude from this that the New York bosses were ignorant of the elements of their profession and stupid concerning their own interests. I also conclude that Roosevelt, even if he approached the denouement with trepidation, made a brilliant ending.

Suddenly the whole country knew that he was anti-Tammany in spite of being a Democratic Governor of New York and an old-time friend of Smith and Wagner. He was an anti-boss man precisely as Wilson had been. The theorist might feel certain that he had copied Wilson's 1911–12 behavior in New Jersey. It looked like it; it seems too perfect to have been improvised; and of course Roosevelt had watched Wilson through his early ordeal, but this is a question of fact. Evidently Wilson's name was never mentioned in the endless discussions of strategy. It was all *de novo*. [2]

Similarly it appears that no one can say for certain whether La Guardia was regardful of the pattern into which he fitted. After watching him for years, I concluded that he had an instinctive antipathy for methodology that would have prevented any conscious

---

[2] There is an account of the New Jersey proceedings, written by the editor of the Trenton *Evening Times*, which throws a flood of light on otherwise rather obscure maneuvers. (*The Political Education of Woodrow Wilson*, by James Kerney [New York: Century, 1926].)

Mr. Kerney knew what was going on from intimate association. Many of the incidents related in his book could be used to illustrate the conclusions here. Wilson meant to get into politics. Moreover, he was at a point in his life when he had to do something. His Princeton string had run out. Coached by George Harvey, who had adopted him politically, he made a deal with the New Jersey bosses, Smith and Nugent, and got to be Governor. They thought him safe and conservative, one of those stuffed shirts bosses require. But the prospect of the presidency became more and more alluring. To get there he had to have the appearance of progressivism. He repudiated a good half dozen of his academic principles and adopted a half dozen new ones. He wooed Bryan, the grand panjandrum of the Democratic party, to good effect, although he must have loathed it. His campaign also involved throwing over the bosses who had made him, which he did. He barely squeezed through; if he had done any less he would have failed. Thenceforth, Mr. Kerney ventures, he was as good an *amateur* politician as ever practiced the art.

This was the year Roosevelt himself was challenging Tammany in "the Sheehan business" at Albany and then moving on to the support of Wilson, which landed him the assistant secretaryship of the Navy.

copying. This was partly because he was not reflective or scholarly by habit and so did not know the precedents too well if they were beyond his own experience; but also it was partly because he had an enormous capacity for busyness, which most political leaders have and which absorbs all their energies. He had it in fantastic enlargement. A swarming multitude of incidents, contacts, agglomerations, associations, and public picturings seethes continually in the brain of a La Guardia. It is the chaotic stuff out of which he selects the materials for his patterns and out of which he makes the meanings for himself that serve as guides for conduct. It is all so fugitive, so swiftly apprehended, so transiently grasped, so mysteriously joined together, that it seems absurd to consider the imposing on it of any retrospective logic, and almost equally absurd to attempt the weighing of influences from the past.

There had been reform mayors before La Guardia, even in New York City; by his time historians had made up their minds why these reformers had been comparative failures: they had not created machines. When the first fervor of reformism had passed, the bosses of the old parties had simply taken charge again by default. There was no one else to perform a necessary function. So far as there was wisdom from other instances, it was to the same effect. Steffens, again, was full of it; and the one competent littérateur among modern municipal reformers, Brand Whitlock, had the same, or about the same, deduction to offer. La Guardia should therefore have concentrated on building a machine, in opposition to that of the bosses, which would have furnished support for himself and made his reforms more permanent. But this is precisely what he did not do, never thought of doing, and, as part of his public attitudinizing, strenuously denounced. The machine was to be La Guardia, as it had been Tom Johnson, Hunt, Jones, Mitchel, Heney, Blankenburg, and other reformers before him. All of them had failed to do more than upset the bosses temporarily, but all had had picturesque careers. I could recall, from my undergraduate days at the University of Pennsylvania, Blankenburg riding down Market Street in Philadelphia on a white horse which was symbolic of crusading purity. At the time I was stirred. But my recollections included disillusion. His reforms disappeared with him after the next election, much as snowdrifts melt in a warm spring wind.

Was La Guardia conscious that he inherited and was the responsible contemporary repository of a reformist tradition? More important, was he conscious that none of his predecessors had "succeeded"—that none had done more than, for the moment, to channel through a group of honest administrators the business of the city? These are not easy questions to answer, but some light is thrown on them by asking the associated question that can with some confidence be answered: Do the incidents of his administration seem to show that there was a rule to which they conformed?

In the first place, La Guardia left the city government better structured than he found it. In the second place, however, the better government was not proof against the mishandling of later mayors— or even against his own. And as to his own mishandling, it is not difficult to demonstrate that he himself was the best exponent of methods for evading the intentions of the City Charter. There was no limitation on himself that he tolerated gracefully and hardly any that he did not break through whenever it became irksome. And very often no more needed to be involved than mere caprice to cause an outbreak of temper, a fracture of regulations, and subsequent virtuous preening as a man whose care for his responsibilities transcended red tape, bureaucratic obstruction, and stifling inertia. There was no sense in him of the value of precedent, of the utility of unexceptionable behavior. He was a one-man government and not to be held to the conduct expected of others. So long as he was there, no limitations were necessary or even tolerable.

Also, it is a sad truth that when he was through, La Guardia left a bankrupt city. On the day his successor, William O'Dwyer, took office several hundred million dollars had to be found to meet pressing obligations not provided for by La Guardia. Debts were falling due; but also, although the city was equipped as never before with public facilities—especially parks and parkways—the adequate maintenance and operation of these pleasant appurtenances had not been budgeted. Not only were the new parks, parkways, playgrounds, and recreation facilities already falling into neglect, all the streets were dirty, garbage was not being effectively collected, children were either not able to go to school or could go only part time, vast hospitals were inadequately staffed and tended—the whole of the city machinery was breaking down from sheer lack of funds. This debacle was in no small part traceable to La Guardia's carelessness in allowing the city's tax base to attenuate. Suburbs outside his jurisdiction had absorbed many of the large taxpayers—a movement facilitated by the expensive parkways—and there had been an increase rather than a diminution of expenses to be met with shrunken income. Old facilities had to be maintained even when new ones in fringe neighborhoods still within the city were being built and staffed.

During most of La Guardia's regime municipal revenue had been supplemented by federal funds—notably from the Works Progress Administration and its predecessor organizations. In 1938, for instance, when I had occasion to examine the matter (as chairman of the City Planning Commission) *slightly more than half* of those expenses were being met from federal or state allocations. There was an end to this as the long depression faded out and war approached. Unemployment was no longer an excuse for asking Washington to support the city. And numerous enlarged facilities, built with relief labor, remained to be supported from revenues cut just about in half. No wonder Mayor O'Dwyer was aghast when he first surveyed the problem he had to meet.

All this is said to show that even a good government can be mismanaged by the most honest of administrators. La Guardia never allowed a cent to be stolen, a favor to be given at city expense, or a compromise he knew to be a losing one to be made with private interests. But when his regime was over, the city's debt to the bankers was larger than it had ever been before, and it consequently carried a burden of interest which in itself would almost have met a reasonable ordinary budget. The only advance toward municipal ownership of utilities had been the taking over of the subways. This was done, strangely enough, at the instance of the financiers, who in former years had propagandized expensively to the effect that there were deep socialistic dangers in such a move. But when subways became unprofitable it was no longer socialistic for the city to take them over. For a system with negative earning power, several hundred millions was paid. This sum committed the city for the next decade and a half—until an Authority was established in a later crisis of virtual bankruptcy under Mayor Impellitteri—to the assumption of an operating deficit ranging up to a hundred million annually which otherwise might have had to be met by the sellers. There was also the interest on all those bonds!

It was obvious from the time when the subways first began to lose, although there were long delays while politicians maneuvered around the issue, that fares would have to be at least doubled. La Guardia was gone, however, long before this public admission finally had to be made. It was not a profitable deal for the city. How La Guardia really felt about it, he did not say. He can hardly have been proud of the result; but if he had had to argue the matter he most probably would have contended that expediency had controlled his action. And he would have thought that a quite sufficient justification.

New Yorkers, in later decades, after experience with O'Dwyer and Impellitteri, looked back to La Guardia with growing nostalgia. A majority of them had been amused by him, felt tolerantly possessive about him, and often said to themselves that anyway he was honest. And he was; they were right. Not one in a million realized how he had pledged them to the bankers, permanently increased the cost of their utilities, and made municipal bankruptcy inevitable; and even if they had they would by then have wanted him back. They only knew that he had been energetic, vigilant in their interest, and, in spite of his sometimes overflamboyant behavior, really dedicated. He was against bosses, crooks, graft, and bureaucrats. They liked that.

Then there was the City Charter of 1936. This made New York's the most effectively constituted of all city governments, past or present. It was an amazing as well as a marvelous achievement. It embodied all—or most—of the devices and arrangements for which theorists and practitioners alike had for a generation been longing. It made the executive powerful but responsible; it confined the legislature (the old Board of Aldermen, now the City Council) to its proper sphere and made logrolling and capricious interference with the executive next to impossible; it provided for long- and short-range planning; it possessed built-in devices for insuring honesty and the careful selection of personnel; it arranged for policy-making at the proper level and with the proper participation, and it gave the city an almost adequate home rule.

La Guardia did not participate in writing this Charter, but when he had finished campaigning for it he had made it his own. He was the first mayor under it and began the shaping of its traditions. There is a great deal to be said about this that would be too detailed for the purpose here. There is reason to believe that he really had understood only the main features, so that when he came to administering it he felt compelled to attenuate some of its best provisions when they proved to be limitations on his own freedom of action. But the most significant fact is that a long effort by New York's most devoted citizens issued in a document that La Guardia adopted before the electorate. This identified him further as a good-government man in the tradition of the municipal reformers—a role he obviously felt himself appointed to play.

The new Charter suited him in one large aspect—it centralized power in himself as mayor. But it irked him in other ways. It interfered with his willful judgments; and no more intolerant public man ever functioned in America—where there has been a succession of obstreperous ones. And when this happened he recognized none of its limitations, most of which were inherent in a government of separated powers.

When La Guardia was gone the Charter remained. It was not so good an operating guide because of him as it would have been had he been more devoted to its principles—he had established some dangerous precedents—yet the residue of credit is considerable. And in all his subsequent machinations to escape from the net woven about him by the provisions of the Charter, he never acknowledged a reversal of his devotion to it. Even serious breaches in its principles he sought to make appear as "improvements." When this interpretation was not accepted by his friends he often became exaggeratedly angry and sometimes accused them of betrayals much more honestly attributable to himself. There were, indeed, many subtractions to be made from the La Guardia reputation as a reformer, and none knew so well what they were as those close to him. They suffered most from his struggles in the net of restrictions required by honest and efficient government.

This side of La Guardia could not be kept secret; but surprisingly little of it reached the public. Loyalty was very characteristic of the substantial citizens who were his sponsors and supporters. They had to deal with a willful, sometimes irresponsible, individual in a position of great—and deliberately enhanced—power; but they had looked a long time for even so imperfect an embodiment of their civic ideals. And to the public he was always the enemy of spoils and of corruption even while his antics seemed slightly ridiculous. In the middle of his career, as I talked with many of his partisans, I discovered that they had not come to any satisfactory conclusions. Some said they thought he had no interest at all in good government. It had merely been a convenient way to get the Fusion nomination and to set up a properly striking contrast with the preceding boss-controlled mayors. Most, however, had quite a different view. They regarded the difficult mayor as a spoiled child suddenly able to impose his will on those around him but basically responsible and with a set toward running the city as a public service institution. As such it had to have honest police and inspection services (the locus of most municipal corruption); it had to perform such duties as putting out fires, furnishing water, and providing schools, hospitals, and playgrounds; and all this must be done better than it had ever been done before. All the La Guardia performances were, in this view, merely calculated to mark him as the embodiment of these aspirations. Notoriety and a reputation for crusading would continue in power the regime that accomplished these things.

This was the view I came to take. It was very hard to get along with him as Mayor. It was more difficult for those who were his associates or subordinates than for his citizen supporters, because he was so often unfeeling, so unwilling to explore facts, and so apt to demand undeserved loyalty in specific and inappropriate instances. We were often on the receiving end of his famous temper, and to the more sensitive or vulnerable this made continuation of work with him impossible. But this, in itself, is not the point here, except as it bears on the question whether his outstanding success was owed in any measure to, or was achieved in spite of, his faults as a chief and as a member of the political profession.

That he invariably knew what he was doing, I became convinced. His tempers were mostly synthetic—to gain a point, to effect a subjection, to exhibit himself in a righteous role. They were part of a whole acting scheme that also included the reward of virtue in conspicuous instances, preferably for the heroism of police or firemen; the treatment with obvious contempt of most associates so that they should share none of his credit with the public; the spectacular emphasis on his jealous direction of city affairs—he raced to fires in helmet and boots, took credit for all the favors flowing from Washington (one reason he petted Robert Moses was that, as a Republican and an old feuder with Roosevelt, Moses obviously had no influence in Albany or Washington), and intervened in time to center attention on himself whenever there was any clear political profit in anything going on—the settlement of a labor dispute, the location of a housing project, a school, or an extension of the rapid transit lines.

In a technical way, all of this is important, just as it was important in the careers of his predecessors. I am quite certain that he, however, as well as they, invented the method for himself and made his own variations on a role that may seem to have been studied but was not. If political observers are struck with the similarities in the careers of some dozen American reform Mayors, they must remember what kind of person it takes to assume and carry out, over a full career, the character necessary to spectacular local leadership. Nothing learned from books or from the study of precedents could produce what New Yorkers recognize as La Guardiaism. And it is impossible to think that a student of government would imagine himself as a La Guardia and study consciously to attain La Guardia's public position. They might want to, and study to, become Mayor; but La Guardia screaming at a meeting of subordinates, running to a midnight fire, scheming to double-cross an associate in such a way as to get public credit—these are not admirable attributes to imitate. They were, however, essential ingredients of the living and acting La Guardia. It was also part of the La Guardia essence that it all came to far less than it might have, because he sabotaged his own charter and failed to map a strategy that would keep his city solvent. In the end he was succeeded by an organization Democrat. If a rule were being made for students to follow, La Guardia, the reformer, if all his characteristics were essential, would be something less than a reasonable example—so much less than reasonable that there cannot actually have been any rule. And if it does not exist, it cannot be followed.

Muñoz Marín, being accurately described as an intellectual, might be guessed to have learned something of his profession from books, from examples, and from storied precedent. This seems the more likely because he was the son of his father, Muñoz Rivera, whose whole life was politics and who had no mean success. Franklin Roosevelt had the example of "Uncle Ted," of course; and the parallels in the two Roosevelt careers are too close to be accidental.

There is a good deal of likelihood that both these professionals regarded with a shrewd and knowing eye what had and had not been found useful by these relatives who had gone just before them. I have made something of the Roosevelt comparison in another place. [3] The Muñoz Rivera-Muñoz Marín relationship may well have been very similar. Uncle Ted was dead before Franklin had got well started on his career. [4] Muñoz Rivera died when his son Muñoz Marín was eighteen and well before the son's political career had begun. The boy had had a rather sketchy education, as his father had moved about; but important years had been spent in Washington while his father represented Puerto Rico there, and in New York after he died. [5] He had moved about in a political atmosphere all his life, partly in Puerto Rico, partly in the national capital. He was too young to recall the occurrences and issues of the easy American conquest of the island incidental to the Spanish-American War, or even the arguments and adjustments that took place as first military and then civilian government was set up; but he heard much about it as his elders argued the merits of the various changes and as they campaigned for revision of the Foraker Act of 1900.

That act was a good deal less liberal in its provisions than the responsible Puerto Ricans had expected after General Miles' brave promises as he had come ashore with his landing party and issued his first manifesto. [6] The Puerto Ricans might very well have had the same treatment as Cuba and have been allowed to organize an independent republic under the hegemony of the United States. No one to this day has been able to say exactly why this did not happen. Instead first a military regime was set up and then a colonial

[3] "Our Two Great Roosevelts," *Western Political Quarterly,* March 1952.

[4] Theodore Roosevelt died in 1919, while Franklin and Eleanor were at sea on the way to the peace conference in Paris. Franklin had by then been elected and re-elected to the New York Senate and was serving as Assistant Secretary of the Navy in Wilson's administration. "Uncle Ted" was actually a fifth cousin of Franklin but an uncle of Eleanor. Franklin, however, regarded him as a mentor. Even after the older man's death he very obviously tested many of his own ventures in prospect by Uncle Ted's suppositious judgment.

[5] Muñoz Rivera was resident commissioner in Washington from 1911 to 1916. During this time Muñoz Marín attended, desultorily, courses at Georgetown University.

[6] Documents on the Constitutional History of Puerto Rico, p. 55.

government on the British model, as modified in American practice for territories eventually intended to become states. [7] In that government, officials appointed by the President had the controlling power. Puerto Ricans were allowed only such functions as were considered innocuous, strictly local, and not likely to affect the interests of the federal union. Such administrative officers as the commissioner of education, the attorney general, and the auditor were also appointed by the President. There was provided an Executive Council with the functions of an Upper House which had a majority of appointive officials. In this way both the executive and legislative branches were controlled from without—the traditional colonial system. [8] Judges of the Supreme Court were also presidentially appointed.

Because no Colonial Office existed to assume the complex administrative responsibilities involved in the relationship, the President was quite unable to see to it that Puerto Rican interests were effectively protected. The power to interfere was willfully retained by the Congress and protected by refusal to establish an adequate office in the executive establishment. Actually a Bureau of Insular Affairs was set up in the War Department to look after both Puerto Rico and the Philippines when they were occupied and military Governors were appointed. That Bureau in the War Department continued, right down to 1934—when President Roosevelt moved it to Interior—to be all there was of colonial administration in the executive branch of the federal government. With a surviving Executive Council to hamper the Governor, and with no agency in Washington to implement executive control, the local legislative politicos and congressional committee members between them made the governmental operations about as difficult to conduct as is possible to conceive. [9]

Before 1934 a certain change had taken place in the formal rela-

[7] Actually and technically this is not quite true. Puerto Rico was an "organized" but not an "incorporated" territory, a fine legal distinction afterward recognized by the Supreme Court, expressing the difference between territories intended for statehood and those whose future is indeterminate.

[8] This last feature was modified in the Jones Act of 1917. A Senate was provided for, but the Executive Council was not abolished.

[9] This relationship was reviewed at some length in various of my annual reports as Governor. Some of these were published in *Puerto Rican Public Papers*, 1946.

tionship—the Jones Act of 1917 had modified the Foraker Act of 1900. As to this, it should not escape notice that 1917 was again a time of national crisis, when certain grudging concessions could be got from an unwilling Congress on the plea of national security. There would not be another change until World War II, when the same arguments would again apply—that the principles we professed to be fighting for were very poorly observed in our own dependencies, and that the loyalty of Puerto Ricans was important.

The Congress, as has been suggested, had a general compulsion to retain its powers without having any of the instruments necessary to meet responsibility—that is, without any means of carrying out the duties it might be presumed to have assumed. This general legislative weakness was never better illustrated than in the long Puerto Rican story of neglect, sporadic interference, irresponsible talk, and disregard for simple justice, which unrolled after 1900.

There were few appointees to any Puerto Rican post throughout the years after 1900 who had more than mediocre abilities. Governors were normally lame-duck congressmen, or sometimes merely minor claimants to patronage, whose talents were anything but administrative; such abilities as they had were political, but they generally tangled unsuccessfully with the Puerto Rican professionals. These wily operators perfected as effective a system of blackmail and sabotage as can have existed anywhere, and Governors were driven frantic by their machinations. Lesser appointments were made at senatorial behest, mostly, and with some honorable exceptions—such as, for instance, in my own generation, the extremely able Justice Cecil Snyder of the Supreme Court, Elections Commissioner Terry, and Executive Secretary Brown—constitute a long list of misfits, incapables, and barely acceptables. [10] The two insular committees, in the Senate and the House, with rapidly changing membership, no responsibility to the Puerto Rican constituency, and incredibly sketchy knowledge of the island's geography, agricultural or industrial interests, and social conditions, used the administrative staff for patronage purposes; they also subjected it to a constant

[10] There were honorable exceptions also in other generations, no doubt, but they have been lost in an unusually misty history. Among Governors, Horace Towner, perhaps, and certainly Theodore Roosevelt, Jr., were men of ability and devotion to Puerto Rican interests.

barrage of irresponsible threats to please their home voters. The sugar industry especially, the island's main support, lay at the mercy of congressmen from competitive continental beet-sugar constituencies. They were always threatening to close or narrow the market for the Puerto Rican product. For fifty years it was a good week in Puerto Rico when some member of one or the other of the congressional committees responsible for insular affairs did not make a speech or introduce a bill to placate home opinion at Puerto Rican expense. Often it was not done with any intent to follow up or even with any specific ill will, but every time it happened the whole island shivered. How was it possible to measure the earnestness of congressional intention?

This shivering was not from empty alarm; nothing might actually impend, but then again it might. The island's Constitution was its Organic Act. It could be changed at any time by a simple majority vote in the Congress without any possibility of real influence from Puerto Rico. The only representation Puerto Rico had was one resident commissioner in the House of Representatives *who had no vote*. By 1934 he was "representing" more than two million American citizens (the citizenship conferred on them in 1917 was very possibly so that they would be subject to the draft for military service—at least their young men immediately *were* drafted). No continental citizen would think himself adequately represented by one voteless commissioner attached to the Congress—and especially if his local government was also controlled by Washington's political appointees.

Puerto Ricans are men and women like any others. If they resented this kind of treatment and occasionally reacted against it with some vigor, it was no more than natural, no matter how it may have been pictured in the States. Actually there was remarkably little knowledge of, or interest in, the island and its affairs—which is why congressional committees could treat it as they did. And this ignorance was a further source of hurt pride for a people of Spanish blood, who had, as a matter of fact, just won a considerable concession from Spain when the American occupation forced them to begin all over again the struggle for autonomy.

Muñoz Rivera had been the chief agent in Spain's softening. After 1898 he had had to deal with the United States. But he had had to negotiate mostly with congressional committees. Their agreements and promises proved evanescent and undependable. Practically nothing was gained during his long endeavors.

All this is thus summarized to place Muñoz Marín in the setting of his beginning, to show the difficulty of the situation he inherited, its opportunities and its almost certain frustrations. Because of these circumstances, he did have one great advantage over my other prototypes: he could become the embodiment of a nationalistic fervor brought to high tension by repeated insults and suppressions. This, as will be seen, was important, but it should not obscure the almost impossible nature of his task. He made creative use even of the obstacles and frustrations, and it takes a touch of genius to do that.

It would be interesting to compare his career with that of Quezon in the Philippines, and especially to evaluate their contrasting uses of latent xenophobia. I shall resist this temptation, except to point out how much more difficult and how infinitely more statesmanlike was the course followed by Muñoz. He deflected a hot nationalism into a demand for responsible association and got from the United States notable recognition and support. He ended by exploiting the exploiter and making the Congress like it.

Quezon succeeded in achieving an independence that gave his people little satisfaction and created an almost insoluble economic problem. It was easier to do, and this was why he did it. It served his political purpose better, because xenophobia is the easiest of emotions to arouse; and he was dead before the consequences arrived. Before he died, however, he knew what the results must be, and regretted, I am quite certain, his weak acceptance of an independence that excused the United States from payment for a half century of imperialism.

This is an interesting contrast. But it probably had nothing to do with the basic decisions made by Muñoz. Neither, I think, did his father's example. His determinations were derived from contemporary Puerto Rican premises. Both his strategy and his political tactics have all the stigmata of originality. They could not have come from books or precedent, in spite of his familiarity with literature and his intellectual bent. If they had they would have been different kinds of choices. So here again is a political specimen that is *sui generis*. Or so, at least, I think.

If the Roosevelt name was something to conjure with in the United States, Muñoz Marín had an even greater advantage of the same sort in Puerto Rico. [11] The situation, when Muñoz came awake politically during the deep depression of the thirties, was a chaotic one in Puerto Rico. The levels to which the economy had sunk would be almost unimaginable to the descendant of later years. The misery of the people was pitiable beyond anything ever known in the United States. The island was still a sugar island, with coffee and tobacco as supplementary crops in the hills. Most of the food, fiber, and building materials used in the island were imported. In this kind of monoculture, estate management can be more efficient than homestead tenure; but in Puerto Rico the enormous birth rate produced laborers at such a rate that competition among them held wages far below what would have been defined elsewhere as a subsistence rate. Efficiency in management did not produce a living wage for the workers.

Perhaps the most moving symptom of Puerto Rican degradation was the nearly complete disappearance of cultural aptitudes among the people. They were losing their arts; but what was worse, for practical reasons, was that they were losing their crafts as well. A worker in a squatter shack with a brood of big-bellied children, a washed-out wife, a diet reduced to the slave fare of rice, beans, and codfish had an awfully slight hold on life. He would die before forty; meanwhile he had only exhausting work to occupy him—when he had work; six or eight months of the year he had none, and had no income in consequence.

The depression in Puerto Rico began—like the agricultural depression on the continent which preceded that in industry by nearly a decade—soon after World War I. In Puerto Rico there was little industry, and the price of sugar was pretty much the measure of well-being. Sugar was literally as cheap as dirt during the twenties. But the years 1928 and 1932 would be noted in insular annals for another reason than that they were the nadir years of a wearing depression. Those were the years of the most devastating hurricanes of a century. For months after each of them the insular economy was

[11] La Guardia also had an advantage of a somewhat similar kind. He did not have a famous "uncle" or father, but he was unmistakably of Italian and Jewish descent, and that, in the New York of his time, was definitely advantageous, especially since he began running as a Republican and therefore had the problem of separating the East Side people from their traditional Democratic affiliations.

paralyzed. The roads were not altogether cleared for weeks; electric power lines were restrung only slowly; there were no immediately available funds for repair and reconstruction of any part of the wreckage. Relief, when it came, was late and inadequate. After the storm of 1932, Puerto Rico was prostrate. Even the will to continue living and working seemed to have blown away on the great wind.

There was a social and economic elite in Puerto Rico, as there always is in distressed places, and Muñoz belonged to it. The young men of the favored families could live peculiarly luxurious lives, tended by a swarm of servants, deferred to by inferiors, educated in foreign institutions. They could, and often did, become very callous. For those who had grown up in a luxury that existed side by side with misery, such a contrast could easily come to be an accepted, unquestioned arrangement. Moreover, the elite tended to suppose that their own luxury was conditioned on the misery of the depressed classes—and they were therefore disposed to regard the relationship as a natural one. The sons of the well-to-do were taught that they were inherently superior; and some such justification being necessary to self-respect, they did not question it. Muñoz was a pampered boy and had no more reason to adopt a critical attitude than had any of his contemporaries. He was sheltered from economic crises as he was from the consequences of such natural disasters as hurricanes. His father had been immersed in politics all his life. He was a famous patriot and a constructive one. He seems to have accepted the change from Spanish to American hegemony as something beyond his power to affect, and to have gone to work to get as much for Puerto Rico out of the new relationship as he could. Young Luis was a looker-on.

It must have seemed to him by the thirties that the American connection had been an unprofitable one for his people. They were in depression compounded by disaster; much of the best land was owned by sugar corporations, several of them controlled by groups of continentals; government was still incorrigibly colonial; poverty was increasing with the increasing population; and every year the culture in which so fierce a pride was felt was a little more diminished.

Resentment among Muñoz's contemporaries—those who, like himself, were aroused from callous apathy—took the very natural first form of conspiratorial anti-Americanism. The United States was to blame. Continental businessmen exploited the workers; the government protected businessmen in their privileges. Both the absentee landlords and the government must be got rid of. Later on this came to seem so naïve an approach that, so far as they could, most of the young *independentistas* wanted to have their part in it forgotten. Changing the ownership of the sugar lands would not make them more productive; rather the reverse. And the profits of the corporations turned out to be not an appreciable per cent of insular income.

Nor did changing the government tend to increase liberty or prosperity, and, when change did come, it created a good many problems for the Puerto Ricans which they had not anticipated. As to this issue, what they were a long time discovering was that their independence was something most Americans, more or less considerately, wanted them to have, not only because Americans abstractly believed in national independence, but because Puerto Rico was more and more an expense and an embarrassment to the nation. An independence movement, if it got wide support, was very likely to succeed. And then what would Puerto Rico be like? The island would have to compete in the open world for the sale of products that now had entry to favored continental markets. And the many assistances that could so easily be overlooked by critical young men, but that actually made the difference between life and death for the economy, would be withdrawn. [12]

Muñoz and his group—there were others of his age who did not follow him—became very discreet about independence when organized relief began to come to Puerto Rico as soon as the Roosevelt administration took over from the less concerned Republicans. It was much more convenient to accept, for the moment, the existing status and to use the flow of funds and the patronage possibilities for building up their "movement."

[12] What these economic aids amount to is interestingly detailed in "The Role of Federal Expenditures in the Economy of Puerto Rico," by R. H. Holton and Jean R. Anderson, *Revista Jurídica* of the University of Puerto Rico, September–October 1953.

A careful and complete assessment of Puerto Rican economic possibilities and relationships is to be found in H. S. Perloff's admirable *Puerto Rico's Economic Future* (University of Chicago, 1950).

6

By that time—1933—Muñoz had had some experience on his own as a politician and was beginning to have expansive dreams. His picture of himself had evidently undergone an almost complete revision. Until then he had lived in the shadow of his elders—first his father, then Santiago Iglesias, and then Antonio Barcelo. This was a familiar followership such as Roosevelt had had under Cousin Theodore Roosevelt (Uncle Ted) and La Guardia had had under the great Progressives, La Follette, Norris, Wheeler, et al., when he was serving with them in the Congress. The Iglesias I speak of was the Socialist leader in Puerto Rico—that is, his party was called Socialist and Iglesias himself had been more or less a devotee of Marxian principle; but actually what the party offered was the necessary alternative to the extreme reaction of the parties dominated by the propertied classes. It was, in other words, comparatively radical and included those who, whether they were Socialists or not, were in revolt on the issue of status. Muñoz joined Iglesias in 1918, two years after his father died. [1]

Presently, however, the young man went back to New York and from then until 1932 he lived sometimes in New York and sometimes in Puerto Rico, a confirmed bohemian, a poet and littérateur, writing a little for *The Nation* and, for *avant-guarde* magazines, verse, reviews, and occasionally an article. He was always a voluble conversationalist, gifted with scintillating flights of fancy, able, time after time, to carry his thought into the illustrative symbolism that

[1] A detailed study of Muñoz's early career and of his relationships with his predecessor politicians has been written by Professor Thomas Mathews of the University of Puerto Rico and will be published by the University of Florida Press.

characterizes all really sublime talkers. He became master of a colloquial English that would always amaze unbriefed visitors and sometimes even his intimates. His English, he was fond of saying, was better than his Spanish; and perhaps it was true that for his freest flights he did find English more suitable. In either language he had an ease and volubility that would always be among his most valuable assets.

It ought to be noted concerning him that he had never gone to Spain, the source of the old Puerto Rican culture; apparently he had never wanted to—something that always seems curious to those explorers of his career who themselves feel the tug of their own roots in the English soil. And indeed Muñoz did and does represent a curious cultural disembodiment that is responsible for more insular phenomena than is usually recognized. The young intellectual in Puerto Rico finds it hard to accept Spain as his motherland. There is too much there which his mind rejects—the tendency to political reaction, or to extreme radicalism, its opposite; the backwardness in science and technology; the acquiescence in poverty; and the isolation from other nations and their civilizations. His defense is to create a cultural-construct for Puerto Rico itself, as apart from Spain, and to dignify it beyond any possible justification.

The American who goes through the usual educational process is apt to look back at the end of his last collegiate year and realize that he has been induced to familiarize himself with several hundred years of English literature but that his formal study of American authors has been very slight and episodic. He may very well never have had a "course" in American literature. He realizes, if he thinks about it, that in the broad stream moving down to him out of the past the American contribution has been a minor and recent one. If he has had an interest in the literary world he has perhaps been able, in most universities, to find "electives" which will have covered the American field; but they were, in proportion, small streams lost in a mighty one. The American literature is an English literature. And not only is there no resentment about this, it is accepted as natural. The college graduate, when he first visits England, is apt to go about in a daze of literary reminiscence, unable at first to separate reality from romance. London is Dickens' London, or Shakespeare's, or Christopher Marlowe's, or Ben Jonson's; Canterbury is Chaucer's; the West of England is Hardy's; the lake country is Wordsworth's or Coleridge's—and so on. He is proud of this tradition because it is his own.

The Puerto Rican, in similar circumstances, has a very different feeling. His family and he very likely may have taken sides violently throughout a generation of Spanish troubles and may have been made ashamed of what went on there—the violence, the intolerance, the disorganization—and the stupid dictatorships. Even if his emotions were reactionary, he cannot be very proud of the Falangista's accomplishments. Going further back, Spain's grandeur, once so refulgent, disappeared as her hold was broken on revolting colonies. Somehow the English made the decline of Empire a matter of moral superiority, and their poverty became the occasion for the emergence of a massive courage. They manage to convey the impression that lesser peoples have been taught by the British to ask for independence and have been tutored in the ways to use it. This blandly ignores many reluctances, attempts at suppression, and revivals of imperialism. But it cannot be denied that a kind of principle has shaped that league of free peoples—their Commonwealth; and that everyone who is or has been part of it—including Americans—has a relation to the achievement which he regards as a personal part of himself.

The Spanish Empire went down reluctantly, miserably, and ignominiously, unable to give freedom or to tolerate equality in overseas peoples, attempting to the last suppressive measures that grew more and more feeble until they were sunk in ridiculous pretension. It was finally exposed in all its impotence at the time of the war of 1898, when the ships of the navy and of the forces on land had wooden guns and the soldiers still wore the glittering uniforms that made them rifle targets. Shrunk to the Iberian Peninsula whence it had emerged, the Spanish power, resting on an impoverished soil, still muttered of past glories as the slow years passed. It was not an inspiring culture to acknowledge as one's own.

Puerto Ricans are largely Spaniards by blood—and also by culture. The blood is not denied, but the culture often is. For it there is offered a fantastic Puerto Rican substitute. The United States is a large country with rich resources and correspondingly rich social appurtenances. If its people have not asserted independence from their British heritage, if they consider English literature their own, and what is indigenous only a small contribution to something much larger and older and richer, how can tiny Puerto Rico have substituted its littérateurs, its scientists, its theorists, for those of Spain? It is a tortured effort. And some of the phenomena associated with this strange and unnatural determination approach the weird and incredible. [2]

This compensatory straining is, however, something with which a political leader must deal. Muñoz's success in doing so was perhaps guaranteed by his early sharing in the pretensions and confusions. Then, too, there were years when he was completely absorbed in other interests, the result partly of cultural orphaning and partly, certainly, of habitual pampering. Somehow, for him, as for so many Puerto Rican boys of well-to-do parents, there had been a fatal lack of that discipline and incentive so necessary to the long ordeal of solid accomplishment. He might have become a literary figure; his talents promised success, or so it seemed to qualified contemporary judges. But he never learned how to—or perhaps was not motivated to—work. He was allowed to shirk every demanding task for so long that any sustained effort came to seem impossible. The first obstacle he met always turned him aside. In all the years that should have been his most creative he produced nothing of any permanent consequence, and not even anything slight that was of first quality—hardly anything that could not have been turned out in one sitting. This seems to me to indicate not that he was lazy or worthless but merely that he had not yet found his métier.

These things are said so that the measure of his later achievement can be seen. How does an apparent bohemian dilettante become a statesman? By what process is a slack youngster transformed into the determined leader of a whole people? Only, I think, by finding

[2] Some experiences of Professor Federico de Onis, the distinguished scholar who arrived in Puerto Rico in the early fifties to become head of the university's Department of Spanish, illustrate this. At about the time he arrived it was decided to change the course in Puerto Rican literature from the "required" to the "elective" category. A group of students concluded that this was an attempt to belittle Puerto Rican culture. They called on Professor Onis in a body and demanded that the course be reinstated as a requirement. The passion and hysterical excitement which governed the interview left the innocent scholar puzzled and shaken.

There was a similarly illustrative incident accompanying the initiation of graduate studies in the same department. Fourteen out of twenty students demanded to be permitted to write their dissertations on Puerto Rican literature.

something in himself when his opportunity appears, something that stirs and is activated by the challenge. Muñoz was to graduate into a brilliant but also a calculating policy-maker. The idealist was to turn pragmatist. He would reject desirable improvements because they seemed innovative and so might offend the congressional sensibilities he felt it necessary to conciliate. Some of these appeasements would be important, but he would not hesitate to adopt them even against the collective judgment of his colleagues. This apparent transformation, which, as I believe, was only the development of abilities latent all along, did seem at the time a most unlikely one. No one could have penetrated to the springs of talent which were to run so free. And acceptance was not easy. Years later there would still be those who could not believe what they saw.

Roosevelt and La Guardia, however, also performed the same prestidigitatorial trick, each in his own way and with his own end in view. Each seemed a most unlikely probability as a future statesman. Each found acceptance reluctant. The one, a pampered only son, exclusively educated, his way smoothed, surrounded by luxury and smothering concern, struck down, moreover, with a crippling disease; the other, a pint-sized, pugnacious, uneducated, and highly emotional young man with an evident talent for nothing but languages. Each came, however, into complete mastery of highly complicated situations in which the qualities of steadiness, persistence, and guileful progress toward a rational policy were the requirements. Each avoided the radicalism that would have alienated a necessary moderate conservative support, although each had strong radical leanings. And each made of himself a central and commanding figure of first consequence to his generation, the focus of a coalition, which, having coalesced, was difficult to pull apart, although not always easy to manage.

Of all of them, however, I should think the student would find the emergence of Muñoz into statesmanlike maturity the most improbable—and therefore the most notable as a personal accomplishment. That is my own conclusion.

Looking back, I suppose it can be said of all three that they could not have risen as they did if the conditions had not been prepared by circumstances quite beyond their control. In the case of Roosevelt, he was ripe for the presidential candidacy in 1932, the first year since 1916 when any Democrat could possibly have been elected; La Guardia was swept into the mayoralty on one of those waves of revulsion that follow in the wake of long-continued and increasingly flagrant municipal corruption, suitably exposed and publicized; Muñoz exploited the misery of his people in the depression and the springing hope that came to them from the New Deal. He deliberately appropriated the New Deal identification in Puerto Rico and was lifted on its powerful swell. This infuriated the federal officials—including Secretary Ickes—but Muñoz won the engagement.

All this may be accepted, but none of it explains why it did not happen to others than my three. There were always competing contenders, sometimes very formidable and likely ones, for the successive positions by which they climbed to higher levels of authority in their jurisdictions. And sometimes they won by a hair or, in the case of Roosevelt and La Guardia, actually lost what seemed like crucial elections, only to come back and win later ones. It is true that each was ready, a logical choice for the crowning position of his career when the opportunity offered; but this should not obscure all that went before while most unlikely human timber was deliberately readying itself, moved by mysterious incentives, for the final test of the future.

Looking at the career of each, it would not be difficult to make a case for the argument that each very early saw himself at the peak he eventually reached. Each undoubtedly did. But it would also be easy to discover numerous others whose intimations of greatness were just as clear and compelling. And *they* did not arrive. No, there were qualities in each of my three which, besides the circumstances, are important in understanding how each one day arrived at the goal he had set for himself. And clear ambition was not the only factor. They, as compared with rivals, had what it took. The others did not.

Some of the qualities they possessed to the necessary degree are not difficult to isolate, it seems to me, when as persons they are sufficiently well known. Each had, for instance, a bulldog determination concerning objectives and a completely contrasting flexibility concerning means. Each, also, was sufficiently vague and obscure, so that diverse supporters could suppose them to have the opinions they wished them to have. Each, furthermore, was a demagogue in the true sense of resting on popular support and maintaining power by the actual or potential threat of electoral punishment for those who refused to consent to his serious proposals. And it is not necessary to reiterate that each, in certain crises, showed the qualities of a strategist in politics, however true it may be that none seemed ordinarily to have an unusual flair of this sort—which is to say that it was strategy and not tactics that won their victories.

These qualities were at least as well developed in Muñoz as in the others. His seemed the least amenable of the three personalities to shape for a political purpose. And the problems he met were more difficult to solve. There had been Presidents before Roosevelt who were able to use the office for supreme national objectives, and reformism in American cities was no novelty before La Guardia, but no one had ever been confronted with Muñoz's complex problem. His approach to it, his attaining of position, and his way of working it out—all had to be *sui generis;* there were no antecedent solutions. It has been said before that none of my three appears to have benefited greatly from such lessons as there may have been, but in the case of Muñoz there was simply no possibility of his having been guided by learning. No one ever before had rescued a backward area from decline, or at least—giving the imperial nations credit they can hardly be said to deserve—no backward area was ever raised so rapidly by such unique methods. One of the more novel of Muñoz's techniques, as it unfolded, could be seen to be that he took advantage of every possible American weakness, every generous sentiment, and that on occasion he even capitalized on some less admirable traits among those who could be useful in his large design.

It must have been far from congenial for the youthful radical nationalist to conclude that an independent Puerto Rico could never become either prosperous or culturally significant. All his sentiments must have been outraged, and the tortuous maneuvers involved must have seemed humiliating in prospect. Sentiment is a controlling emotion in the Latin make-up, and humiliation is something hardly to be borne, even if the sacrifice of important rewards is involved. Nevertheless, Muñoz achieved it for himself and, moreover, forced it upon his supporting elite. There were defections. Many Spaniards in Puerto Rico could not make the adjustment any more than they had ever been able to in Spain. But Muñoz ruthlessly exiled from the party those who could not conform and went on without them. Eventually they formed an *Independentista* party of their own and attracted most of those whose fierce patriotism seemed to require separation from the United States at any economic sacrifice. But the number of votes they commanded, when their ideas were brought into actual competition with Muñoz's realism, was always minor. [3] A large majority of the insular electorate knew themselves strong in association with the United States and saw themselves ruined if that association should be ended. Muñoz finally brought himself to the position of representing to his people the strength of continental America, while remaining incontestably Puerto Rican. He was at once *criollo* (native) and *yanqui* (American).

This was more than an amazing tour de force, because he carried with him all the sentiments of proud separatists, who, however much they appreciated being able to lean heavily on the strength of the United States, had an uncontrollable dislike for all continentals. It was made possible by such developments as the elective governorship which preceded the Commonwealth. Patriots were no longer required to accept a continental-appointed governor in order to secure American economic assistance; by a miracle, one of their own now stepped into the role of representative. Muñoz's feat was amazing in another way: he usurped his representative role, stole it from a group of those who had for a generation made a profession of friendship with the powerful on the continent. These "petityanquis" had long sought to persuade the Puerto Rican electorate that their most desirable future lay in statehood. The trouble was that they were the insular reactionaries, and the thirties was not the decade for reaction. Affiliation with the Republican party was no guarantee of influence in Washington—beyond that of being a nuisance —or of bringing any good thing to the island. In retrospect, it almost seems that their own stupidity defeated them and discredited their leaders; but of course it is partly the cleverness of Muñoz that makes them seem to have been so obtuse.

Muñoz let them cling to statehood and identified it for the electorate with reaction. He adopted a new status, which eventually came to be called "Commonwealth," and showed his people the

[3] This leaves out of account the small band of nationalist terrorists who gave up electoral methods for violence and sought to force compliance with their will by indiscriminate shootings. But these never had much electoral following, nor did they seek it. They were not democrats.

neatest political trick of all—how they could have their cake and eat it. They could rid themselves of "foreigners" and yet have all the assistance, on which they had become dependent, as a right. They could even benefit from the Social Security System and receive state aids equally with the states, and without any obligation to pay Federal income taxes. How could the *independentistas*—who would have thrown away all these gifts—or the statehood party—who would have involved Puerto Rico in paying its share of taxes—compete with the status represented by Muñoz?

7

This legerdemain was not perfected quickly or easily. It required thought, flexibility, endless ingenuity, and iron determination. For what Muñoz set out to do was patently impossible. No one could have believed that what came about was something he had had in mind all along; it seemed incredible. But, fantastic as it must have appeared, it was apparent afterward that he had maneuvered into being precisely the status he wanted to attain, and had done it with intention and design. It was an accomplishment that required skill of the first order.

I myself was caught one time in a typical—and perhaps crucial—incident in Muñoz's difficult grand maneuver. I knew more or less what was happening, because I had begun to see what the design was. But the affair was delicate for me because of divided loyalties —often a difficulty for the public servant who reaches a higher echelon. I have told something of this incident in the book which recounted my adventures in the governorship of Puerto Rico, [1] and I shall repeat only enough to illustrate my difficulty concerning the progress of Muñoz.

My governorship was fated to be an unhappy one as it progressed, although, as later events showed, it was a uniquely creative period for everyone concerned. I was faced with all the necessities of a poverty-stricken land—that I expected—but in addition to that, the very beginning of my term coincided with the oncoming of war and blockade. How the needs of that time were met I shall not recount again. It is more important here to say that I had an additional ambition. I wanted to be instrumental in advancing Puerto

[1] *The Stricken Land* (New York: Doubleday & Co., 1947), Chap. 28, pp. 537 ff.

Ricans toward the full citizenship implied in complete local autonomy and eventually statehood. It was clear enough that immediate statehood was both impossible and undesirable—impossible because the Congress would not consent (the continental beet-sugar lobby was influential enough to stifle any movement that would have resulted in two senators and six representatives from another sugar area); and undesirable because the burden of federal taxes could not be borne. The Jones Act of 1917 had modified the Foraker Act of 1900 in important ways: citizenship had been granted and more local autonomy in government had been authorized. But both these had important limitations, and I thought a significant further step might again be taken, short of statehood, one clearly in the direction of advance, and one consonant with the national interest. The time for it had arrived, I thought, and I wanted to assist in its realization.

My own difficulty, it will be understood, was that as Governor I had a duty to Puerto Rico, and that as the President's representative I had a duty to the United States. I had to be loyal to both at once. I had no difficulty with my conscience about persuading Washington to give Puerto Rico all the economic assistance I could manage. It seemed to me that this was owed to a people who had been taken in charge involuntarily and had been allowed to fall into the direst poverty. Thinking also that the responsibilities of local government ought to be enlarged, I conceived that the enlargement might be achieved by providing that the Governor should be elected and that the sovereignty of the United States in Puerto Rico should be represented and symbolized by an official who, whatever he might be called, would be in effect a High Commissioner.

The High Commissioner would most importantly be a symbol, but he might also preside over and co-ordinate the multitude of federal functions still to be carried out on the island. They ran all the way from lending agencies to the agricultural extension service; from grants for vocational education to the Public Health Service. Under the appointive governorship, federal sovereignty was centralized in the Governor's person, just as in Washington it was centralized in the President. But if the Governor were elected, he would and could represent only the people who elected him. He would in no sense represent the federal government.

The President—Roosevelt—was persuaded; but he made much

more than I had of the point that there must be a representative of national sovereignty; in fact, he made it a condition of consent on his part. Between us we determined that the way to approach the matter was by way of a mixed committee to make recommendations which the President could then transmit with approval to the Congress. The committee—including Muñoz—was appointed and was called to meet. Muñoz, to my surprise, was reluctant. He thought at first that he would not attend at all. Then he decided that he would. Then he delayed, and until he turned up late none of us knew for certain whether or not he would be present. During the weeks of this uncertainty I learned new lessons in political behavior.

It should be understood that since the appearance of the *Partido Popular* (Muñoz's political party) on the Puerto Rican scene, its professed aims had been deliberately confined to economic and social betterment. The question of status had been held in strict abeyance; party members were forbidden to discuss it in public, and if they did they were repudiated. "That," Muñoz had said, "we will turn to when we have made some economic progress." This had not been easy to do, since the active workers of his party were mostly *independentistas* in sentiment; moreover, the usual political polarization had set their party off against the *Republicanos*, who were for statehood. If you were not for statehood, it was the general opinion, you must be for independence. There was no middle ground.

Nor was it yet known that Muñoz had marked out the middle ground for his territory. His critics said that his former known *independentista* affiliation was merely in suspense and waiting a favorable moment. When everything else possible had been got from the United States, it was whispered, independence would be demanded—with subsidy. This was what Sumner Welles called "divorce with alimony," showing that he too assumed, as did most other knowing observers, that the *Populares*, when they finally revealed their attitudes, would ask for endowed separation.

But Muñoz was evolving something far subtler and more favorable both to Puerto Rico and to himself—a situation in which the United States would stay tied to Puerto Rico, with himself in a position to represent the source of subsidies at the same time that he also represented the claimant for them. He was to be both patient and doctor.

Just here I must digress to say that three responsible Puerto Ricans —Rafael Cordero, Enrique Campos del Toro, and Miguel Guerra Mondragón—had, somewhat before then (in 1942), called on me at La Fortaleza to present a scheme they had been evolving for some time. It was a scheme for an in-between status, neither statehood nor independence. They called it an "associated state," as I remember; and Cordero actually, in 1943, in speaking of the scheme, called it an *estado libre asociado* (which means literally "associated free state"). I was interested and discussed it with them at some length. Two of these proposers were lawyers, one was a university professor, and all could be called liberal progressives. They were strongly against independence; but they saw that statehood, if possible at all, would only be feasible in the relatively far future. The interests opposed seemed to them much too powerful to be overcome within a foreseeable time. My own attitude, as I recall, was that for the moment the more moderate proposal for an elected governor was all that could be expected from a Congress that had expressed such uniform hostility to any change. Cordero and his friends acquiesced, but with the notation that more would shortly be demanded.

The relevance of this is that this is the scheme Muñoz in due time adopted and made a central *Popular* doctrine. The invention was thus not his own, but it may well have been that something of the sort was germinating in his mind as well as in the minds of others. [2] The constitutional format of the *estado libre asociado* remained to be worked out in a future Assembly, but the outline existed already in the papers of the group I have mentioned. I suppose the translation

[2] It is well to use extreme caution always in allocating credit for social ideas and inventions. Their germination in an individual mind may have started long before any overt sign of acceptance is apparent. Frequently they fall on stony ground and are lost altogether. Sometimes they lie ungerminated until the climate becomes favorable. For a long time I attributed the origin of the *estado libre* to Cordero and his friends of those early days. But much later I discovered that as early as 1922 the then existing Union party had had as the principal plank in its platform a proposal for a *libre estado asociado*. The text clearly anticipated the later development. Cf. Antonio Barcelo, "El Partido Unión de Puerto Rico" in *El Libro de Puerto Rico* (San Juan, 1923). I am indebted to Professor Henry Wells for calling this earlier invention to my attention. Who furnished the idea to the platform-makers in 1922, I do not know. But it is also to be noted that Muñoz's father was always careful not to commit himself to independence and that he always had in mind something he and others spoke of as "autonomy" but did not further define.

of the three Spanish words into one English word was Muñoz's idea. The word "Commonwealth" is no translation at all, as anyone can see, but rather a presentation to each public of the same legal instrument under a name expected to be acceptable.

Muñoz undoubtedly had this already in the back of his mind as the presidential committee I have mentioned met in Washington, and this probably accounted for what seemed to me so strange a reluctance. He knew that the auspices for such a scheme as he had in mind were not yet propitious. He was not anxious to reject the President's offer of an elective governorship, but he would rather not be forced yet into any commitment.

When the committee met he put forward a proposal of his own that thoroughly confused matters. He asked for a grant of funds without strings attached; he had in mind an amount large enough to effect an economic tour de force; it would simply be given to the government of Puerto Rico in exchange for an undertaking not to ask for further financial support. [3] The committee, ignoring this suggestion, made its recommendations without Muñoz's agreement. But his diversionary effort succeeded; the Congress did not act. And it was not until after President Roosevelt's death and my leaving the governorship that an act was passed changing the office to an elective one. By that time Muñoz had persuaded everyone involved that the high commissionership about which President Roosevelt and I had felt so strongly was an insult to Puerto Rico and odiously reminiscent of British imperialism. A federal co-ordinator, low-sala-

[3] It is interesting to note that Muñoz's grant of funds was made—not by the Congress, but by the circumstances of war. The revenue taxes on goods shipped from Puerto Rico to the U.S. are returned to Puerto Rico. Whisky-making was stopped during the war, and rum from Puerto Rico largely took its place. At the same time taxes on all spirits were increased. For several years, as a kind of gift of the gods, Puerto Rico had a return of revenues that about doubled the insular income. When I left the governorship in 1946, there were substantial sums tucked away in various pockets, most of which Muñoz inherited when he became governor in 1948. It took some ten years to empty these pockets, and by that time the economic spiral that characterized the late forties and early fifties in Puerto Rico was well begun. It had been measurably assisted by the fortuitous gift of revenues during the war years.

This might go to show, I suppose, how lucky great politicians have been when their careers are examined in retrospect. Muñoz got his fund; but when it was used up he was still getting all the assistances from the Congress that he would have got anyway. He had not had to trade future subsidies for his lump sum.

ried, without place or perquisites, was provided. The position was never filled.

There was now no federal representative, the governor was to be elected, and no question had been raised about the continuation of all the existing assistances. The logical candidate for the governorship was none other than Muñoz. The maneuver was complete—or nearly so.

No disaster resulted. Muñoz was elected and re-elected. He was a model executive. He worked hard; from continuous study he knew everything that went on. He used his intellectual gifts in the service of his people. No one questioned his authority. Federal aid went on and was actually enlarged. Its generous continuance supported his position. Best of all, there was no Government House elsewhere. Puerto Rico was, in effect, independent; but Puerto Ricans were United States citizens; they received several Social Security benefits; their roads, hospitals, airports, and low-cost houses were built with federal aid; they had an agricultural extension service. And presently (four years later) they would have a commonwealth, an *estado libre asociado*. Having cake and eating it too was not after all impossible if you happened to have the requisite political genius.

It would be expected, it seemed to me, that in the writing of the new compact between the United States and Puerto Rico, in 1952, there would have been some recognition of federal generosity. The obligation of the federal government was made clear. Puerto Rico was to have full local autonomy. Only as to foreign affairs was there any restriction. There was even an implied understanding that for the future no unilateral change would be made in the relationships now being established. In other words, any revised arrangements would require mutual consent. This had the effect, if strictly interpreted, of making permanent all existing relations and transforming them into treaties that would require renegotiation for revision. [4]

The new "constitution" of the Commonwealth was approved by referendum in Puerto Rico and ratified by the Congress. Its initiation was solemnized in July 1952 with impressive ceremony which

[4] The financial obligations of the United States in Puerto Rico ought not to be made to seem greater than in fact they were. In the fifties, for instance, a large percentage of the payments to Puerto Rico was for veterans benefits. This was not a gift. Puerto Ricans had served in the armed forces; the veterans were entitled to the same benefits as any other veterans, Puerto Rican or not.

included the adoption of a flag. The object of all the ceremonial, it might be suspected, was to make such a record that it would be very difficult for future Congresses not to honor the compact made by the Eighty-first Congress and make unilateral changes. It is an established principle that one Congress cannot commit succeeding ones. There is no such thing as an enforceable contract, and treaty status for a legislative undertaking is not possible. Nevertheless, in the eyes of Puerto Ricans, a treaty now existed, and there would be trouble if it should in any way be altered. A succeeding Congress would presumably at least hesitate before entering on such a course; and the more seriously it was regarded by Puerto Ricans, the more hesitation there would be.

The constitution was not very old when Muñoz began tentative explorations of further possibilities. These looked in the direction of further autonomy. He would, for instance, like to control and administer the state-aid programs and cause the withdrawal of the various departmental representatives who reported to Washington. This was obviously not because it could be done better by Puerto Ricans. Such a removal would indeed excise the tissue of mutual aid that had done so much to advance the backward states of the union and bring them into conformity with the best practices. It was rather because Muñoz wanted to edge closer and closer to independence without losing financial aids. More than anything else, these tentatives, after the Constitution was adopted, indicated what actually was his ultimate goal.

The decision here both about politics and ethics is irresolvable because it turns wholly on intention. If Muñoz intended that sometime Puerto Rico should accept the obligation of association, there was no objection to the constitution.[5] If he intended the status

---

[5] There is some reason for believing that he recognized this obligation. At least twice in public statements he has spoken of the need for recognition One of these statements was explicit. It occurred in his annual address to the legislature in 1952.

. . . *Puerto Rico [when able] ought to pay its share into the Federal treasury . . . in the same way that it is now contributing morally to the democratic reputation of the Union. . . . When that day arrives we ought not to wait until we are asked to share in the expense; we should rather be the ones to propose the sharing and to pay for it ourselves in the exercise of our own democratic authority and our own sense of responsibility as members, in a new way, of a great Union.*

defined by it to be permanent, or if he intended modification in the direction of independence, there was the grave objection that it was an exploitation of some citizens by others. In such an adventure no morally sensitive person could have a part. Admittedly this last is an ethical matter and has no place in a discussion of politics as technique—that is, unless the unethical quality of the arrangement should ultimately interfere with the working out of the technique. Then the ethics becomes part of the politics. In this case I believe that this will in the long run prove to be true.

The result, if this is so, will be that, whatever Muñoz's actual intentions were as to status, and whatever he may attempt, his successors will someday find it expedient to move for modification. If they do not, they will begin to lose the benefits which the bargain with the Eighty-first Congress sought to make permanent. This is because no patently one-sided agreement can endure. When Puerto Ricans have been raised to the level of well-being maintained by citizens in the States, it will become, however gradually, impossible to preserve the one-way arrangements frozen by the constitution. The choice which will then confront Puerto Ricans will be this: They can move toward statehood and mutual sharing in obligations and benefits, or they can move toward independence, giving up, even if gradually and reluctantly, the benefits of association. If this latter choice is made, there will be a presumption that this was the intention all along; and the Commonwealth arrangement of 1952 will be regarded as a hoax which the Congress was duped into accepting.

As a tour de force, looked at in the limited perspective furnished by the circumstances of the fifties, the Commonwealth arrangement is a remarkable achievement; looked at from farther away, it will inevitably become one landmark among many in a people's progress. It will be a good or a bad landmark—and its author a good or bad political strategist—by the standard of intention that is then apparent.

This would seem to contemplate not a request that federal taxes be levied in Puerto Rico but that Puerto Rico should make a grant, determined unilaterally, to the United States.

8

The books ought not to be closed on political achievements until all the returns are in, and that may be in a quite distant future. Practicing politicians are apt to rate far too high simple electoral victories and not to admit to the accounting what is gained or lost to society from success at the polls. What is distant is easy to sacrifice, and even a statesman who thinks of posterity will forget it when "running scared." It happens that all three of the examplars under discussion here reminded me on occasion that it was a politician's first business to win elections. That I can recall successive and similar reminders from all three indicates a like valuation among them of voters' approval. It indicates also that for each I furnished a provocation for such a defense.

My leaders were alike in overrating majority support, or, perhaps I should say, in attaching to it a value it cannot have. And I did remonstrate with each for paying what seemed to me too high a price in compromise for victory. Whether or not I went on in each case to say that it still remained to be seen what had been gained, that was what I meant. In any long evaluation it has to be said that it is of no use to win if winning does not make it possible to accomplish something of importance. Presumably I implied—or said—that the contest had not only been one between personalities as such but also between candidates who had stood for something. My politicians, however, in the euphoria of victory, were prone to accept what had happened as an end, a satisfactory completion; and in the short-run sense they were right. The electorate had chosen them much more than their policies.

The truth may have been—it often was—that they had yielded point by point, as the canvass had developed, all or much of what they had stood for in the beginning. They had come down with fear-sickness as the enemy's attack developed and as the election loomed over them. And when they were finally victorious they could hardly claim to have stood on any platform. At best they stood on one that had nearly vanished in a fog of equivocation. They consequently had little leverage on the legislature elected with them; and on all but the most overriding policies—such, for instance, as those having to do with recovery from depression or defense measures for the nation or similar weighty issues for cities or states—they had advertised no commitments to which they could now appeal as they tried to shape a program and force its adoption. Legislatures, elected from geographic districts and owing their campaign funds to special interests, have to be severely disciplined if measures of general interest are to be got through. And there has to be potential punishment for recalcitrance, with rewards for good behavior. Plain commitment in anticipation of victory furnishes an elected leader the strength both to punish and reward. Thus equipped, he can demand and get support for this program. Without this support he is likely to be ignored.

The Chief Executive—President, Governor, or Mayor—in the American system of tripartite government, is sometimes also spoken of as Chief Legislator. [1] The function of Chief Legislator can be carried out successfully only by a determined leader armed with a mandate. The mandate can easily be frittered away in the process of conciliating special-interest groups in order to make certain of election. In extreme cases of this sort the candidate may have won for himself, but he will not have won for his cause. And in the long run he will find that he cannot get done what he knows to be necessary.

There is a view of this, put forward by Mr. Walter Lippmann among others, that it is a very good thing to have no discernible differences remaining between candidates by election day. That makes the elected Chief Executive, whoever wins, a representative of all, or nearly all, the people. It is this, the argument runs, that is responsible in the United States for an admirable submission to the rule of the majority, so much in contrast with some other nations

[1] Cf. Louis Brownlow, *The President and the Presidency* (University of Chicago, 1949). Others have also used the phrase.

that either have only one party to begin with or whose minorities resort, if they are able, to force when electoral results are unsatisfactory.
A revolution to reverse an election is common procedure in Latin
America, there is seldom a serious movement toward one in the
United States—some high and violent talk, sometimes, but soon
stilled for lack of support—the Civil War, of course, being the most
monumental of several exceptions.

I think Mr. Lippmann exaggerates the benefits from almost indistinguishable parties and platforms. It inevitably means that progress is made more difficult; and overlong resting in the status quo
may result in an accumulation of maladjustments and wrongs whose
correction may sometime be forced in a near-revolutionary overturn.
Such an overturn occurred in 1932, for instance, after three reactionary Republican administrations. It was only because an exceptionally skilled leader succeeded Hoover that the change was not actually revolutionary. Roosevelt had avoided asking for a mandate,
but the seriousness of the times frightened the Congress into consent
to his extemporized demands, and he got done what was necessary.
Similar tactics in the succeeding campaign (1936) had reverse results. A mandate was not asked for then either, and since the Congress was not frightened, the requests made of it were refused,
sometimes in humiliating fashion. In fact, in Roosevelt's case the
low point of his presidential years immediately followed his most
resounding victory.

The choice is between peace and a program: The leader need
not go to extremes, but he is foolish to deny himself the backing
he must have if any accomplishments are to be credited to his regime. There can be too much peace in politics if politics is to serve
a public purpose and not merely keep an individual or a party in
office.

The outstanding Presidents—and other Chief Executives as well—
are marked by historians as "strong" when they have prevailed in
the inevitable clash of the Executive with a recalcitrant or hostile
legislature. The most notable ones have had this success because
they represented some definite cause or program—Jackson, a return
to Democracy; Lincoln, indestructible union; Theodore Roosevelt,
an assertive nationalism; Wilson, the Democratic progressivism he
called "The New Freedom."

When the conduct of candidates is studied, an evident, compelling urge to compromise and conciliate is to be seen at work. Each is likely to start out as the emphatic representative of a point of view and to end up having frightened no one and having promised heterogeneous—and perhaps inconsistent—benefits to many interests, but without having taken a firm position on any crucial issue. This is less true of the strongest leaders, but even of them it is visibly characteristic.

All my politicians did this. Of the three, Muñoz was the least culpable, President Roosevelt the worst offender, and La Guardia somewhere between. The weakness of Muñoz was evident, for instance, as he hung onto the support of the numerically unimportant *independentistas*. They were his old friends and companions, of course, once the center and not the fringe of the *Popular* movement, and there may have been some sentiment about this—except that long observation has taught me to be skeptical of apparent sentimentality in politicians. It is more probable that he was stretching his political personality widely in response to the law of conciliation. The intransigent *independentistas* in his party—a number of whom rose to positions of influence—were a constant source of embarrassment. But he could not bring himself to believe what most others knew, that these extremists had no following.

The old elite whose members had brought Puerto Rico to the demoralized state that gave the *Populares* their opportunity were not really very much afraid of Muñoz. His alliance with labor would involve some raises of wages; and the land program would alienate some larger estates owned by absentee corporations—who, it turned out, were not seriously averse to selling anyway and who got a very good price indeed. But otherwise they suffered no damage; and they shared in many benefits.

By 1952 little was left in Puerto Rico of government enterprise. But Muñoz had been, as always, lucky. The post-war years had been ones of continuous prosperity, and this had involved a sustained market for sugar and a vast increase in tourism. Also, in Puerto Rico as elsewhere in the American system, unchecked inflation of prices caused no revolutionary reaction because wages also went up and because benefits of various sorts were concurrently increased.

Not all benefits came from outside. There was, when Muñoz came to the governorship, a stiff income tax, well administered. And the yield of this was useful in carrying out many programs of assistance which, in other circumstances, would not have been possible. Close figuring to maintain a certain level of well-being was not necessary. The "national" income of Puerto Rico doubled in the decade after the war. In the later years of this upward surge the collectivistic ideas that had marked the early *Popular* challenge to the insular reactionaries were abandoned as not essential to reconstruction. The government began to subsidize new *private* enterprises, and it disposed of those public ones that had been begun earlier. Republicans in Congress had nothing "socialistic" to complain of when the Constitution was up for ratification in 1952. They were, indeed, so well satisfied with Muñoz's conservatism that the act was more a Republican than a Democratic measure.

This might seem to indicate that Muñoz's caution was justified. Perhaps it was. The result was what he most wanted, and it was achieved without too great trouble in this way. But the costs of compromise are not wiped out by the achievement they may have made possible. They are still costs; and a proper social accounting, if one were ever possible, would deduct the costs from the gains. Only in that way could the net of the profit be determined. That this never was and never will be done, it is not necessary to suggest. What is being dealt with in all such cases is to an extent imponderables. Values that are mostly subjective cannot be weighed with any precision.

Muñoz's soft policy toward the reactionaries in Puerto Rico, his giving up of governmental economic interferences—either ownership or effective regulation—may very possibly have been important in conciliating the Eighty-first Congress and in creating the atmosphere in which the last act of his grand maneuver could be carried out. To go further with assessment it would be necessary to attach a value to the grand maneuver and other values to the sacrifices. It will be a long time—as I said—before the returns are in on either the profit or loss side of this balance sheet.

Meanwhile the basic fact was that Muñoz was occupying the governorship with satisfaction to himself and, apparently, to most others concerned. The government was extremely well run as to administration, and the budgetary planning was effectively done.

The whole picture, with the exception of agriculture, was one of careful foresight, imaginative and sustained development, and progress toward standards comparable with those of the mainland. And the dramatic change, within a decade, in the Puerto Rican scene was attracting attention from all those who had an interest in induced economic development. Resident on the island, as students or interns, were hundreds of learners from all over the world. Some were even sent or directed by the Department of State—in itself a significant difference from former days.

The obvious conclusion is that his grand maneuver was not only a successful political venture, in strict technical terms—because it had won elections for himself and his party and because it had set him up as Governor in amazingly favorable economic circumstances—but also because it had a desirable result from the point of view of the federal government. I was compelled to acknowledge that the forebodings I had expressed on leaving the governorship in 1946 [2] had so far been mistaken. Muñoz had no writ for representing the interests of the United States and he made no pretense of economic interest in anything but the welfare of Puerto Rico; but his pride in Puerto Rican achievements had led him to develop, at some pains, a new picture of Puerto Rico in the minds of Latin Americans— something of importance to the nation.

Communists had an interest in representing Puerto Ricans as a people betrayed, kept in subjection for the benefit of American capitalists, their liberties truncated, and themselves sunk in misery. "Puerto Rico Redivivus" was Muñoz's theme. And since he was a Latin speaking to Latins and bore an honorable name among Spanish Americans, his propaganda made progress. The small group of remaining *independentistas* found it more difficult to maintain eagerly sympathetic groups in Cuba, in Brazil, or in the Central American countries than it had been when the apparatus of colonialism still existed. Puerto Rican progress, with Muñoz presiding over its incidents, was an irrefutable fact that enfeebled even the naturally impassioned oratory of the Iberians. [3]

So the grand maneuver was turning out to be in the interest of

[2] In *The Stricken Land.*

[3] The *nacionalistas*' resorts to violence, first the attempt on President Truman's life, and then the promiscuous shooting up of congressmen in session, were a measure of Muñoz's success. They were rapidly losing their small remaining following, and only martyrdom could re-establish their dwindling prestige.

the United States as well as of Puerto Rico. My divided loyalties need not have given me uneasiness. And there was another thing about it that began to seem, if not at once practicable, to have possible significance for the future. This aspect of it rested on the American undertaking to intervene against men's miseries wherever they might be found, but especially in the American neighborhood. "Point Four," in President Truman's 1949 inaugural address, won more friends for the United States, I should say, than any other presidential pronouncement in our history. It indicated that officially we would not be indifferent, ever, to suffering. We knew now, after our own experience, that poverty was never necessary. Admittedly part of our own success in abolishing it, even if by no means all, had been owed to an unexampled richness of resources. Even more important was what we called "know-how" and what elsewhere was called "expertise." But even if it was wealth and "know-how," joined, that constituted the secret, others still need not despair. Out of our stores of both we were disposed to distribute what we could well spare and what others cared to have.

We could spare a good deal if it would gain for us some good will, some lessening of tension. For our rival imperium, Russia, was finding it all too easy to play on the very human sentiment of envy among those who were less well off, and was even able, in many instances, to turn it into active fear and preventive revolution. Old exploitations by American interests in Latin America were called up, ghosts from the past, to torment a nation now embarked on a "good-neighbor" policy. It was not always easy going, even with fairly lavish use of funds, to transform ill will into good will by propaganda. The Point Four idea was a brilliant and timely one. It proposed to substitute deeds for protestations and even to improve the deeds—for the federal government had been informally exporting technicians and maintaining them in Latin America for years, and to this extent Point Four was nothing really new.

Could it have been wholly luck, or was it subtle planning that brought Muñoz's grand maneuver to a climax just at the time when there was intense interest in proving the propaganda claims of the Communists to be wrong and in showing what a good neighbor the United States actually was? At any rate, there was this concurrence. The establishment of a Commonwealth of Puerto Rico showed that the United States was not only disposed to increase the well-being of Puerto Rican fellow citizens but was willing to allow them to define for themselves the relationship they would establish with the federal Union.

This seemed to say—merely as a whisper, an intimation—to others: You may also, by being friendly, be so joined to the American system that the blood of our prosperity will flow from our veins into yours as it does into Puerto Rican veins. And you need not become a colony; you need not assume the posture of a potential state of our Union. You can become, like Puerto Rico, near us but not of us.

In an address at the University of Florida in 1952 [4] I suggested this extension of the good-neighbor concept, and I was given the opportunity of summing up the situation in a volume devoted to Puerto Rico in 1952. [5] Those two occasions marked some advance in my own perceptions. In one—the Florida address—I pointed out how much farther our money and effort would go if instead of periodic transfusions of assistance we arranged for a steady flow outward from the existing technical agencies that had been responsible for our own success. [6] I had done some figuring and I had made certain that the cost of this kind of thing would not be significantly higher than recent undertakings of a more sporadic and far less effective sort.

In the *Annals* article I addressed myself mostly to the economic situation, pointing out that Puerto Rico was coming into the ambit of those economies that shared the spiral of prosperity and saying that policy should now be changed to implement the new possibilities. As to the new Constitution, I said rather casually that it was another long step toward union and that it would probably not be long before the statehood step would open out as a possibility. I had thought of outlining another possibility, but it was one I did not take very seriously, and I lacked space. I meant to say that the Constitution might prove so satisfactory that it would arrest

---

[4] "Caribbean Obligations," *Papers of the Latin American Conference of 1952* (University of Florida Press).

[5] "What Next for Puerto Rico," *Annals of the American Academy of Political and Social Science.*

[6] The agricultural college-experiment station-extension service system, the Public Health Service, the Bureau of Public Roads, the Bureau of Standards, vocational education, and even certain Social Security titles were the examples I used.

further progress toward union, at least temporarily, and would also make it impossible for Muñoz's successors to press farther toward independence. If that should be so, its significance for others than Puerto Ricans must be considered. Perhaps something had been discovered that would make possible the series of economic unions I had felt were the only reliable assistance we could actually hold out to our neighbors as practicable.

9

Obviously I was late in getting around to my appreciation of Muñoz's maneuver. When its significance dawned on me I was inclined to retitle it in my own mind the "Grand Conception of Muñoz Marín." I catalogue it now under that title. His Commonwealth has, I really believe, a genuine claim to be rated as a first-rate political device—one to be ranked with our federal Union and with the British Commonwealth.

The satisfactoriness of any such tour de force is measured by the way it fits the demands upon it. And see how the *estado libre asociado* answers to such a test. In the first place, the people involved are "free"—that is, they have local self-government. The defender of the old colonialism would say that all this really means is that the local politicos are free of supervision and can carry on as high-handedly as they like. [1] And it is true that most peoples emerging from colonialism have a worse government for a long time than was maintained by the metropolitan power. [2] But this is not an argument that has sufficed to arrest a separatist movement in any instance within my knowledge. And in any case the Latin Americans

[1] This is what Nicholas Roosevelt would say of our withdrawal from the Philippines, for instance (cf. *Front Row Seat*, University of Oklahoma Press, 1953), and it was what the Dutch said about the Indo-Chinese, and the French about the Tunisians and Moroccans, not to mention the British opinion of various wards (Ceylon, Malaya, the Sudan, Ghana, and India) which have been advanced toward local autonomy at a rate far faster than seemed wise to experienced colonial officers.

[2] This was demonstrably true, I believe, of Burma, of the Sudan, and, in another way, of the Gold Coast and Nigeria. India is a special case but, strictly speaking, the British administration was probably more efficient than any government will be for decades to come. And when the Dutch left Indonesia, the supervening chaos was only by exaggeration to be called government at all.

who are the neighbors for whom we feel most responsibility have long since escaped from colonial status and have had thoroughly corrupt and inefficient governments most of the time for a century. They have endured successive bullying dictatorships, however, without petitioning for a return to Spanish affiliation. And their relations with the United States have been a curious mixture of envy, reluctant acceptance of favors, and exasperation. No politician below the Rio Grande or on the continent of South America has ever thought of furthering his fortunes by suggesting any closer relationship with the United States. Many have claimed to be responsible for aid or favors, but none has ever claimed to have given aid to or done a favor for the United States, much less moved toward a closer liaison of any sort.

The Puerto Rican arrangement seems a more practical way of channeling American expertise and capital into the economies of the smaller nations than has yet been found elsewhere. The sporadic and specific attempts at betterment represented by "missions" have all been relative failures. They have helped temporarily, and occasionally have left a residue of improvement, but after withdrawal has been made the effect usually is very like abandoning a well-tended field to weeds. In a few years the effects of cultivation are nearly indiscernible. I would contend that attachments to the American system through the Washington departments would make it as unlikely that Mexico, San Salvador, Peru, or Chile would regress as that Oklahoma or Idaho should. They would become parts of the most effective mutual-aid system ever devised, with a nourishing stream of capital and expertise circulating continuously.

And see how the conception fits the patterns which the national strategy must assume. Other peoples must not be held to us without their consent—even if it is only without the consent of their demagogues; they must, however, be brought within the circle of those who have a reasonable well-being, because only such peoples are safe to live with even as distant neighbors. The fact that political hegemony is renounced frees us from fear of revolutions or the need to suppress them. The politicos can carry on pretty much as they like, provided they leave the joint services alone—just as no state governor can go too far in using federal state-aid funds for his own purposes.

Poverty-stricken neighbors belong back in the same era as exploited factory labor. Both are poor customers, poor co-operators, and unreliable citizens. Americans need to have the underdeveloped people in the world advance so that they can live with them in mutual respect and security. If they have some feeling about gratitude, they had better give it up. It will not be forthcoming. Moreover, their own interests are involved. If thanks are given, good; but if they are not, the operation is still a necessary one with which sentiment ought not to interfere.

That this will cost a good deal is generally acknowledged. But that the cost will be less than periodic intervention is obvious; it will even be less than the sporadic assistances which will inevitably be made from time to time as crises have to be met. But there has not been a unanimous agreement as to how the job ought to be done. To the discussion about this, Muñoz's conception has made a significant contribution.

President Truman's proposal turned out to be no more than a vague idea. He did not know whether what he had in mind could be done or how it ought to be done. And because of this he allowed the whole matter to be confused by those who thought they saw in it the chance to revive the old financial imperialism. In the climate that soon supervened, this persistent longing for the old satisfactions of isolation, in an age when there could be none, perverted the whole movement. Actually very little of permanent benefit came of it. This petering out was unfortunately what had so often happened. What was lacking was a sound and practicable device for the close association that would increase others' well-being in a way and at a cost acceptable to the recipients and to the givers as well. The way was found in Puerto Rico; it was found, moreover, without any deliberate approach to an invention that would suit American needs. Nevertheless, the device is now in being and waits further use.

What is of greatest interest here is how this really amazing achievement was conceived and by what manipulations it was brought about. When this kind of reconstruction is attempted several difficulties arise. For example, Muñoz could not let anyone know what his ultimate purpose was: neither the continentals, because they would conclude that what he had in mind was independence under another name and would resent the exploitation of American generosity; nor the Puerto Ricans, because they thought in stereotypes—statehood or independence. Besides, a politician cannot afford to risk very much on a venture whose outcome is doubtful. If it goes wrong, his identity with it can cost him his leadership.

Muñoz therefore had to fall back during all the preliminaries on vagueness and indirection and leave most of the preparatory moves to those who would make them for other reasons. He could restrain here and push there, feeling for one opening after another, but he could not disclose his intention and lay out a program. The whole approach had to be opportunistic and apparently purposeless. It is doubtful whether, until the last moves became possible, he could have felt that the whole design would really work out in his time. It required so unlikely a concurrence of events, so general a contribution to the scheme by many who were not aware that there *was* a scheme, that he can hardly have been sure of a quick or complete success. Yet, a review of the events shows that the developments followed each other in mounting sequence until the climax was reached in the Constitution of the Commonwealth and power slipped into his hands.

It is one of the necessities of such an enterprise that its manipulator shall keep himself free of all entanglements that might interfere, and that he shall, with the utmost vigilance, guard himself on all flanks. So Muñoz used men and groups of men as expendables. This included the inventors of the *estado libre* idea, who would never be credited with their contribution to political engineering. His view must have been that if his party members were loyal to Puerto Rico they required no reward, and if they were loyal to him they were simply more dependable and useful. In any case, for so overmastering an objective no one had any right to expect the ordinary rules of conduct to govern the master manipulator. So by the time the accomplishment was complete only a few were left of the original members who had joined to start the *Popular* movement.

These old-timers were still alive—most of them—when the Commonwealth came into being, but they were in exile from the policy centers and knew themselves for discarded instruments. They met sometimes and talked over past battles, living again the excitements of insurgency. Some of them had sacrificed years, some fortunes, in what they had thought of as a cause. Strangely, now, they realized that, although their loyalties had been engaged so deeply as to jeopardize any other career they might have had, although they had neglected families, businesses, or professions, and although they had worked through months and years of tension, they would be hard put to say just what they had suffered all this for—what, exactly, had been their motives.

Only a few, even after the most outrageous treatment, became embittered, and only a few ever thought of challenging Muñoz's leadership once they had accepted it. It is true that this seems to be a characteristic of all "movements," especially political ones, whose members have emerged into the possession of power. There is, in the end, only one survivor. He has used and discarded, or submerged and humiliated, many of those who began with him and were fired by the same beginning zeal, and even those who joined somewhere along the way with all the fervor of converts. Zealous fellows are not trustworthy, and trusted ones begin to understand too much of the whole design. Unless they are unquestioning and at the same time usefully shrewd manipulators, they sooner or later must be excluded from the leader's confidence.

Muñoz was like La Guardia and Roosevelt in this. There might appear to be a good deal of camaraderie in that agreeably fierce back-to-back fighting which men love, but sooner or later the circle narrowed, or another formed to which some old members were not admitted. They might go on enjoying the retrospect of mighty engagements with a common enemy, but actually they were has-beens and they knew it. La Guardia, like Roosevelt, had fewer friends with every year he lived, as ordinary men know friendship. And Muñoz, because he was like the others, only more so, also had few. He had followers; he had temporary confidants; he even had a very few colleagues who seemed to survive through the years. But hardly any of them thought that the leader would defend them, reward them, be grateful to them, return their loyalty, or hesitate to punish or to exile them whenever it would be convenient to the cause or to himself. And there was almost complete acceptance of the necessity for this ruthlessness. Politicians understand politics, even lowly ones who ask only the privilege of serving.

Detachment is a characteristic of leadership, and a very necessary one. It may be so essential that it conditions political achievement. But this, like other elements of success, can be identified; but not too definitely. Measurement is hardly to be thought of. To every apparent trait many exceptions turn up, and their elusiveness is exasperating. The present case is typical. The conception was generated in a solitary mind, scheming complicated schemes, allowing them to half materialize and be studied in prospective reverie, trying and fitting them in a kind of vision to the imagined circumstances of the future.

This is the creative political process. It differs somewhat from many other creative acts; it has no physical manifestation and is not associated with manual dexterity as is painting, writing, or designing. It has to have time and scope. Many elements go into its making, much experience, judgments concerning acceptability, practical estimates of its utility, and so on. But political creativeness is facilitated by consultation perhaps more than any other kind. Not only can assistance be helpful in tracing precedents and formulating devices, but the idea trying to be born can be eased into the world more smoothly if its originator can talk about it over and over. The necessities of communication help what is coming into being to find its final shape.

But a political leader is deprived of most of this assistance in his really large formulations. He is the center of interested attention. It is worth something to many people—and it is vital to the interests of some—to be able to know what he is likely to adopt as policy. They will be vigilant to further or to circumvent, as their own interests dictate, anything he may suggest. He must guard himself, therefore, from that penetration of his mind that will be the chief preoccupation of many of his helpers and associates. Often he will have to take the immense trouble involved in elaborate deception.

These are inevitable handicaps. The political chieftain lives within bindings that are never loosened and under stresses that are never relieved. There are, of course, always parts of his intention that can—and, indeed, must be—discussed, first with intimates, and then, if they develop so far, with the public. For it is seldom that anything of importance can be done, especially if it is novel, without preparing opinion to receive it. This may involve a routine of considerable complexity. Even the reactions of trusted advisers have to be shrewdly regarded and assessed. The closest intimates may have standards of judgment the leader does not want used in the particular case, and he cannot always say so. He may have to guess, to translate, and to transpose if he is to learn what he wants to learn. Then there may follow serious consideration of the means for introduction to the public. This may be also by indirection; in fact, the older and therefore the more involved the leader is in a web of loyalties, commitments, and half-realized projects, the more cautious and tentative he will be. And then it may seem expedient to entrust the introduction of a near conception to no more than one subordinate, who can, if necessary, be repudiated. This device is so often used that it has a familiar name: "the trial balloon."

Only when public reception is judged to have been favorable will the novel suggestion be cautiously acknowledged by the leader. If the reaction is enthusiastic, the acknowledgment of authorship will need to be accelerated. There is, indeed, a very nice calculation involved here concerning timing, for which there is, so far as I know, no guide. This is one of those rule-of-thumb techniques that the politician exercises instinctively, although it must be said that with none of them is the instinct infallible. It often has to be said of their performance that it could have been better done.

This is one of those illustrations, frequently available in the art of politics, of apparently inevitable but annoying inefficiency. There is nearly always gross waste: the waste is traceable to infirmity of judgment; and infirmity of judgment is again traceable to the almost completely subjective nature of the elements that operate in the deciding process. Too much is given for what is gained. The effort expended in contriving, in maneuvering, in securing approval is far more than is necessary to the result. There is no trustworthy measure, until afterward, of progress toward acceptance; and as submission to decision—electoral, legislative, or merely in public opinion —approaches, there tends to be a panic conviction that more must be done. The worst of this is that any newly adopted effort to overwhelm indifference or opposition is apt also to overwhelm scruple and be put into effect by the use of doubtful means. These may return sometime as torments. This is when compromise and concession take command and the scheme is modified.

What a life! the ordinary man will say. Yes, what a life! But many men feel an irresistible compulsion to enter on it and to fight their way to its upper levels with the hope of reaching a position of power. It is not by any means always those who are best equipped who reach the top echelons. Accident and circumstance play a part —sometimes, it seems, a preponderant part. Political history is full of "stuffed shirts," stooges for powerful bosses or interests who need a "front." There have been many such Mayors, Governors, and even Presidents. My three, however, will never be numbered among this list by anyone. They will be in quite a different list: Johnson, Hunt, Jones, Low, Whitlock, Heney, Mitchel—Mayors; Randolph, Henry, Pinchot, Hughes, Smith—Governors; and Washington, Jefferson, Jackson, Lincoln, Wilson, and Theodore Roosevelt—Presidents. The differences here, difficult to identify as generalities, are yet recognizable when what is looked for is likeness of habit, of social skill, political effectiveness, and public support.

Muñoz will no doubt wonder in age—as La Guardia and Roosevelt must have done, although neither of them lived to be old enough for real contemplation and assessment, when a man sits in the sun and fights over old battles in his mind—whether his pains and sacrifices were worth what he gained. He had to give up so much, contrive so constantly, submit to such demanding disciplines! And for what? So that, at the peak of power, he could go on with the same regime, grown now more taut and routinized, knowing that every month and every year he grew less rather than more effective, being thus the victim, as others were the beneficiaries, of his sacrifices and efforts. And yet, confined as he was, he had always to find new resources of imagination, to invent new devices, and to exert exhaustingly the magic of public persuasion.

The trappings and routines of power, after a while, are not the compensation that they were at first. Gradually they become bindings and ties; finally they become something submitted to and undergone with apathy, even with resentment. The horrible fatigues of ceremonial, fiercely resented as they often are, finally have their way and are no longer even evaded. The man has become the prisoner of office. The small, nagging urge that started him off has landed him in a padded cell—a cell padded with plush, it is true, but one in which he must perform, it seems to him, as an animal does on his treadmill, routines prescribed by tradition and circumstances.

Considering, if he ever has time any more for considering, how the achievements came about for which he will be blessed by posterity, or how the mistakes were made for which he will not be forgiven, he is likely to be almost as puzzled as the observer who is unable to reach any conclusions because he can never uncover the hidden processes he would need to know.

With all three of my specimens of the political genus, I was at one time or another able to sit down and try to carry back to its origins and trace through to its conclusion some policy of importance. I found them not much more certain than I myself, after I had studied the matter, as to why the process had been conducted as it was. And I have the feeling that if I had tried this with the greatest achievement of each—Muñoz with the Grand Conception, La Guardia with the Charter of '36, Roosevelt with Social Security or the United Nations—I should have had less success than I had with the relatively minor matters about which I was able to inquire and to which I could direct their reminiscent probings.

10

Take the Grand Conception as a political tour de force and imagine
a re-creation of its progress. Puerto Rico was in limbo when Muñoz's
imagination must have begun to evolve the preconfiguration of the
later scheme. Long before the idea began to take shape it must have
existed in embryo in his mind, perhaps as something whirling and
twisting just beyond reach, perhaps as a half-recalled suggestion of
his father. Or it may have been inspired by the Cordero group's
suggestions; very likely they were at least a stimulus. Puerto Rico
at that time, as some wit described it—referring to an old melo-
drama revived in the twenties—"was neither wife, maid, nor widow."
There were always a few members of the Washington government
who would have made an honest woman of her; but there were
difficulties about either of the obvious extreme choices—statehood
or independence—that made progress toward either very difficult.
And inertia was a weight no casual interest could lift. For Muñoz
these were years of inertia too.

The first appearance of his *Popular* party was not until 1938; its
first victory was in 1940. [1] The organization and growth of the
party were coincident with and dependent upon the New Deal
in the United States. Muñoz realized that something basic had hap-

---

[1] When he joined the Socialist party of Iglesias in 1918, nothing came of it. He
went back to New York and stayed there until 1932. In that year, again in
Puerto Rico, he made up with Barcelo, the *Liberal* leader, and was elected to
the Senate. But he could not stay long in the shadow of so old-fashioned a
politico; he was soon restive. He broke with Barcelo, was expelled from the
Liberal party, and formed the *Acción Social Independentista*. This was composed mainly of strongly pro-independence *Liberales*.

Even then, however, he was shy of outright independence. That his co-
expellees were *independentistas* made them his companions, and they were the
nucleus of the *Popular* party formed in 1938, but he did not accept commitment
to their definition of status. He evidently felt that there was no future in it.

pened in 1932 and he soon saw in it, after his long wait, the possibility of achieving his first goals. If he could identify himself and his group with the new Washington forces, he would leave the old politicos, and especially the *Republicanos,* in an embarrassing position. They would have been maneuvered into opposing the sources of aid. This is pretty much what happened in the years 1936–40. Harry Hopkins' successive relief organizations burgeoned in Puerto Rico as they did in the States; so did the agricultural agencies; and because Puerto Rico was in more misery there was more to be done and they assumed a greater importance. This involved considerable employment in government agencies, not to mention work relief. And it was the first expansion of this sort in Puerto Rico for many years. Control of the appointments to these agencies could make or break a political leader, and a reputation for influencing the distribution of relief could give him immense influence. Muñoz set out to gain control. His struggle was ferocious but indecisive.

It was not until 1941 that a New Dealer—myself—was sent to occupy the governorship. The first Governor to be sent by Roosevelt in 1933 had been one of those fantastic characters who turn up once in a while in such posts. He had been given the job on the recommendation of Ed Flynn in return for a campaign contribution and because Flynn conceived that being a Catholic was the only qualification necessary. He took his place at once as an example of the ineptness of democracies in colonial affairs. He did not last long; and because of the row he caused, the President appointed—as he was inclined to do in a tight spot—a retired Army general. This was Blanton Winship, who, with the best intentions, failed to establish himself in Puerto Rican regard as a friend, except, of course, of those conservatives who were losing their grip on insular affairs. After six rather troubled years he was succeeded by a retired admiral, William D. Leahy, who soon left to become Ambassador to France. Finally, for a few months, Guy Swope, a lame-duck congressman from Pennsylvania, held the post. He found the difficulties unpleasant and preferred a job in Washington. I became Governor in September of 1941, Muñoz's first real ally as head of the executive branch, after Roosevelt had been President for eight years.

This curious series of inept appointments would have caused a revolution in Puerto Rico if it had not been for the operations of the relief organizations. The Roosevelt Governors before 1940 were allies of the old elite, that combination of landowners, capitalists, merchants, and politicians, which had had the insular economy as well as the government in their power for so long. Muñoz could do nothing with them, and especially when he had not yet got control of the legislature. And how could he ever get a majority there unless he could build up a party? To do this he needed patronage and some basis for promising to better the lot of the miserable masses to whom he must appeal.

Beginning in 1934, a really vigorous attack on the causes of poverty had been started, not nearly extensive enough, but still properly conceived and capably directed. The agency for this was the Puerto Rican Reconstruction Administration (P.R.R.A.), and it planned extensive public works which the relief organizations, even under the sympathetic and imaginative guidance of James and Dorothy Bourne, Hopkins' representatives, could not undertake. After the transfer to the Department of the Interior in 1934 of the Division of Territories, this organization came under the general aegis of Harold Ickes, and its immediate contacts with Puerto Rico were made by another old-time Progressive who became director of the division, Ernest Gruening. Muñoz, desperately disappointed that the executive branch should still rest firmly in the hands of the old elite, set out to capture the new emergency organization. Gruening co-operated with him at first, but what he felt was a thoroughly reprehensible greediness on the part of Muñoz offended him presently, and he felt forced to set up relations with Governor Winship and his friends. Muñoz's use of the emergency organization seems to have been considerable—or his claims were considerable—but it was far from being his to dispose of as he liked.

Winship as Governor had been so unpopular, even with the copious flow of relief funds to the poor, that he was often in physical danger when he traveled about the island, and twice there were outbreaks of a violence that was always smoldering just below the surface. The *nacionalistas*, so called, were able to say that what they had continuously contended was obviously true—no matter what the regime in the United States, Puerto Rico would be treated just the same. There was no solution but independence, and that status could be reached only by force. President Roosevelt, in the press of other affairs was insensitive to what was going on in Puerto Rico and slow to appreciate its causes. He was inclined to resent what seemed to him an ungrateful treatment of his Governors, one after the other.

Winship and Leahy did not contribute to understanding. They were obtuse and conservative. They pictured the Puerto Ricans to the President as unruly and anti-American; and he was inclined to some such solution as was being so irresponsibly reached—with his complete concurrence, it must be said—for the Philippines. But Puerto Rico, he felt, was not nearly so likely to make any kind of showing if turned loose and was likely to become one more troublesome independent nation in the Caribbean. He was obviously, in these years, temporizing. There was a conflict in his mind also between two of his strongest instincts—the one for the freedom of all peoples, a very American feeling, and the other for the tradition of colonialism, which he got from his aristocratic origins and his Navy affiliations. Also, from his Navy traditions, he had the strong view that the Caribbean was an American lake, its islands a shield for the Panama Canal, and Puerto Rico, with its military and naval establishments, the key to the Canal's defense. He had had some Haitian experiences when he had been Assistant Secretary of the Navy which seem to have influenced his view of Puerto Rico. This was a mistaken judgment but one he was not to give up easily; Puerto Ricans were far from being Haitians.

Muñoz did not know about this semi-imperialist Roosevelt. He knew the President only as a New Dealer, and he was baffled by his tendency to appoint military reactionaries and to support them in anti-New Deal measures. He was certain that he saw his way to success with Ickes, but even there he was defeated by Gruening's reaction to his political demands—which, it must be believed, were far from subtle or reasonable. He was a young man in a hurry, and such young men are not very nice. [2]

[2] It may be necessary to explain further that when the New Deal began in the United States and relief organizations began to be set up it was soon acknowledged that Puerto Rico needed the same sort of assistance and needed it worse. The unemployment and the miseries of poverty were called to everyone's attention by Governor Winship, who, if he felt that people should be docile and orderly, felt also that they should be fed and clothed. Two separate undertakings were begun. Hopkins' emergency relief organization established a Puerto Rican branch at once, and a little later a Puerto Rican Reconstruction Administration was established with a more fundamental purpose—to see whether something could not be done to stimulate economic activity, to start new

It was far from clear to him how he could proceed. But anyway he was committed to the struggle; and his only chance, even though he lacked any of the supports he ought to have or any of the access to jobs or funds so necessary to organization, was to identify himself as a New Dealer. He had nothing, but he must go on. If he was at first defeated by his own awkwardness, he nevertheless persisted. The dilettante in every other pursuit now found in politics reserves of stubborn determination.

In spite of—or perhaps because of—his dedication and single-mindedness, these were uneasy years in the wilderness for Muñoz, much like those both Roosevelt and La Guardia also had to endure. Such interludes are important to political figures. They either contribute to maturity or lead to degeneration. They are often the decisive testing times. There is an epic quality to the tales told by the old-timers among the *Populares* of the struggles, during this period, to become established, of the expedients adopted, and of the sacrifices of the faithful. There is also a curious ambivalence in what they have to say about the role and the behavior of Muñoz. They see quite clearly, even through the mists of nostalgia, that there were ignoble passages, that a certain amount of double-crossing went on, and that supporters were made use of whose aims and motives were questionable. For much of this they now blame Muñoz. He was likely to be at one moment abnormally pessimistic and at another unreasonably cheerful and careless. He would not or could not help in raising funds; when something had been gathered together with the most sacrificing effort, he squandered it regally and without much relation to its bearing on the cause—often for his personal gratification. This is what they are apt to say.

And yet, if one or more of them can be caught in a reminiscent mood, all these doubts and questions are sooner or later overridden by their certainty that there was a *cause*, even if it was not yet defined, and that it was worth working for even if the immediate aims were mostly negative—such as overthrowing the old politicos and taking their places. In bitter moods they feel that they were used

---

industries, to diversify farming, to carry out public works—power plants, sewage and water systems, housing, schools, roads, hospitals—and much of value was accomplished. Unfortunately the problems were of such a magnitude and politics was such a problem that what was done was lost in the rising volume of need.

by Muñoz to further his appetite for power; in more reflective and judicial moments they see that much was gained for Puerto Rico even though they themselves were expended.

There was a kind of informal *Popular* headquarters at a resort near Cidra in the interior of the island. This was not a plush place. It had cabins for overnight visitors and an outdoor *cafetín*. There were not many such retreats in those days in so poor a country, and this one was popular. Curiously, it was owned and operated by a continental —Elmer Ellsworth—who, in spite of having a foreign origin, was a long-time resident and, what was more relevant, a man of indignation. The irresponsibility of upper-class Puerto Ricans had long seemed to him intolerable. The plantocracy exploited those who worked in their enterprises, and they were vigilant to prevent any change that would disturb these arrangements. It was a case, unfortunately familiar in social history, of putting individual interests above social ones. And although Ellsworth was a landowner and planter himself, he joined eagerly with those who were conspiring to overthrow the regime of the old elite. He was one of the first and most effective of the *Populares*.

There was Jesús Piñero, also, who was often among the crowd at Treasure Island. He was a landowner but similarly disaffected, and he became, in the early days, a kind of partner with Ellsworth in working for the cause. Together they collected funds and got signatures to petitions, for which purpose they traveled endlessly, organizing the faithful and making converts. Then there was Antonio Fernós Isern, a doctor who had been assistant commissioner of health under a former administration but was disillusioned concerning any possibility of betterment without political overturn. Also there were several lawyers; for instance, Benigno Fernández García with the fire of righteous anger burning in his slight body; Rafael Buscaglia, later to be the first *Popular* treasurer; and the youthful Jaime Benítez, future Rector of the university, who was the intellectual shadow of Muñoz throughout the difficult years. Among the other lawyers were Samuel Quiñones, Benjamín Ortiz, and Ernesto Ramos Antonini. Manuel Pérez, the gentle, scholarly student of labor conditions, supplied such ammunition as was needed concerning conditions everyone knew about but very few troubled to define. Then there was Manuel Seoane in Caguas, superbly knowledgeable and effective local leader who became Mayor of his city and, because he felt his duty lay there, refused larger responsibilities; Grillasca in Ponce was another local politico who became and remained Mayor of his city throughout the formative years.

Besides Jaime Benítez, there were others who, because they were young and ardent, were useful to Muñoz as no older ally could be, among them Roberto Sánchez Vilella, Sol Descartes, Rafael Picó, Rafael Cordero, and Victor Gutiérrez Franqui. Most difficult of all to work with, because hardest to control, were the crowd of intransigent *independentistas* who had formed the *Acción Social* and who would rise to power along with Muñoz and never cease plotting and intriguing for his permanent commitment to their movement. For to them the party was everything—as it is to Communists—and individuals nothing. The others were patriots but they did not confuse ends with means. They were willing to allow Muñoz to define and redefine the means so long as they could be confident that the ends of economic and social betterment were being sought.

After the years of struggle, very few of the young people—mostly university instructors under the old regime—would have survived into more serene years. Picó would be treasurer; Descartes, Chairman of the Water Resources Authority; Cordero, Controller. Of the older allies, several would have died, but most of the rest would have been discarded. Piñero, after having been interim Governor, would have died in disfavor; Seoane, Ellsworth, Gutiérrez Franqui, and Jaime Benítez (after having so brilliantly brought the university into good repute) would have been ousted. Quiñones and Ramos Antonini would be legislative leaders still and Fernós Isern would be the Resident Commissioner in Washington. But no more than could gather in a small room would still be in office.

This tendency to slough off or to divert supporters who are troublesome is characteristic of politicians who rise to power. There have been some in American history who would have done better to slough off more of their followers—Grant, Harding, and Truman, for instance. It must be said that it is only the less notable leaders who have been faithful to their friendships. My three were ruthless discarders, although sometimes cowardly about administering the ouster themselves. It is a useful political generalization that notes the frequency with which the successful follow the rule of punishing friends and rewarding enemies. The friends, it seems to be concluded, have nowhere else to go, and the enemies can perhaps be conciliated.

The electoral victory of 1940 was, in spite of all the difficulties, a decisive one for Muñoz, and that of 1944 almost unprecedented in the history of representative government. Even in 1940 the *Populares* won control of one house of the legislature and lacked only the few votes of the *Liberal* remnant to control the other. They were on their way to the overwhelming victory of 1944 which left their opponents with two representatives in each House.

II

Muñoz offers an interesting illustration, quite typical, of a leader who attained the goal he had set for himself relatively early in his career and then was forced to resort to spectacular invention to avoid retirement, his work completed long before he was ready. La Guardia to a less degree had the same experience; after achieving the Charter of 1936, everything was anticlimactic for him in New York. So much so that entirely new ambitions shaped themselves in his head. He never attained them, but they were completely formed. Roosevelt never really triumphed over depression, but he conquered the fears it laid on the American spirit and in 1936 got the electoral ratification of his efforts. By that time the defeat of the dictators had displaced the New Deal as his goal; before victory arrived, organization for peace had become paramount in his mind. He died with both these last achievements in sight but not yet secure. Roosevelt did not invent war to replace depression. But war did make him indispensable again as he had been before. They were both inevitable, perhaps, but more inevitable because Roosevelt was President.

Richard Hofstadter [1] has pointed out how characteristic this was of Roosevelt. The New Deal did not turn out to be what he intended, although he never admitted it, nor was the United Nations his conception of world organization. He was an opportunist—that is, he was indifferent concerning the means to his ends. Mr. Hofstadter had some difficulty with this and so failed to rate highly enough Roosevelt's persistence and determination in pursuit of his real objectives. These, it is concluded, really come down to personal power. And it is easy to interpret the careers of most successful politicians in this way. All of my three were suspected of this duplicity. It is, however,

[1] In *The American Political Tradition* (New York: Knopf, 1948).

far too simple a formula. Each had objectives of vast importance quite outside his own interests. He may have become identified with these interests. In fact, all of them did. But the objectives were, nevertheless, important.

Muñoz was thus more or less at a loss after the Commonwealth came into existence. Nothing was in sight that was worthy of his powers. He could devote himself to administration, which he did; but for politicians with statesmanlike stature, that kind of thing is never enough. He had now to ask himself: What further?

Leading public men are driven by compulsions which they themselves may very well not understand, since few men can be their own analysts. But it cannot be accidental that issues of first importance turn up one after another in their careers. The suspicion that they are induced is perhaps natural; no less a person than Charles A. Beard was convinced that President Roosevelt deliberately brought on World War II. He stopped this side of attributing a political motive—that some issue was necessary at that stage of the Roosevelt career and that the war was invented and provoked. But there were plenty of others who did not hesitate to make such a suggestion.

I should like to advance the tentative idea that what the political careerist will do when one much-advertised goal is attained, and a flat and uninteresting period follows, is likely to be one of two things —to which I shall come. But I must first remark that I exclude settling down to routine. Prodigies of detailed work are possible, evidently, to the most unlikely of men. None of my three, for instance, was notably industrious before he came to the work to which nature called him. On the contrary, all of them had the opposite repute among their acquaintances, one in one way, the others in other ways. Roosevelt slacked his law work and was more industrious at his hobbies than at his profession, and this was true in the out-of-office interludes on his way to the presidency. La Guardia interspersed the activities of a one-man legal-aid bureau with intervals of indulgence when he was out of a job. These were completely at variance with the prolonged spells of intense application to his job which became legendary among his associates in office. He seemed to change personality too. The La Guardia of congressional days was a warm and outgoing person always at the service of friendship; thoughtful, kind, modest, inclined to hero worship, and ready at any time to share a good dinner and to exploit the companionship of the bottle. The La Guardia who was Mayor was very often dour and suspicious, inclined to tantrums at the expense of friends, puritanical, extremely critical, and with his mind centered more than he realized in himself and his fortunes, because he so fully identified these with the interests of the public.

Similar observations can be made about Muñoz. The bohemian who, above all else, loved a *pasadía* with friends, allowed himself such a pleasure only occasionally after he became Governor. Of the old easy days when he was not yet in office, or when he was a legislator, there are innumerable tales. He could outtalk, outdrink, and outstay the hardiest of his followers or any visitors there might be. Company was furnished for him in relays. He was seldom ready to go home before the rising sun reminded him that another day impended. It seemed to him a godly gift to be able to sit in a large circle, on the sand or the grass, on the beach or in the hills, trade wind susurrating in the palms, an ample supply of variegated liquors within sight, someone to fill his glass before it emptied, and just to talk. Some people are born talkers, and he was one of them.

All this changed when he became Governor. His associates told me of his reform as though they spoke of a miracle. And in this he was like the others; all my three became literally prodigious workers in office. This does come to an end, however, when all is set and on the way. Politicians are not happy administrators. They can do it. But they will not keep it up if no new undertaking is involved.

The two sorts of enterprises a politician of the order I am here considering may enter on when he suddenly discovers himself to have attained the goal toward which he has for a long time been striving are (1) a new and more honorific office, or (2) a new and more grandiose undertaking. He must have in prospect one or the other. He may not stand still. If he does he will not only be bored to distraction but will also be likely to decline very quickly as a politician. This is because an opportunity will be given to some creative and ambitious rival. The general apprehension that a leader is not moving quickly communicates itself to numerous would-be contenders for his office who have hitherto been discouraged or deflected by the obvious impossibility of displacing him.

This may be something he will have to contend with anyway, no matter how vigorously he may be acting. His position will be so much envied that it will be remarkable rather than otherwise if some challenger within his own party does not arise. There will almost always be someone whose ego has been enlarged by lesser victories, who has marked out for himself the premier place, and who realizes that delay will be fatal. Good judgment may tell him that success is unlikely; nevertheless, he will be moved to try. La Follette furnished this kind of opposition to Coolidge, Huey Long offered it to Roosevelt, and McCarthy to Eisenhower. La Guardia himself was a Republican maverick. Muñoz played this role in his early days, and when he was Governor his most serious problems of rivalry were within rather than without the party.

But Muñoz, having the soundest of political instincts, did not allow events to reach that state of rest which invites competition. That he had not attained his ambition only to enjoy the serene joys of office was demonstrated again and again. His associates were always conscious that his mind was moving restlessly and that he was exploring possibilities. No one in Puerto Rico knew so quickly when dissatisfactions began to form; no one was so clever in creating diversions. But these were not always merely diversions. They might be in pursuit of defensible objectives, ones people would understand and approve, and ones he could win after a clamorous battle.

The undertaking of most consequence in the years following the establishment of the Commonwealth was that of raising the level of living. In most instances the process of economic development goes along beneath the surface of political events, and only its more dramatic aberrations furnish political opportunities. One such opportunity in recent years had been furnished by the Great Depression of 1929 and after, which had unseated Hoover and given Roosevelt his chance. This kind of thing had happened before in American history but was not so likely to happen again—not, at least, in such dramatic form. The bulwarks built by Roosevelt were not altogether proof against conservative sabotage, but it was unlikely that after his work was done such a calamity as 1929 would happen again. The improbability of disaster might prove to be a severe handicap for the Democrats, since the Republicans had pretty well established their claim to be the party of prosperity.

The Republican claim was thoroughly phony; reactionary administration in Washington had been responsible for allowing the events of 1929 to run into those of 1932, when all the banks had had to close at once; but in these matters facts and logic are of less weight than popular misconception. Americans were convinced that the Republicans were safe and sane; they were conservatives. The Democrats were less reliable; they had ideas; they were, in a later phrase, "eggheads." They had, when President Truman retired, bequeathed prosperity to Eisenhower and the Republicans. The general impression was that it was only necessary not to disturb it, which the Republicans were not likely to do. So they were given power in 1952, and they would keep it unless they took liberties with Social Security or allowed administered-price inflation to create social pressures they could not check, and so brought on another sort of depression.

I mention this because it was a major conditioning factor of the climate within which Muñoz moved. The Republicans were likely to be in power in Washington for some time to come. But this would be by a narrow margin. Probably the Democrats would control the Congress while the Republicans controlled the Executive. He must therefore move cautiously, offending neither, yet commending himself to both, especially since his next major move at home was to be in the direction of more autonomy. These conditions called for a delicate and interesting series of maneuvers. They were carried out almost perfectly, and several of them at least were not only delicate but breath-takingly bold. It is demonstrable, on the whole, that Muñoz's was a career of classically irregular regularity.

I 2

It is a source of regret to me that I did not know La Guardia more intimately before 1938, when I was appointed by him to be head of the Planning Department of New York City and chairman of the Planning Commission. We regarded each other as friends, but actually we knew each other only casually, mostly as like-minded progressives, only occasionally as leisure-time companions. When I joined his administration he had already been Mayor for four years and was one of the best-known figures in American public life. He could be said also, at fifty-six, to be an old hand at politics. Besides his stormy presidency of the Board of Aldermen (1919–21), he had been elected no less than seven times to the Congress, and he had been defeated in strenuous contests twice for the Congress (1914 and 1932) and once for the mayoralty. His score, finally, was three defeats and eleven wins. In 1938 ten of these were behind him; there was one more victory to come. He was an old and experienced hand in the latter part of his career.

One of his defeats had been at the beginning, when he had been a brash youngster. The nomination in the 12th New York District had been given him because no one else would run—it was fantastic to think a Republican might win in lower Manhattan! His loss by a narrow margin had been almost as good as winning because he had multiplied by several times the usual Republican showing. Also, his strenuous campaign had got him the attention of the professionals and he was given another and better chance. His other loss was accounted for by the Democratic landslide of 1932, but for which he might have won in that year. So it could be argued that he had lost only once in circumstances that made winning at all likely. That was in 1929, when as the Fusion candidate for Mayor

he lost to Tammany's Jimmy Walker, then at the height of his popularity and not yet discredited by the inexorable exposures of Samuel
Seabury, the distinguished counsel for the Hofstadter Investigating
Committee of the New York State legislature. Even this loss was
no disgrace, but a win would have been not quite impossible.

This was the only one of La Guardia's contests of which it had
to be said in retrospect that it ought not to have been undertaken.
There were several others that in prospect seemed so to nearly
everyone except himself; but those he won, showing that his electoral instinct was much more reliable than that of his advisers. He
was not so happily selective in seeking and taking appointments. He
became, late in his career, too eager for preferment; but as Mayor
he had the sense not to seek a fourth term, and that must be
counted as discreet. He might not have won that contest: there
had been many disaffections, his machine had broken down, and in
those post-war months the city's affairs were in very bad order.

La Guardia by then had given what he had to give; conditions
had changed and he was no longer adaptable. Besides, he was disappointed, sick, and irritable. His ambitions in New York had long
since been sated, and opening after opening to larger Washington
enterprises had closed in his face. The war had run its course without him (except as chairman of the American section of the U.S.-
Canadian Permanent Joint Board on Defense and as director, for a
while, of Civilian Defense). He had found it very hard not to have
a more prominent part in the vast mobilization and felt himself
ill used. He went unhappily into retirement after a few months as
head of the United Nations Relief and Rehabilitation Administration (UNRRA) and an ambassadorial assignment at a temporary
post; but he did not go without a noisy show of carping. It was
typical that he made life miserable for his successor until death took
him in September 1947.

When I worked in the city administration he was not yet resigned
to holding on in New York. Indeed he was just approaching his bid
for assignments of a grander sort. He was definitely hopeful of
recognition by Roosevelt. And I am still at a loss to know just why
his ambitions were not satisfied. The President told me more than
once while the unsatisfactory Woodring was Secretary of War and
the responsibilities of a very probable conflict were being piled on
the department that La Guardia was just what was needed. He was

a spectacular success as Mayor of New York—a vast operation; he was a figure of national prominence, almost as well known as the President himself; he was not a Democrat but a Progressive-Republican with a majority following of his own in the country's biggest city. He was known to admire the President extravagantly, even if a little enviously, and could therefore be used in the rough and ruthless way customary with senior politicians. He himself was rough and ruthless with his subordinates and would therefore understand. On the whole, the balance was very much in Fiorello's favor, the President said. But he also said that not everyone agreed that this was so—"the Democrats," he added with a rather tired smile.

Of course Stimson was chosen instead, a very different kind of man. La Guardia was made director of Civilian Defense and chairman of the American section of the U.S.-Canadian Joint Defense Board, but these were consolation appointments. The work with the Canadians had dignity and circumstance, but the Civilian Defense job went wrong from the first. Within a matter of months it had somehow become a subject of ridicule and had done him no end of harm. This was partly because he was so obviously anxious to inflate its importance. He used somewhat the same methods which in New York had won him that curious affectionate but disparaging respect that made competition with him so discouraging for all the other politicians. Running to fires in helmet and rubber boots, answering police calls, wielding a sledge on confiscated slot machines, and screaming at his commissioners or his colleagues on the Board of Estimate—these were well-publicized characteristics of his behavior. [1] He was a scold, a nosy interferer, a quick-tempered tyrant to

---

[1] Robert Moses catalogued them as follows: . . . *rushing to fires, reading the comics, leading the band, helping Grover Whalen to greet trained seals fresh from swimming the English Channel, jeering at stuffy tycoons knee-deep in soft rugs in Park and Fifth Avenue clubs or at "tinhorns" in the less elegant bistros, crucifying a market inspector for accepting a cheap necktie from a pushcart peddler, acting as a committing magistrate to pillory a welfare inspector who did a favor for somebody on relief . . . firing a faithful, if sometimes sappy, secretary for getting tight, driving the gay hurdy-gurdies from the streets, screaming obscenities at Mussolini's Virginio Gayda over the Italian trans-Atlantic radio, denouncing the Greyhound bus officials as "Grey Muts"* . . . *berating offending City Hall reporters, taking away the policemen's clubs, directing traffic, laying out airports, acting as impresario of the City Center, proposing with impish glee to hang the wet wash in the back of Gracie Mansion where everyone in Carl Shurz Park could see the short and simple flannels of*

all his subordinates. But he was impervious to any interest but the city's; he led an almost puritanical existence, he sweated over his budget, and he struggled visibly to increase the amenities available to citizens. These were also well-publicized habits.

No one who really knew ever said that La Guardia was an efficient administrator; but it was something in New York, after years of Walker and O'Brien, to have an intelligent, honest, and devoted one. And allowances were made. During his first two terms the city was his. He played on its emotions, amused it, abused its crooks, built up its services, and watched its funds. He was the first reform Mayor ever to be re-elected. He appeared to achieve his success without making any commitments or incurring any embarrassing obligations. He shouted picturesque denunciations at all politicians and meanwhile operated as slick and economical a vote-getting device as an American city ever saw. His hard core of foreign-born support grew rather than diminished, and the alternatives were such that respectable higher-income citizens voted for him faithfully.

When I joined his official family his notoriety was at its height. He had been re-elected the year before; the new Charter, for which he had campaigned so strenuously as to make it seem his own, had just gone into operation. He was president of the United States Conference of Mayors (whose headquarters in Washington gave him a convenient *pied-à-terre* in the capital and an excuse for frequent White House visits); he was a follower of Roosevelt in spite of his Republican supporters' protests; and he was actively campaigning all over the country for war against the dictators in Europe.

This last made him one of the few prominent politicians who were furthering the President's campaign to persuade Americans that there were dangers to be faced. He was already more a national public figure than Mayor of one city. And it must be admitted that his interest in the city had fallen away. It was a conquest completed; he needed another venture that would try his powers. He looked longingly toward Washington.

At that time he was a man driven as by whips. In my first year with him, before his hopes were diminished, he talked with me by

the ruling family, and beating his breast and quoting Timothy that he had fought a good fight and kept the faith. "La Guardia—A Salute and a Memoir," the New York *Times Magazine*, September 8, 1957, p. 17.

the hour about national affairs, political grand strategy, and his own chances of moving up. I found the same fascination in these conversations that I had had in similar talks with the President. There is, in first-rank politicians, a concentration which, once it is grasped, furnishes a kind of atmosphere in which they can be understood. They are possessed, these people. They have been seized of a destiny—and that destiny calls them to occupy the center, to be the cynosure, to capture attention, to possess power. There is never any question about their own capability or suitability, no doubt that they can find the answers to the most complex problems. [2] They have identified themselves with a people. In a sense the people have entered into them and they offer themselves as the embodiment of popular aspiration. They feel this coalescence to the extent of living in a world of their own whose inviolability is protected with the utmost diligence. It is so much a shock not to be accepted by the majority that they do not really acknowledge defeat when it comes—not in their hearts. It was all a mistake. They try again and perhaps succeed.

At the same time they have minds of a peculiar sort which stand apart and appraise events and people, estimate confluences, and judge changes. But this intelligence is so oriented that all its operations serve the burgeoning ego that is moving along a predetermined way toward a climactic end. La Guardia's climactic end was not, in his estimation, the New York mayoralty. That was preliminary, a trial run, which now he judged had been wholly successful. But it had gone on too long. [3] There must be a way out and up. Every waking moment of every day his sensitive feelers were out, groping for the situation that could be taken advantage of, the man who could be persuaded to help, the thing he could invent or do that

[2] To Richard Hofstadter this seemed important in Roosevelt. He speaks of his "confidence that he could do no wrong, make no serious mistakes . . ." Cf. *The American Political Tradition,* p. 311.

[3] Just as Roosevelt had felt that his assistant secretaryship of the Navy was going on too long. He too sought escape almost annually and was frustrated. It was only long afterward (in 1928) that progress was resumed; and it is possible that if La Guardia had not died prematurely his progress might have been resumed. The presidency, by the time Roosevelt left it through death, would not have been available, probably; he was unfortunate in being Roosevelt's contemporary. But he might well have had years in a senatorship.

would contribute. His body might be in New York or on the road, but his heart was in the capital.

As we got off a plane together in Washington one day in 1939, after a flight from New York, he stopped still on the tarmac, drew a great breath, and said, "Rex, the air is better down here. This is the only place I can really breathe." I believed at that time that his affair was progressing well, and he thought so too. I was confident, because the President had said so, that he was to be Secretary of War. I had even asked if I could discuss it with La Guardia. There would be much to arrange in New York, I said. There was no successor. The Democratic machine might win again, and some kind of control over its behavior ought to be devised. The President said that he would like me to explore it. There were some problems, but they were not to be worried about.

We did talk about it, and Fiorello's hopes were so high and his eagerness so apparent that his ambition became more and more evident to others. It was discussed in wider and wider circles, including those in the capital. One much-copied cartoon at the time showed him attending lackadaisically to city business while one vastly enlarged ear was turned to the Washington telephone.

From time to time, also, there was talk of his running for the governorship or for a seat in the United States Senate, but there was never much chance of this in those years. Farley, Flynn, and other Democrats would never have yielded him the nomination, and the upstate Republicans were not the La Guardia sort. Socialist, Labor, or Progressive labels were all very well in the polyglot metropolis, but they were anathema in the rural areas. Bert Snell, the Republican leader in the House of Representatives, as hard-shelled a reactionary as ever lived, was shaped to the upstate pattern of an ideal candidate. He was a power there and in the House of Representatives. Into such a pattern it was fantastic to think La Guardia might fit and such leaders would never have accepted him.

I do not know whether there ever was a time when the apotheosis of his career may have seemed to La Guardia to be represented by the mayoralty. I think it quite likely that he settled into the charmingly colonial surroundings of New York's genuinely lovely City Hall, after he was first elected in 1933, with a kind of delight in the incongruity but with a determination to show the supercilious that after all he belonged in such a place. It may be that he thought of nothing further for some time—perhaps until 1937 or 1938, when the presidential nomination for 1940 began to be discussed and it seemed unlikely for many reasons that Roosevelt would run again.

Certainly his satisfaction in that classic room in the southwest corner of the old Hall was a deep one. The uneasy little Italian bandmaster's son, after an extremely undignified scramble, had emerged in full control of an actual center of power. Its dignified and sedate air did seem to fit him ill, but actually he was more at home in these surroundings than any of his immediate predecessors. They had really had the gamin backgrounds La Guardia only seemed to have. He had a sensitivity to beauty and style which none of them had had. And by now he was tired of his masquerade and wished that it might be forgotten. Frequently he seized a baton and led a band or an orchestra, and he supported artistic projects of all sorts as city public works in defiance of the rule that politicians must be as scornful of art as of ideas.

Even under the old Charter the Mayor had been a chief executive *par excellence;* presently, under the new Charter, his personal prestige would be greatly enhanced. The city by then had become a billion-dollar enterprise, and he was in complete charge. There need be no more fly-by-night law offices with an uncertain income from fees; the constant harassment of the life of a congressman—who had to get himself re-elected every two years—was considerably diminished by the Mayor's four-year term. Best of all, for a person like La Guardia, he could do things directly and today without asking leave of anyone. There was a run-down city to rehabilitate. There were grafters to uncover and punish. He must have regarded the prospect with satisfaction. And the way he proceeded to function shows what zest there was in it for him. He became a whirling dervish of a Mayor. The police, the firemen, the various inspectors, the garbage and waste collectors—all of them he regarded as an extension of himself. A job undone or badly done was a fault of his own. And he could preen himself and purr like a cat when new police cars, refuse-collection trucks, or fire engines were lined up in the square outside his window for inspection, with men in uniform at the salute.

He boasted to the newspapers that his appointees were serving with him for other reasons than the salaries paid them by the city. He did not say that he often treated his commissioners like dogs, nor did he call attention to a turnover among them that must have been unprecedented in municipal history. In my time there were, as I recall, thirty-two executives who were of roughly equal rank, either line or staff officers. [4] They had a luncheon once a week in the office of the commissioner of sanitation, an affair that La Guardia did not encourage and never visited. He and he alone was the embodiment of the city's ethos. His commissioners were helpers, but they did not share this ethos. He held them accountable to himself. He was incorruptible and infallible.

It would be almost but not quite fair to say that he was an instinctive dictator; he was certainly dictatorial. Nevertheless, with all his unforgivable boorishness, his ungrateful acceptance of proffered affection and co-operation, his incredible ineptness as an administrator, he would be looked back on for at least a generation with reminiscent regret. No one could take his place in New Yorkers' regard. Although he withdrew from the campaign of 1945 at least partly because he feared that his following had fallen away from neglect, his later indifference was soon forgotten in the recollection of his best days in City Hall.

Very few of us at the top of his administration were chosen for strictly political reasons; many of us were there because we were regarded as expert; some were not even New Yorkers. All of us had seen a challenge in the job there was to do and had been told that we were to be completely independent of bosses or, indeed, of any responsibility having to do with votes. We soon discovered that we were expected to do a good deal of humiliating kowtowing, to give many of La Guardia's favorites jobs, and to respect without question whatever capricious notions the Mayor might have about our work. This was because it was *his* work, not ours.

Naturally, with men of reputation, independent disposition, and perhaps more than average self-respect, there was resentment. And not infrequently there were scenes in that dignified room in City Hall that comported ill with the décor. Often those who were given unreasonable or even downright silly directions refused to accept them. The number who walked out and never came back was con-

[4] Under the old Charter there had been 142 by La Guardia's count—at least he cited that number in a campaign speech in 1933. This statistic illustrates the advance made in the Charter of 1936 toward the centralizing of responsibility.

siderable; but there were more who, when tried too far, lost *their* tempers too. Sometimes the slanging match could be heard outside in the halls, to the consternation of the devoted secretarial staff, who knew, however, that any caution would only turn the erupting wrath in their direction. They closed doors, kept visitors away, and tried to pretend that nothing unusual was going on.

Those who shouted and swore as loudly as La Guardia usually got a compromise. They never got an apology, but then they never expected one. On occasion, however, such a scene would end in a mirth as hearty as the previous slanging. But that was when the mayoral anger had been simulated for effect. I would not quite say that Fiorello liked a man to talk back to him; but if he did not want to lose him, he allowed it and appeared to harbor no ill will. With some—like Robert Moses, for instance—he gave up after a few trials and left them strictly alone. Moses, he felt, was valuable; he was also every bit as irascible as La Guardia. Their first few set-tos are said to have been epic. But in my day they had come to a stalemate. They pretty much ignored each other except for necessary technical communications. Moses was an exception to all rules. He was not sent for and lectured; as a matter of fact, he was not sent for and would not have gone if he had been. If the two met it was by some arrangement that evaded the issue of protocol.

There was, indeed, much to be explained by anyone who set out to defend La Guardia in New York. A not inconsiderable number of influential people—not only those who had worked for him, but others as well—had opportunities to see his displays of arrogance, his offensive manners, and his ingratitude. They despised him so thoroughly as a person that they could barely tolerate the thought of him as Mayor. I do not suppose they voted for Tammany candidates in 1937 and 1941, but I imagine they stayed home on election day.

There can be no question, I think, with La Guardia, as with Roosevelt and Muñoz, whether their characters and their behavior were of a piece with their political abilities. Could La Guardia have been a kindly, tolerant, and reasonable individual who made people love him rather than become infuriated with him, and still have fought his way to the mayoralty and then to re-election in boss-ridden New York? Very probably he could not. Moreover, it has seemed to me that the mayoralty was the same kind of complete fulfillment for La Guardia that the presidency was for Roosevelt and the governorship was for Muñoz. La Guardia never accepted this as his terminal situation; but such it proved to be, and although his further ambitions were formative ones and even affected his career as Mayor, still the mayoralty can be taken as a quite sufficient climacteric for a man of greatness. And his conduct of the office sustains such a judgment.

I should perhaps note that all my specimens, when they got where they were going, savored success only temporarily—that is, for a few years—and then, in response to political law, upset the static situation into which they had fallen as a result of the completion of a program—or such completion as could be managed—by creating or accepting a new issue that could then be pursued with the old fervor. The fighting and sweating to get somewhere are activities that generate strong satisfactions. Just having power is not nearly so heady an occupation as is the getting of it. Nature made politicians love what politicians have to do, just as she made mothers love the caring for children.

It can even be said that the qualities required to reach the top positions in democracies are disqualifications for carrying on many of the duties they involve. Leaders know this, and it is no accident that they again and again set up the situation in which they function best. If politicians had to be judged by efficiency in office, they would be failures. The administrative duties devolving on the chief executives of modern governmental units are such that they can be carried satisfactorily only by trained and experienced experts. Geniuses at public persuasion, such as candidates for office have to be, may also turn out to be gifted administrators; but it is extremely unlikely, and it was certainly not true of La Guardia any more than it was of Roosevelt or Muñoz. It is the sad experience with elected Mayors that has been responsible for the city-manager movement. What is sought is a separation of duties that will allow business to be carried on by the manager while the Mayor goes on with his politics. This is more possible for cities than for larger governmental units, which is too bad, because the disparities between necessities and qualifications are even greater in the larger ones. There is a higher proportion of business in the city that is obviously routine and so easily assigned to an administrator; but state and national responsibilities tend to be wider, and if the ordinary duties of such offices are more infused with policy they need even more that expertness which the politician usually lacks. He is a happy boss-in-office who discovers a man Friday whose talent is for administration.

There were some mayoral responsibilities which La Guardia carried superbly. He was an educator, a morale builder, and an inventor. He taught New Yorkers to work with him for civic betterment. He made them proudly conscious of New York's premier position. And in every dispute within the city that touched at all any of its vital functions he intervened even at some risk of losing face. He was almost always on the right side, and when he was not, he was usually able to make it appear that he was. These were demanding and exhausting duties, but he throve on them. He could make three or four public appearances a day, say something each time, submit to being photographed and interviewed, and consistently make a telling point looking toward the structure of confidence and co-operation he was always building. That is to say, he could do all this at first—during his first term and on into his second.

When he tired of it finally and looked elsewhere, only the good will of his best years carried him through the last ones, and in the end it had been exhausted. He had gone on too long and had lost the zest. While the mayoralty was new to him and the sense of victory strong, he was aflame with vigor, tireless in persuading citizens to follow him, a Jeremiah in his denunciations, and a righteous commander of his battalions. But all this did not make him an acceptable administrator. He was required, because he had chased out some old rascals and laid down some new directives, to be the head of a vast machine he was not fitted to run. The new City Charter said that he had to assume responsibility, and no provision was made for a managerial executive besides. So he struggled with unsuitable activities. [5]

It was at least partly because he was an uncertain administrator that La Guardia became dictatorial. It may be that imperious personalities develop in such situations because it is inevitable, given the kind of person successful candidates have to be and the nature of the duties thrust on them as executives. Good administrators know how to sort out more important from less important decisions, how

---

[5] That the Charter did not really forbid such an arrangement was shown when a later Mayor—Wagner, in 1953—turned over to an executive manager all the business affairs of the city. La Guardia did try delegation, to Henry Curran, for instance, but he found it temperamentally too difficult.

to find effective subordinates and charge them with responsibilities, and how to follow their performances without interfering. La Guardia knew none of this and never found any of it out. If he found good subordinates it was because his ego required important men under him; if he got effective service, it was in spite of his own part in the operation. He interfered, sometimes publicly and often without cause; he tried to make all decisions and so failed to make the important ones with due care. He used methods of fear and irritation, instead of those of encouragement and support. He believed in no one's loyalty and respected no one's abilities. Mr. Moses has referred to this:

> When the Mayor was mad at me, which was not infrequent, he would say, "The only boss you ever had whom you really respected was Al Smith. You think he was a better executive than I am. What's he got that I don't have?" And I always answered that I admired both of them but thought Smith a better executive partly because he had more loyalty to his men.
>
> My wife once charged the Mayor with lack of loyalty. He replied, "I'm loyal to principles, not to men," a very cute rejoinder but one which still horrifies me, because all genuine loyalties in affairs of moment must run to individuals. The bred-in-the-bone, unswerving personal loyalty of leaders like Governor Smith to old friends and followers as well as administrative aides—which no doubt sometimes caused tough predicaments and incomprehensible decisions—was a thing La Guardia did not comprehend. [6]

La Guardia's lack in this respect was often the subject of cautious discussion among his commissioners. Some took it as Bill Carey did, who was a contractor with a large business and was sanitation commissioner on the side. To him the Mayor's antics were more amusing than anything else. They were not allowed to interfere with the cleaning up of the city. But there were more vulnerable and more sensitive souls who after a typical session with the Mayor were likely to emerge either purple with suppressed wrath or reduced to a pulp by abuse. Moses speaks of this too:

[6] Op. cit.

In my book, the most glaring example of the Mayor's in-difference to personal loyalty was in his failure to support the municipal employes who were badgered and frightened at pri-vate hearings by Paul Stryker, without counsel or advice, in the witchhunting aldermanic relief investigation headed by Ber-nard Deutsch. I cannot forget the impish, almost sadistic, qual-ity which led the Mayor to humiliate a department head by calling in a stenographer and shouting at her, "If you were any dumber, I would make you a Commissioner." [7]

There was never a better illustration, I suppose, than La Guardia's mayoralty of the confusion into which our political theory has led us. Here was a man superbly equipped for leadership, who was not only allowed to become but required to become a caricature of the great executive. He felt that he had to be a bigger tycoon than those a half mile south of him in Wall Street. He so continually confused his caprices with the public interest that presently the metropolitan sense of humor, as was inevitable, began to work on such suitable material. The little giant was in danger of becoming a clucking busybody. When he rowed with his commissioners, the press and the public were likely to conclude at once that he was merely behaving childishly again. And his prestige melted away.

Yet it is a fact that he was re-elected even after the concentra-tion of powers in the new Charter had devolved upon him and he had used them without the wisdom or dignity they demanded. In 1938, when I joined his official family, he was already tired of it; he knew he was not doing so well but was unable to change, and he was hoping rather desperately for rescue before his credit should be exhausted. He had been too long in New York. He thought his relief might come by way of Roosevelt, and he hoped to move to Washington. He was re-elected in 1941 not because of, but in spite of, his executive behavior; because of his performances in public, not because of his efficiency in office. He was still dedicated and still colorful; he was against the bosses and had convinced the peo-ple that the bosses were their enemies as well as his. La Guardia, absurd and childish, was better than scoundrels and wasters.

[7] Ibid.

13

Very possibly I exaggerate La Guardia's incompetence in administration; it was less incompetence, really, than perverseness. Or it may be that he could not believe housekeeping tasks to be important. Or again he may have felt the lack in them of the spectacular for which he thirsted. Yet again, he may have sensed the wastage of great talents for one occupation on another occupation for which they were unsuited, without proceeding to an understanding that something remedial could be done about it that would enhance, not diminish his prestige. He certainly worked very hard and was as earnest as a man could be. Also, he was always fascinated by details, even if without any competence in their disposal. It made him genuinely happy to feel that his municipal organization was giving good service, something everyone understood. So he cannot have been quite so bad as those who had to work with him thought he was. The record of his administration is one of considerable progress, especially in public works. Many projects had been talked about for years and deferred time after time as Tammany Mayors fell farther and farther into fiscal chaos. Most of the old ones and many new ones were undertaken and promptly carried through, some under the direction of the redoubtable Robert Moses, but many under other auspices. The difficulty with awarding La Guardia credit for this physical progress is that he was just in time to cash in on the federal aids that were part of the New Deal. These aids were not only extended generously for building public works but also could be used for maintenance.

His fiscal failure in the long run is at least to be condoned by mitigating circumstances. The underlying problem of New York was shared by other American cities; all of them were in effect bankrupt by 1930 because the municipality was not coextensive with the metropolis. Disaster had crept upon them unaware, and there was by no means a wide acceptance of the drastic cure that was indicated. La Guardia can be blamed for not having grasped his opportunity, but not so much as he could have been blamed if there had even been one example to follow. For another thing, much of what needed to be done would have had to be authorized by state law. [1] He could not have extended the city limits to include the suburbs which were parasites on the city; nor could he have accomplished other reforms—alone. But he might have furnished the same sort of leadership as had put through the Charter of 1936. If he had I have no doubt he would have prevailed. The trouble was that he seemed not to be convinced that the diagnosis was correct. Anyway, he could not be roused. What was expected of him by the city's older first citizens, he accomplished. He provided a reform administration on the traditional model, defended it, perpetuated it in a new charter, and transformed New York from a notorious Tammany playground into a place of pride and civic energy.

For still another thing, it can be argued that La Guardia went as far in reform as he could and that if he had tried to do what I suggest he would have failed; he might, moreover, have jeopardized more than he could have gained. Rescuing New York from the money-lenders and reducing the predations of the real estate interests would have involved a struggle in which all the conservatives, generally on his side as things were, would have united against him. This would have included the press, always so hot for reform until reform touches an influential interest.

La Guardia was entitled to say to me—as others had said—that his justification was that he won elections; and if I retorted that an election won was a victory only if it resulted in the gaining of some objective beyond an office for a politician, that was merely a matter of opinion. It is impossible to say for certain in his case that further objectives were attainable. It will always remain a matter of judgment.

There had been times in La Guardia's political career when he

[1] In the case of New York, there was also the problem of New Jersey across the Hudson River and even Connecticut a few miles to the north.

appeared to be something of a Socialist; he had even run for the Congress on the Socialist and Progressive tickets in 1924 when he was denied the Republican nomination. It was during this term that he formed his first alliance with La Follette, Norris, Wheeler, and the other western Progressives with whom he felt so much at home. In 1924 he campaigned as intensively for the La Follette-Wheeler ticket as for himself. The Progressive program for the nation stirred him more, I think, than the program of municipal reform with which he was later identified. This, of course, involved public ownership of most utilities as well as many electoral and governmental reforms. So far as he could, La Guardia fought for that program throughout his congressional career. Not much of it was realized—at least none of the major items—but the struggle toughened the little congressman from New York. He became nationally known as well as popular among his Harlem constituents. They were proud of his reputation.

It has to be recalled what the United States was like when he was being re-elected time after time. These were the notorious twenties—the Republican boom years that ended in the great bust of 1929. And if any one person typified the reverse of conservative smugness during the "new era," it was that other kind of Republican, La Guardia. No one—not even the mighty La Follette himself—so often embarrassed the apologists for the big-business regime, so often spoke up about the squeezing of consumers between low incomes and high prices, fought so effectively for labor's right to protest, or more often displayed a healthy indignation at the frequent violations of civil rights. Strangely enough, too, considering that he represented New York, he fought and bled along with the farm bloc for agricultural relief measures vetoed repeatedly by Coolidge and Hoover. On the surface it was a strange alliance: the Wisconsin, Nebraska, and Montana Progressives with the representative from the city slums. It annoyed the metropolitan press, which was unsympathetic toward agricultural relief measures and skeptical of progressivism in general. But it did not annoy La Guardia's constituents. They seemed to understand well enough, when he explained to them—even if the New York *Times* could not—how depression in agriculture could spread to the rest of the economy. And as for the rest of the Progressive program, they were probably ahead of their congressmen. Many of them were socialists in fact if not in name.

La Guardia's kind of statesmanship lifted him above the ordinary levels of representation. He had a constant consciousness that all national life was a whole. Again and again he fought for what seemed remote and even irrelevant causes for a New York congressman to excite himself about. But it was seldom long before his wisdom was recognized by an appreciative constituency. And his reputation as a statesman grew year by year until it was country-wide.

There can hardly ever have been a better illustration of one of my underlying generalizations here than La Guardia's decision-making. This is true both of those choices that had to do with his own career and those that had to do with public policy. These were often, but not always, indistinguishable. But, in any event, they were made so nearly *de novo* that they seem never to have proceeded from analysis. This is to say, I suppose, that politics, at any rate at this level, is an art, and perhaps incorrigibly so; it is pursued by instinct rather than reason. This does not imply, however, that decisions are necessarily irrational or unrelated to desired objectives. Politicians are, in fact, notoriously cold-blooded and unsentimental, though the reverse kind of impression is sought to be projected in all that affects their strictly political function. They almost never act in ways unrelated to the furtherance of their careers, and this furnishes one point of reference of which their biographers can be sure. There is an exception to this generalization as there is to most others. This is that the picture politicians have of themselves, and by which they live, may become dangerously confining. And it is very difficult for them to behave in ways inconsistent with this stereotyped and habitual pattern. A politician who is a conservative, a liberal, a progressive—or who bears any other such label—will be reluctant to cloud the picture. Somehow his self-consideration is seriously involved and he will regard criticism on this point as more damaging than most other kinds he may be subjected to. The necessary accommodations are often far too long delayed or even rejected, and this can be fatal.

It is true that there is so usual a change as a result of success, however, that this seems almost as regular a matter as the regard for the self-photograph. Success involves the holding of office, the carrying of responsibility, and identification with a governmental organism—a commonwealth, a city, a nation. Holding together or reshaping, in accordance with preconceived views, such an organization as a government is a formidable enterprise in conservation as well as group initiative. The politician seeking office is pretty free with criticism, and charges of this sort are apt to extend some way beyond the observation that present incumbents are incompetents or even rascals. The attack is likely to involve government itself. And the candidate who allows himself the leeway he thinks he needs for his campaign is subsequently apt to find that he has said far too much on this subject for his subsequent convenience as an administrator.

No vast and ongoing enterprise involving hierarchies of bureaucrats carrying out a multiplicity of duties can be changed overnight. In fact, the extent to which it can be changed at all in any short time is very limited. Yet candidates for office, if the office is one possessed by the opposition, are almost invariably committed in the public mind to drastic revisions; and quite often, realistic as politicians usually are, they nevertheless fall into the trap of believing their own claims. I would contend that Muñoz, La Guardia, and Roosevelt were relatively immune to these fallacies and that they experienced fewer torments in office from promises made beforehand than most other politicians, this being one mark of their claim to genuine greatness. Yet each did at times claim too much, each followed the usual course of turning—or appearing to turn—conservative, and each became, in the end, the defender of a governmental regime not markedly different from that against which he had led a revolutionary attack. It is only the degree of difference that marks them as superior.

There is nothing so absurd in the record of any of my three, for instance, as Eisenhower's commitment made in the campaign of 1952 to "keep the long nose of the federal government" out of private affairs, or his assertion that the return to Republican reaction was properly to be called a "crusade." Harding's "return to normalcy," Coolidge's *faux pas* concerning intergovernmental debts, Hoover's commitment to "keep government out of business" are illustrations of extreme foolishness which were soon proven to be so and which returned to haunt their authors. But they could be matched by illustrations from the careers of all amateurs who have

found themselves in positions beyond their competence as politicians. [2]

There are such incidents to be turned up even in the careers of my
three if close enough attention is paid to detail; and sometimes
there are uglier incidents, ones that approach the indefensible. The
mistakes and the unfairnesses may have been lost in the larger
judgment after a few years, but they are undeniable. And some of
them were of the sort that are disagreeable to record. "When I make
a mistake," La Guardia himself said of an appointment he should
have known better than to make, "it's a beaut." But this was a flash
of unusual, even if charming, candor. The truth was that La Guardia
was more apt than the others to make unwise remarks and to resort
to doubtful tactics. He was more temperamental, more irritable, and
perhaps less scrupulous. This last would be more difficult to document; but certainly the digging up of a ten-year-old statement of
McKee, one of his opponents in the 1933 campaign, which could
be interpreted as a slur on the Jews, was hitting below the belt; and
his treatment of Bertrand Russell, in a famous education incident,
was utterly inexcusable on any grounds other than truckling to
Catholic prejudice.

These were unscrupulous resorts, but only in the very long-run
sense can they be said to have been poor politics. The campaigns in
which they were used were hard-fought and were successful. They
may or may not have contributed. But they are incontestably part
of a successful record. It may well be, however, that when Roosevelt
had to choose—which is what it came down to—between Stimson
and La Guardia for Secretary of War, Stimson's elevated and dignified demeanor (a newsman once said that Stimson was the only
individual he had ever known who could look pompous *sitting
down*) as against La Guardia's peppery temper and reputed unreliability, as well as his party irregularity, La Guardia's apparent
lack of poise and judgment counted heavily against him.

He had, it may be, exhibited his notorious Italian temperament
too often. His argumentative methods when he was a congressman
had made him well known; the fact that he was almost always

[2] In this connection I may recall that Al Smith in 1933, in a speech at the
Chicago Exposition, said something of the sort. "The heavy, cold clammy
hand of bureaucracy," he said, had done much to hamper industry. The New
York *Times*, October 24, 1933.

on the progressive side and that what are usually called "the interests" never had any influence with him certainly endeared him to a wide following—and to Roosevelt as well, who always recognized in him a companion in progressivism. Exhibiting a loaf of bread and crushing it in his hands to show that it was mostly air, thus illustrating the middlemen's fakery, was effective, and for twelve years he was undoubtedly the most feared of all the anti-prohibition agitators, but his public defiance of the Anti-Saloon League by making beer in public was, even if hilarious, certainly not dignified; it was, besides, an incitement to lawlessness, even if the law in question was unpopular. At one time or another he attacked the Steel Trust, the New York financiers, and practically all the other most powerful Republican supporters. And he was usually intemperate about it. If Roosevelt was after a Republican for Secretary of War, La Guardia was not—and Stimson was—among those in good standing.

La Guardia's dearest hope by then, probably, was that after 1941 he might be made a general. He would have traded anything he had or hoped to have for such an appointment; he thought he had a good case, and Roosevelt undoubtedly promised it to him—partly to compensate for the bitter disappointment over the War secretaryship. On exploration it was discovered, however, that confirmation was extremely doubtful and would, at the least, involve an embarrassing disturbance which the President could not afford just then. Curiously enough, the strongest objection seems to have come from Senator Harry S. Truman, then making his reputation as head of the Senate committee on the conduct of the war. Truman seems to have felt that so obviously political an appointment would reflect adversely on the whole military establishment. It may be that the senator was overly influenced by the cries of outrage from the professional military men who were riding high in those days and thought their prestige very precious. At any rate, La Guardia's reputation as a mountebank, in however good causes, undoubtedly lost him his last and dearest wish. Robert Moses decorates this incident with a nearly forgotten arrangement by which La Guardia would have had his military cake and eaten it too:

> La Guardia always wanted to be a general with one star (to begin with) and President Roosevelt agreed to nominate him and assign him to Italy. So sure was he of the job that he

rearranged his pension, ordered his uniform and canvassed the selection of a temporary successor. He had no thought of retiring as Mayor and didn't like the applicable provisions of the City Charter. So, with the help of some upstate officials with similar ambitions to eat their cake and have it, an extraordinary bill was passed at Albany under which an elected official could accept a commission in the Army, meanwhile holding on to his local office and picking a temporary successor who would be turfed out as soon as the elected incumbent chose to come home. Any ambitious student interested in the fine art of bill drafting can find this gem. It was Chapter 26 of the Laws of 1943, repealed in 1948 by Chapter 687.

This strange act superseded all statutory and charter provisions about absence, incapacity, retirement, etc., of the incumbent. The bill, which was entitled "Absence from Public Office for Military Duty," was so drawn that its real purpose was unrecognizable—just another bit of patriotic legislation to help win the war. There were plenty of rumors floating around as to the Mayor's departure. They were confirmed when he sent for me and said he had picked me to act in his absence, Judge Thomas D. Thacher having declined this dubious honor. I asked him what about Newbold Morris, who as President of the Council was designated in the Charter to pinch-hit for the Mayor when he was away. He gave no responsive answer.

I told him I wasn't interested in any such shenanigans and didn't believe anyway that he was going to be confirmed by the Senate. Actually, Judge Samuel Seabury, Charles C. Burlingham and other mammoths of civic uprighteousness rushed to Washington and protested to Secretary Stimson who had already told the President he didn't think the Mayor's fiery, provocative presence in Italy would be helpful and that he could not recommend confirmation. The nomination never went in. The Mayor stayed on at City Hall. I never heard what became of his uniform. [3]

That La Guardia was treated badly by Roosevelt in these and other instances is a tragic reminder of practicality in politics. It is

[3] The New York *Times Magazine,* op. cit., p. 118.

difficult to find any adequate defense at this distance if there is admitted to the judgment either gratitude for loyal support or consideration of competence. La Guardia would have been, in my opinion, a better Secretary of War than Stimson, even if he might not have been recognized as a veritable Republican hostage in the Democratic ranks. There are many reasons for believing he would have done a commendable job. He was, for one thing, more vigorous. Stimson was, even in 1941, suffering the first onsets of a senility that left much of the responsibility to his assistant, Robert Patterson. If La Guardia could have had Patterson to manage the administration while he furnished the leadership, Roosevelt might have been very well served indeed, and there would have been far less of the kind of conduct that identified the war effort as the private possession of favored businesses.

When it is said that La Guardia's conduct was characteristically such that he could not be taken seriously for the high appointive posts he wanted and which the public interest would have been well served in his getting, something more than technical politics is involved. None of the performances for which he was so well known ever prevented him from being elected to the offices for which he ran. I do not believe his idiosyncrasies would have prevented him from being elected to the presidency if he had had the luck to be available in non-Roosevelt times or if Roosevelt had stepped aside in 1940—always granting that he could have been nominated. Whether he could have got either party's nomination is quite another matter. Here too his notorious unreliability in party matters would have been a handicap of immense weight.

But there was an even more considerable difficulty than that he was thought to be erratic and unreliable. This was that many of those who would have to support him if he was to succeed on the national stage had suffered from his ill-governed tongue or been the object of his dramatic tricks. Such injuries are not quickly forgotten. The man responsible for them has little chance of finding supporters even if he promises victory. For, paradoxical as it may seem, the professional who is not a candidate may have more important objectives than the winning of elections. Or, to put it another way, some of the objectives of bosses are not furthered by winning elections they do not control and from which they cannot profit. They would rather lose elections than lose control. These people profoundly distrusted La Guardia, so he cannot be said actually to have got anywhere near the presidency.

If La Guardia's career as a whole is reviewed it can be seen that he made two mistakes he could not recover from. One was substantive; the other was a miscalculation in timing. It may be that what happened might have happened anyway; it is impossible to be certain. But each *may* have been avoidable and each *may* have had a material effect on his failure to rise beyond the mayoralty as he was ambitious to do. One was his affiliation with the Progressives in 1936; the other was his thinking that 1936 would be the last Democratic-Republican contest. By 1940, he believed, there would be a Progressive-Conservative polarization. As was proper to his career, he had begun to think of going farther almost at once after election to the mayoralty. And by the time his first term was in its last year, he was making a radical shift in affiliation.

It must never be forgotten that La Guardia was actually a Westerner, and typically western in his intentions and reactions, even if with an Italian overlay of temperament. His was a breed familiar to American politics. Among his contemporaries—some actually older, some younger than he, but active at the same time—were Wheeler, Norris, the two La Follettes, Floyd Olson, and numerous associates in the House, such as Tom Amlie; and these were the people with whom he felt a close kinship, with whom he liked to be, and whose motives he understood and approved. His New York career as "the little half-Jewish wop" was mostly a masquerade, except for the occasional lack of control which gave away his ancestry; and to sustain the role was a trying ordeal.

One term as Mayor would have been plenty; four years as a Republican were too many. With Roosevelt in the White House, how could he pretend to belong to the same party as the Republicans among his Fusion supporters in New York, from whom, in all respects except a desire for good government in the city (meaning, mostly, economy), he differed as much as it is possible for a man to differ from others. They hated Roosevelt immoderately; he admired and envied the President and would have served him gladly in any post and at any time if only the command had come. To live with Roosevelt-haters galled him, and he would have escaped if he could.

Naturally, with this irritation tormenting him, he spent a good deal of time and attention on the possibilities. He made up his mind, very likely because his judgment was a little warped from wishing it were true, that a party realignment was in process and that it would be consummated in 1940. Thus it seemed that 1936 was not too soon for him to take his place and begin to work among those who, he believed, would command the greatest prestige in the future and with whom, fortunately, he felt at home anyway.

If he must run for a second term in New York—and he saw that he must—he felt that he was now in a strong enough position to repudiate his affiliation with the reactionary Republicans. He could run as a candidate of the local Labor party, stressing his independence. If this was possible, then he could begin to renew his national affiliation with the Progressives. Thinking of this, and watching developments, he concluded that Roosevelt himself was in an impossible situation with the reactionary Democrats. The President might run again in 1936 as a Democrat, but he would not run for a third term in 1940; and during his second term he would gradually turn more and more to the Progressives. By 1940 the taking of sides would have reached the point of regrouping. The Republican and Democratic parties in 1940 would have dissolved and become on the one side Progressive-Labor and on the other side Business-Conservative. He would put himself in a position to be the person most eligible for designation by his own people—the Progressive-Labor group. How could he do this better than by openly joining the Progressives-for-Roosevelt in 1936 and in 1937 running for Mayor again on the Labor ticket?

This cannot be said to have been an unreasonable calculation. His own part in it was carried out. He did affiliate with the Progressives in 1936, he was re-elected as Mayor in 1937 without any debt to the Republicans, and by 1940 he was precisely in the position he had intended to reach. Roosevelt's decision to keep the Democratic coalition together by an appeasement policy that required the sacrifice of most of the New Deal was something La Guardia could hardly have foreseen; nor could he have guessed that Roosevelt would have felt compelled by the war in Europe, the necessity to marshal American support for the Allies, and a growing sense of his own indispensability to run for a third term. He was even entitled to feel, right up to the last year, that he could perform the rallying function as well as Roosevelt. In fact, his part in it, unasked and unwelcome, was not inconsiderable as things were.

There was no secret about the beginning he made in 1936. He signed, with several others, all like-minded Progressives, a call to a conference in Chicago on September 11. What this meant was clear enough to everyone. For instance, the story in the New York *Times* had this to say:

> *The action of the Mayor in signing the call for the conference was considered his decisive act in thrusting aside his past associations with the national Republican party and allying himself with New Deal fortunes . . . The organization Republicans will take his action as a formal renunciation of Republicanism and on that ground will seek to deny him endorsement in the Mayoralty contest next year. The Mayor, however, is understood to be taking the step with this possibility in mind and is sounding out the chances of becoming a candidate of the Labor Party . . .*
>
> *The Mayor is said to feel that major political realignments are due in the nation and desires to associate himself with progressive and labor groups in the belief that such a coalition may become the dominant force by 1940.*

On September 12 there was a story about the meeting, noting that a National Progressive Committee had been formed and a resolution adopted for the support of Roosevelt. La Guardia was mentioned as the chairman of the resolutions committee. A letter from Senator Norris was read and a comment of La Guardia was quoted to the effect that the Progressives were merely doing "what the other crowd did at Detroit last week." This referred to an enthusiastic meeting of anti-Roosevelt Democrats. The inference was that a realignment was indeed in process. [4]

In the same and near issues of the *Times* the headlines were mostly monopolized by Landon and Roosevelt. But it was noted with intense interest by everyone that the *Literary Digest* poll was

---

[4] The Chicago meeting was a really representative one—representative of both Progressives and Labor. Young Bob La Follete was made chairman and at once appointed La Guardia to draft a resolution supporting Roosevelt. The meeting was attended by Senator Bone, Elmer Benson (then a Farm-Labor candidate in Minnesota), Adolf Berle, Frank Walsh, and altogether four senators, two Governors, twelve representatives, and twenty-seven labor leaders. Among the latter were John L. Lewis and Sidney Hillman. Berle was there, of course, as La Guardia's second.

giving Landon an almost 2 to 1 advantage. There was quite some belief that the Republicans would win. The support of the Progressives cannot have been unwelcome to Roosevelt, and he must have known that La Guardia was burning his bridges with something in view beyond re-election to the mayoralty. They were both politicians.

La Guardia was thus irrevocably affiliated, and it turned out to be a mistake. That is, the realignment on which he counted did not take place. No national Progressive party arose. And Roosevelt, although he must have been moved by La Guardia's Progressives-for-Roosevelt activities in 1936, when for the moment it looked as though Landon might be winning, was not moved enough to draw La Guardia into his Washington family and give him an opportunity to be a successor. There was not going to be a successor, and La Guardia was reduced to the fortuitously humiliating position of hoping for the favor of an appointment that also never came.

This sad history can be attributed either to bad judgment or to bad luck; perhaps both. I am inclined to think that La Guardia miscalculated Roosevelt's political toughness—his imperviousness to sentiment. And although he was strenuously opposed to the totalitarians in Europe, he did not understand what national political purpose they would serve at home—that they would, in fact, keep Roosevelt in the presidency. He ran against them and they made a perfect foil. There was thus some lack of perception which compounded the ill fortune of that time.

I have already indicated why La Guardia's appointment—and so the renewed chance to move up—never came. It was because he could not or did not escape from the "little wop" masquerade. And also because, when Roosevelt needed a Republican for Secretary of War—to emphasize unity in foreign policy and the approach to war —La Guardia had made himself ineligible by guessing wrong on the prospect of realignment by 1940. He was no longer a Republican. Possibly, also, Roosevelt was responding to the law that, however great their services to a common cause, likely competitors are not given conspicuous public favor.

It was a tragic outcome, one hardly deserved, and one, moreover, as I felt, that was a loss to the nation. La Guardia's leadership was never made available. He is remembered as New York's best Mayor when what he longed to be was America's first Progressive President.

14

It is far from original to remark that even the most successful politicians are slow to recover from the disease of legislative irresponsibility once the infection has been contracted, yet I venture to insist yet again in this context that the difficulty is important. The best practitioners of leadership have had either very brief or, for some reason other than brevity, not very significant careers as legislators. Or, to put what I mean to convey more exactly, the acquired habits of representative lawmakers interfere with rather than further success in the executive offices which are the politicians' supreme objectives.

The observation is nearly as true of Mayors and Governors, who have actual and heavy policy-making and administrative responsibilities, as it is of Presidents, who have heavier ones. The difference is of degree, not of kind. It was this responsibility that La Guardia rose to, as it was that which Muñoz rose to also, out of long and formative legislative experiences. Each suffered from his conditioning as a legislator. Not Roosevelt, however; his short service as state senator in New York, back in 1910–12, had definitely not given his mind that hardened legislative cast which is so difficult to break. He had gone on from the Albany legislature to seven and a half years of executive work in most demanding circumstances—during a world war, and under a chief who was disposed to require that he carry the really wearying administrative work of a huge department—and it was this experience that shaped his attitudes, not that of the legislature and its committees. Then there was, as well, the four years of governorship immediately preceding his assumption of the presidency. And in this experience he had occasion to become the executive, pure and untainted. He had, during his four years in Albany, not only a legislature to subdue, but one with a Republican majority.

There was little about legislative failings that he did not know by
1932.

More than any other President in our history, he came to the
office conscious of the need for exercising executive leadership and
determined that the Congress should follow and not lead. The
Roosevelt clarity about this contrasts vividly with the muddiness of
such other Presidents as Harrison, McKinley, Taft, Harding,
Coolidge, and Truman. Of all these, Harding and Truman were the
worst; they came from the Senate. Both of them frittered away the
precious months of their presidential honeymoons in self-education,
reiterating at every opportunity the fatal fallacy that the Congress
made policy, the Executive only carried it out. By the time they
had awakened to their responsibilities it was too late. Neither got
anything done. In this, Roosevelt resembled such predecessors as
Lincoln, Cleveland, and Theodore Roosevelt, who began as they
knew they would have to end—in conflict with the Congress, and
making full use of a victorious candidate's advantage to coerce it
into implementing a program.

It is not, of course, implied that *lack* of legislative service guarantees leaderly qualities in a President. This would be both illogical
and unhistorical. Such recent illustrations as Coolidge, Hoover, and
Eisenhower would confute such an inference. But I think it is amply
true to say that lack of legislative indoctrination is an advantage,
especially in the precious initial period, when so much can be got
done if the initiative is really seized and pressed. Generalization
here is, however, not less subject to exception than it is in most
other political rules. Coolidge, Hoover, and Eisenhower were all
capable executives with long training but no enfeeblement from
congressional experience. But they were Republicans; and they believed, as other Republicans did, that a strong presidency was inimi-
cal to the national welfare. This was because the well-being of the
whole was regarded as additive—that is, they accepted the conception that when many or most of the nation's corporate concerns
were prosperous the nation must be prosperous too. It was their
view that the government fulfills its highest purpose if it contributes
to business prosperity. This, by an easy transition, comes to be stated
and believed in another and more significant form and context.

It is honestly accepted that the policies formulated for their own
prosperity by the business leaders of the country are policies that

ought to be furthered and supplemented by national action. This may seem naïve; it may seem, moreover, to have been confuted in the most devastating of national disasters—the Great Depression of the thirties. It is, nevertheless, the most influential article of faith among industrialists, financiers, and merchants. And these, with their dependents, their followers, and their political allies, make up the Republican intelligentsia and determine Republican policy. Their minds are simply closed to the inevitable succession of events that lies beyond the freedom of each to make himself and his organization prosperous. This succession determines that the courses pursued will conflict and that the stronger will suppress or dominate the weaker. But well-being not only is not to be achieved by additive policies, but requires precisely the opposite ones; it is to be attained only by cooperation and by the voluntary subordination of all to the minimal governing requirements for the whole.

The holistic conception implies the formulation of goals and targets and the discovery of what contributors ought to produce; also it implies that each will join in an effort to reconcile his policy with that of others. This must all be done under government auspices— unless a combination of businesses becomes a government itself, and this to a democracy is—or ought to be—intolerable. Government is not, in this effort to give direction, required to "take over industry," to "run business," or really to interfere intolerably. But it is required to control the strategic junctures. It must set the goals; it must allocate duties; it must require a certain conformance with rules that are for the general good. Businesses, for instance, must not exploit each other, their workers, or their consumers, if the entire national organization is not to be slowed down and brought eventually to a stop by such exercises of individuality. For only by each making things and rendering services to others, on such terms as can be supported, can the whole be kept going at all. And it is the object of the responsible modern government to keep the economy which functions within its area up to a level of satisfactory activity. Otherwise the responsibility falls on it, as has been amply demonstrated, to set things going again—after they have halted. And not only that, it must repair the damage and support the injured!

Repairing such damage as occurred in the free-enterprise debacle of 1929, and going on to support the injured, is something that could not occur very often—say once in a generation—without involving revolution and chaos. It happened in 1929 that the party required to furnish the alternative to the Republicans' additive conceptions, not given up even with the lessons crashing in their ears, was the Democracy whose ready man was our Roosevelt. He identified the fallacy that had brought the Republicans to grief, but he also understood the reluctance of almost every one of his compatriots to recognize that the alternative was collectivism. Economics was one thing, therefore, and politics was another. Economics required collectivism; politics required that collectivism be camouflaged as competition. Actually the situation is not too inaccurately described by saying that the presidency of Roosevelt represented attempts to find a congenial collectivism and that the contemporary Congress represented atomism—or "freedom," as its proponents preferred to call it.

La Guardia stood with Roosevelt, was his parallel, and had a problem that was, in a modified sense, similar. Nowhere in the nation were the results of Republican policy more fatal than in the city La Guardia became mayor of in 1933. He was stirred by the challenge of chaos and worked ardently for relief and recovery. The difference between his problem and Roosevelt's was fixed, again, by the fact that New York was only part of the whole which was the nation. The whole determined the prosperity or poverty of the part; the whole could give it relief or withhold the necessary support. La Guardia had to spend much of his time in scheming and supplicating for the well-being of his subsidiary and vulnerable realm. He had time for few large or well-considered designs for the whole. He did not have to bring into being an NRA or an AAA, to create a Civilian Conservation Corps or a TVA, as Roosevelt did. He did, however, have to invent or adopt various expedients suitable to the city's situation. He probably went on being an atomist at heart while he participated in collectivist measures—like most of the other contemporary Progressives. He had no occasion to make commitments.

I have proposed La Guardia as a first-order politician, not as a consistently statesmanlike thinker or even always an adequate one in smaller matters. He was extremely sensitive to suffering and to injustice, and his indignation was at times almost uncontrollable. Anger very often caused him to react in ways his reason would not have approved. It was at such times, mostly, that he behaved in the indecorous ways for which he became notorious. This was especially true while he was a legislator, and it is indeed impossible to find, all during the nearly two decades of his public life before he became mayor—those being his legislative years—an occasion when his anger overcame his judgment in other than a public cause. He served no private interest except when some injustice was involved. He was probably no more impervious than others to reflections on his integrity, but he could ignore such attacks or meet them with reason, wit, or indignant retort as the case required. The exploitation of the poor, the undermining of civil liberties, the corruption of public office, the pretensions of the rich or the noble, or the prostitution of democracy by would-be or actual dictators who held power by force—these were the causes that roused in him a rage he was utterly unable to control.

It is true that anyone subject to this kind of seizure learns after a while the results it gets. Most of these may be bad because they are not weighed in advance, but some of them may be good because genuine indignation is frightening to the corrupt. And in his later years La Guardia's rages came frequently to have a calculated incidence in his own mind, which, to the student of his career, is a welcome comic relief even if it does appear that such resorts prevented the full development of his public usefulness. The worst feature of his temperamental popping off in the early period before he had learned to control it was that such occasions were public and, being public, constituted a show. Shows have to sustain interest if they are to have a long run, and an old actor tires.

It is true of most public men that their course comes to have a line that can be extrapolated. Their reactions can therefore be predicted, even if only roughly, by those who have something in mind to be done in which their concurrence or their opposition may be important. But there are degrees of this possible prediction from charting former positions. Of La Guardia it could be said that it would be very easy to predict. Roosevelt was certainly at the other extreme; of very few public men was it possible to say, with so little confidence, what his course would be, until he was entirely ready to let it be known. And his readiness to share it with anyone—except the close associates involved in its formulation or execution, and a very few others—was precisely the readiness he had to share it with those he knew would try to prevent its success. His confidence in the keeping of secrets was almost nonexistent—except, of course, among his official household. And even with them he was a judicious and sparing sharer.

This was a way in which these two contemporary political practitioners stood in very vivid contrast. But both changed in respect to this characteristic. La Guardia became more cautious; Roosevelt came to value hard commitment, in certain cases, very highly. And both are methods that require discretion.

The difference between Roosevelt and La Guardia is very well illustrated in their attitudes toward atomism and holism. Roosevelt was a wholeness man who, out of discretion, gave ground to atomism; La Guardia was an atomist who learned something of the nature of wholeness. But Roosevelt's commitment was never clear or complete; he never admitted to having a philosophy, and his policies could never be predicted; he made wide detours and long backtracks; and, even to the end, his most perceptive opponents were not certain where to have him on any specific item of this large issue.

La Guardia stood where he stood, his indignation ready and quick, his preference clear and open. He proclaimed from any and all available forums what he believed and what he thought. He scorned the art of timing. He challenged, and he threw everything he had at the challenged, seeking to overbear by the sheer weight of his attack. But as he became older, or perhaps as the responsibilities of executive office took hold of him, his style changed noticeably, at least with respect to his own responsibilities—he still exercised the old freedom concerning those of others. For instance, he was equivocal as Mayor about public utilities in New York. He had advocated public ownership at an earlier time; as Mayor no one could find out what he really intended. And it was the same about financing and the long-run development of many facilities. But he was very free about what ought to be done to and with European dictators. He made speeches all over the country about the federal policy in depression, and often his suggestions turned out to be not those the President had in mind. These, it will be seen, were a long way from his immediate duties and responsibilities. He could speak freely.

Roosevelt never objected to this activity of La Guardia's any more than he did the similar activities of others. It was part of his general method to encourage many suggestions. Reaction to them enabled him to make a shrewd guess as to which ones would be generally approved. It also served to confuse the members of the opposition. Various pronouncements were always being made by those who might be supposed to be confidants of the President—like La Guardia —that turned out to have no place whatever in any presidential scheme. The truth was that Roosevelt held his supporters, especially those of the urgent and forthputting La Guardia type, at long arm's length. They could get themselves out on any limb they wanted to, but they risked having it sawed off.

La Guardia had many falls from sawed-off limbs. But this was in his role as national statesman. In his later years as Mayor he followed somewhat the same method himself. Many a commissioner was unable to find out what the Mayor had in mind and, becoming impatient, said too much and found himself ignored or even repudiated.

La Guardia, however, never really learned that it was better not to rebuke his rash subordinates, something Roosevelt did only on the rarest occasions, such, for instance, as the Morgan contumacy at TVA or the Jones-Wallace row in the midst of the war; and then what he did was mostly for the public effect such a rebuke would have. Far oftener he allowed differences of policy, sometimes extremely important ones, to go on and on, becoming more and more widely known, even notorious, without taking sides himself. He seemed to enjoy the role of sphinx. At any rate it was one he habitually played, to the intense irritation of his more impatient subordinates, but also to the discomfiture of enemies who would have liked to know, even more avidly than his supporters, where he stood.

There were involved in this a sense of timing and a calculated weighing of effect of the sort we have seen Muñoz using in the matter of status for Puerto Rico. La Guardia either did not possess or did not use such a calculation, and he was too impatient to enjoy the waiting out of an opponent.

This waiting and allowing differences to boil up, and even to become fierce and notorious, rose, in Roosevelt's case, to the status of a recognized technique. It put him in a strategic, even if sometimes a rather embarrassing, position. When the controversy had run its course and opinion had jelled he could shape his policy to suit the outcome without having run the risk of favoring the wrong or unpopular side. He could jump into, sidle into, or even pretend always to have been in the group which had the best of it. [1]

[1] This sometimes went to the length of something very like betrayal. Ed Flynn in *You're the Boss* tells somewhat resentfully, although he himself recognized the necessity involved, how Roosevelt sent for him in 1933 and persuaded him to have McKee run for mayor of New York. This became the famous three-sided campaign which La Guardia won because McKee took votes from Tammany—which was what Roosevelt had intended. Flynn, acting in good faith, and presently bogged down in his campaign, begged a word from the White House in support of McKee. Only then did he realize what had happened to him. The White House was deaf and dumb. La Guardia won, and Flynn was made to look absurd—although, as he admitted, his Bronx machine came out of the ordeal stronger than ever because of Tammany's defeat.

15

La Guardia, like my other politicians, for all his ready indignation and his unrestrained expression, was capable of harboring a kind of affection for the professionals on the other side as well as in his own camp. This often seemed to resemble the respect and liking military commanders develop for their opposite numbers. Indeed I think it could well be said that professional politicians, like professional soldiers, have no enemies, only adversaries. Generals like nothing better—most of them—than sitting down, when the battles are over, with those they have fought. They relive their campaigns in retrospect with intense mutual interest. I have a vivid picture of Muñoz sharing experiences with Celestino Iriarte and several others among his most implacable political enemies midway in a career that ended in their relegation to the political scrap heap and his occupancy of La Fortaleza. The *simpático* atmosphere of these occasions was unique. No one but complete insiders could possibly have understood many of the allusions. The world outside—the world of ordinary folk—was altogether excluded. Nervous but obviously pleased hangers-on kept the chilled champagne coming, the trade wind rustled the coconut fronds, and bitter enemies sat in unbuttoned familiarity, savoring their mystery, obviously the more precious for being open to so few.

The relations of Muñoz and Iriarte were not very different from those of La Guardia and John P. O'Brien, his predecessor in the mayoralty and a faithful retainer of Tammany. If La Guardia believed half of what he said about the Tammany crowd he was bound to regard O'Brien with contempt. But O'Brien had done him the honor of respecting his motives as few of the other bosses had professed to do, and La Guardia many times went out of his way—even at possible political expense—to express his regard for the bumbling

Tammanyite. And their intimate exchanges, especially when recalling La Guardia's maneuvers while filling out the unexpired term of Al Smith as president of the Board of Aldermen in 1920 and 1921, must have been at once highly technical and very satisfying. O'Brien liked La Guardia, and La Guardia reciprocated. Yet there can hardly ever have been campaigns with more concentrated bitterness than that of 1933, when they opposed each other. And I am quite certain that the majestic Seabury, La Guardia's principal respectable sponsor, would not have been seen in O'Brien's company, if he could have prevented it, for any reward whatever.

In 1933, however, both Tammany's candidate, O'Brien, and Fusion's candidate, La Guardia, could find some common cause in attacking Joseph V. McKee. McKee was the front for a daring raid in force by Ed Flynn, boss of the Bronx. After Walker had left office in disgrace, in 1932, there had been a special election, one feature of which had been an impressive write-in vote for McKee, who was not even a candidate. This had been interpreted in the same way by both Roosevelt and La Guardia. They saw in it a useful popular disillusionment with Tammany. Roosevelt convinced Flynn that the voters could be got to accept an alternate boss—himself; and La Guardia thought they wanted to get rid of bosses altogether, or at least that they could be persuaded that that was what they wanted. So it was a three-cornered fight. La Guardia regarded the Flynn-McKee effort as the most threatening, and Tammany was outraged by the treason of the Bronx boss. Both candidates lit into McKee and somewhat neglected each other—a lucky circumstance, considering their mutual affection.

La Guardia must have guessed, if he did not know, that the McKee candidacy was a Roosevelt idea. And he must have been grateful—perhaps to the point of presuming on the presidential favor. He may have mistaken what was convenient for Roosevelt as a kindness to himself. This may have aroused assumptions concerning Roosevelt's friendship for him that were unjustified. They would lead him into trouble in due time. But for the moment the intervention seemed like the beginning of an alliance.

From the start of the campaign it appeared that La Guardia was likely to be elected. He could therefore conduct what for him was a dignified canvass, talking learnedly about the need for a new charter, detailing the reorganization needed for several complex departments, and dwelling on the fiscal crisis (it was clear even then that bankruptcy impended although he did not realize how deep the causes lay). These speeches were the work of Berle, Seabury, Windels, and others of what later would have been called a brains trust. It was only when La Guardia was seized with the familiar last-minute panic that he published the eleven-year-old McKee article, dug up by some rascal in his entourage, which seemed, in advocating more Catholic fervor in education, to claim that the Jews got more out of the school system than they were entitled to.

La Guardia was elected, and O'Brien was not disgraced. The Tammany defeat was blamed on Flynn, who had split the Democratic strength. Roosevelt was far above the battle. It was said by mutual friends of O'Brien and La Guardia that the subsequent conversation of the recent political opponents had all the relaxed satisfactoriness I have referred to as characterizing the Muñoz-Iriarte meetings. [1]

Roosevelt allowed himself the same indulgence and perhaps found the political talk in some way valuable as well as agreeable. But there are not many equals for a President to converse with—fewer than there are for a mayor or a governor, even if the likely aspirants are counted who are benignly viewed. Besides, all Cabinet members and most legislators are ineligible, even though they have ambitions, as most of them have, or perhaps I should say *because* they have ambitions. This leaves almost no one. In Roosevelt's case, however, there were a few others who seemed to qualify—professional politicians, mostly from New York, who had been through old campaigns with him. These battles were lived over in recollection at every opportunity, with obvious pleasure if not with profit. A few of these confidants were in the position of not being by any possibility rivals,

---

[1] Ed Flynn's comments on La Guardia in *You're the Boss* (pp. 138 ff.) follow his account of the election in 1933. They are, however, directed to La Guardia in general rather than solely to the campaigner of that year. No one was ever in a better position for appraisal, but then Flynn was not necessarily being utterly frank:

The new Mayor, Fiorello La Guardia, was always an interesting character. As it turned out, his administration was generally beneficial to the city. It was certainly beneficial to him, for he had always known how to turn situations to personal account. He used Tammany Hall and the "boss system" as whipping boys. Yet he set up one of the best political machines that ever functioned in New York. Unquestionably, in his first campaign he was the beneficiary of gangster support. Once elected, of course, he disowned the gangsters.

and a few were entirely trustworthy after the way of dumb experts. Bob Wagner was one of the political equals. He was a senator from New York and, although a Tammany protégé, nevertheless an ardent progressive when the New Deal was new. In fact, before the New Deal was named, Wagner had advocated many of its measures. And he was ineligible for the presidency, having been born on foreign soil. His memories went back to Roosevelt's very first appearance as state senator and the instructive incident of the holdout against Tammany's senatorial candidate, "Blue-eyed Billy" Sheehan, which Wagner had helped to compromise. Roosevelt could reminisce with Wagner.

Then there were Herbert Lehman, Judge Mack, Tom Lynch, Frederick Green, and a few others from upstate New York, not often seen, but thoroughly trusted. And, young as Bob La Follette was, the President had a fondness and respect for him that were equaled in only a few other instances—Harry Hopkins, of course, Sam Rosenman, General Watson and Steve Early, and, until he died, Louis Howe. But these last were not equals. And I think that after he became President there were only a few people and only a few occasions when intimacy was possible. Like all other first-rank leaders, he had almost no actual friends among his many acquaintances. And his most intimate exchanges had limits that he did not allow to be breached. As to strict equals, there was no possibility of coming close to ex-President Hoover, sour and offended as he was. And Tom Dewey never rose to anything like equality in Roosevelt's esteem; indeed he regarded him as a despicable character altogether, hardly to be tolerated in decent society, an opinion that came from watching Dewey's political behavior and that of some of his managers.

For only two of his presidential opponents did Roosevelt have the requisite respect. Those were Landon and Willkie. Landon was so thoroughly beaten in 1936 that he retreated to the deep shadows and was heard of no more; Willkie, until he became a candidate in 1940, was a utility executive with a grievance that effectively prevented communication. He affected to consider that the President, acting through TVA, had wronged both him and his concern, the Commonwealth and Southern Corporation, and his often-voiced opinion of Roosevelt was unprintable. Their few personal communications in New Deal days had been acrimonious in the extreme. Of all kinds of people, also, the President was least likely to trust utility men.

I heard one of the acid conversations, and I thought then that Willkie's expressed disrespect not only for Roosevelt but for the office, which to me was shocking, would keep the President from ever having further exchanges with him. But later, after Willkie had been a candidate, had been beaten and assumed the posture of loyal oppositionist, I think they came closer together than anyone else at his level ever did with the President. About this Sam Rosenman had something to disclose that no one else knew before Roosevelt's death. [2]

I might perhaps add, though it has only limited applicability here, that Roosevelt was quite prepared to accept Landon as an equal and, in fact, on one occasion did so. It is possible that they had exchanges after their campaign. Of those I do not know. But, as I have recounted, I was present at one in the summer of 1936, when both were already nominated candidates. This was the meeting at Des Moines. The affair, for most of those present, had the flavor of high comedy; but Landon, I suspect, had quite another view of the proceedings.

How this kind of exercise bears on the art of politics seems to me obvious—obvious but not measurable. I suppose many conclusions are not objective in the sense of counting or measuring, and because these qualities are regarded as being associated with science, politics is not a science, although Gouverneur Morris did speak of it as a "sublime" one. Perhaps it is not an art either, but we have fallen into the way of designating anything not science an art, so I follow, perhaps indefensibly, this lazy fashion.

I have made something of contending that politicians seldom learn anything useful. But, like all my generalizations, this one has been qualified almost out of existence. I am now qualifying further. As everyone knows, the earnest devotee of any art is tireless in perfecting himself. He practices endlessly. He discusses, reads and studies, and goes over and over his experience; but, most of all, he practices. He can be said to experiment, as well, if by experiment is meant that he projects the consequences of proposed actions and tries them in imagination to see whether the useful will outweigh the danger-

---

[2] This was the project for forming a third party. Cf. *Working with Roosevelt* (New York: Harper, 1952), Chapter XXIV. It was also referred to in my book, *The Democratic Roosevelt*.

ous. Much of this is not conscious or consciously pursued. The easiest lessons are those got from talk. The hardest are those got from books. This is because conversation is congenial to the gregarious person, and most politicians are gregarious, even though usually frustrated because of the need for caution. Books are difficult because politicians are infrequently intellectual or even, in the real sense, literate. It is not their métier.

Still they do learn. They acquire a vast store of knowledge about their trade. But I should still contend that, to their fine perceptions, no situation, coming upon them in full career, seems precisely like any in the past. Nothing they have gone through, heard or read about, or practiced can seem entirely relevant. And I am quite sure, human beings and their societies being what they are, that variation is so nearly infinite as to preclude repetition or exact prediction.

This the practitioner knows. The sense in which he uses any learning or intelligence is very different from the usual meaning of those words. It is true that he did not get his skill from nowhere; and if he did not get it from nowhere he must have got it from somewhere. But the source is genuinely mysterious. This being so, there is no school and no course of study really to be recommended for aspiring Mayors, Governors, or Presidents.

The most successful among the professionals regard their activities as having a very large technical content. This is not secret knowledge because it does not consist of tricks; but it is mostly created anew in each situation or is so adapted as to seem new. There are tricks and they are often used, such as the discrediting of opponents, if possible indirectly, or by using someone from outside. This has been an element in many American campaigns and is sometimes thought by the historians to have had considerable effect. "Rum, Romanism, and Rebellion" is supposed to have helped Cleveland to win in 1884, but the illegitimate child which turned up in the same campaign had no discernible effect. In 1944 the Republican whispers about Roosevelt's physical disability rather reacted against Dewey. Muñoz was accused in the 1952 campaign by his opponent Travieso (who had been Chief Justice of the Supreme Court of Puerto Rico and ought to have been above such a resort) of irregularities of conduct that by no stretch could have any bearing on his fitness for public office; and, if anything, it added to Muñoz's majority. The conclusion about the use of such means is not at all clear. But there are evidently many professionals who believe them to be effective.

None of my three was much addicted to tricks. Roosevelt used almost none, if a rather narrow definition is accepted, and I know of many he rejected. It is relevant that the reason for his feeling that Dewey was an unworthy opponent was Dewey's tendency to lean on cleverness of a doubtful sort. He was an inveterate insinuator; and he and Herbert Brownell, his manager, finished their campaign with a reputation for unscrupulousness seldom exceeded in the not-too-scrupulous campaigns of the past. Muñoz's campaigns tended to heat up unnecessarily toward the end, and in all of them he said things he perhaps need not have said; but their level was, on the whole, high. He stuck to the issues, not using much more exaggeration of consequences, either, than was warranted. La Guardia was most susceptible and departed oftenest from political rectitude. But then he campaigned oftenest in risky circumstances. This may have been his own fault, and it can be said that part of a politician's competence is picking his fights; but he was not that kind of politician. It is impossible to believe that he did not enjoy his rowdy exchanges in the sense of finding the satisfactions in them that were necessary to his completion. It undoubtedly filled him with delight when his own gang of hard-fisted hoodlums, the "Ghibones," [3] bested the Tam-

[3] Not very much is actually known about the Ghibones—that is, for the record. Mr. Lowell Limpus, in his *This Man La Guardia* (New York: Dutton, 1938), pp. 185–86, etc., speaks of them and offers the translation "swashbucklers" for the term. "Bravos" might be better. At any rate, they were "led by the brilliant Marcantonio," and what respect Marcantonio had for American institutions was made amply clear by his later career as congressman. But even though La Guardia cannot, in later years, have approved Marcantonio's conduct, he was tied to him by bonds that went back to the younger man's fealty as a Ghibones leader. This is explained by Limpus' remark: *This organization, of which most New Yorkers never heard, was a secret fraternity, the members of which took a secret oath of personal allegiance to Mayor La Guardia* And: *This secret fraternity, unknown except in Harlem, was composed of a cross-section of Italian-American life . . . They were crusaders and they followed their leader blindly"*

Ernest Cuneo, in *Life with Fiorello* (New York: Macmillan, 1955), p. 143, speaks of the Ghibones in a rather muted way; he makes them seem to have been harmless crusaders. They were, he says, *half-clown and half bully-boys, who were uncritically devoted to Fiorello They were not unlike the early New York City volunteer firemen of a hundred years before, being long on gusto, in boisterous good health, and anxious to plunge into any fray offering good clean fun. Fiorello paid little or no attention to them except in the election season, but they were invaluable as organizers and guards during the actual contest. They were, in a sense, Fiorello's Minute Men.*

many thugs who had usually had their own way around Manhattan's polling places. But actually in his campaigning there was a maximum of fact and sense, conveyed to his constituents vividly and forcibly, and a minimum of the hokum resorted to by his opponents, some of whom were supposed to be very respectable citizens.

Anyone who will read in the files of the New York *Times* La Guardia's speeches in the mayoralty campaigns, which the *Times* reported faithfully, as is its way, and his congressional campaign speeches, will come, I believe, to the same conclusion I came to: that he was a wonderfully effective educator at the same time that he was making his plea for votes. Year after year, battle after battle, he spoke exhaustively of the relevant issues it was his responsibility to explore. In relatively few instances did he make ungenerous or personal attacks. He sometimes used undignified methods or found overvivid illustrations, and he was thoroughly demagogic and hypocritical about bosses and bossism. But, to excuse this, it must be added that he was always fighting Tammany. There were bosses to beat, even if he was obviously an unorthodox one himself; and he had the kinds of constituencies in which vividness was appreciated.

It is hard to estimate even roughly how many words La Guardia devoted to telling New Yorkers about their city and its operations. There must have been millions about the budget alone, and anyone who thinks it easy to talk about finances and hold the attention of voters is innocent indeed. And especially if budgets are not your own best subject.

It is easy to see how this is done, and La Guardia does not deserve all the credit. It is unlikely that he ever wrote one of the sober and well-reasoned speeches himself. But, like all prospectively successful candidates, he could call on plenty of expert assistance. The budget speeches were written by bureaucrats or by Berle, the reorganization dissertations by Paul Windels or by Lester Stone or Jim Kieran—as able a group as could have been got together in the United States. It is only the rough-and-tumble street-corner speeches that are pure La Guardia. They were not usually reported in the New York *Times*. They could not be. They were often incoherent. They always became impassioned. They were repetitive in subject matter and highly personalized. They also revealed, to those who listened critically, some of La Guardia's shortcomings. He had an unmistakably defective command of English, a long way from the cultured product Seabury, Berle, Windels, Morris, or others of his supporters could have produced. But none of *them* could have been elected mayor of New York. Newbold Morris was not convinced of that until he tried for himself and was thoroughly defeated. [4] None of the others ever ran for anything.

[4] Cf. Newbold Morris, *Let the Chips Fall* (New York: Appleton, 1955), especially Chapter 10, which bears the plaintive title "God Made So Few Republicans."

16

There was no concealing La Guardia's recent-immigrant look, even if he had wanted to assume another guise, as in his later years—in contrast with his earlier ones in politics—he undoubtedly did. So Neapolitan did he appear that it was widely assumed that he was himself foreign-born, something not at all unfavorable in his successive congressional districts and even, perhaps, in the city at large. For the foreign-born voters seem to favor a foreign-born candidate, even though his origin is not their own. La Guardia, for instance, was always a favorite among the Jews. But this last was, in his case, to be accounted for on other grounds as well. He spoke a certain amount of Yiddish, and in his ancestry there was a Jewish grandmother he had never seen.

He looked and acted polyglot. And since in his circumstances such an appearance could be politically useful, he exaggerated it; and those who knew him best were well aware of his innocent fakery, so much more attractive than the pseudo-aristocratic pose assumed sometimes by Americans. Actually he was as American as Al Smith or any of a number of others descended from recently come families. He had been born in New York, but his Italian-immigrant father had been an Army bandmaster, so that Fiorello had spent the years of childhood and youth on various Army posts. The one of these he always recalled as home was at Prescott in Arizona. There he went to public school until the Spanish-American War took his father away.

When he was sixteen he was undoubtedly as typical a small-town American boy as could be found anywhere in the wide West. He was small and excitable, and he had an olive complexion and dark, liquid eyes; but even in Prescott he was not thought to be much out of the ordinary. It was remarkable how little he was affected by the Italianism of his family. He even escaped learning the language. But he did become familiar with the horses and guns of the West and presently moved on to automobiles and airplanes.

After his father had gone off with his regiment, Fiorello staged the first of those imaginative performances that were to characterize his whole career. He turned up one morning in the office of the Phoenix *Morning Courier* and suggested himself as a war correspondent; he offered to write without pay if his expenses were met. I would give something, as an observer of his progress, to have a recording of his conversation on that morning with the *Courier's* editor. He must have made a fantastic representation, because actually his offer was accepted. At sixteen he went off to Tampa, where his father was serving with the 11th Infantry, to report the war.

In that hot, confused, and unsanitary staging base an event occurred that may very well have had a good deal to do with the transformation of young Fiorello into a lifetime radical. His father was one of the victims of the notorious embalmed beef that was so much deadlier to the American soldiers of 1898 than were the Spanish armies in Cuba. He never recovered from the poisoning and presently was invalided out and in a few years died. An anger centering in his father's betrayal by commercial exploiters of the war struck into Fiorello's soul. I think it never left him. At any rate, when I knew him he still had the easiest indignation to arouse about such things of anyone I have ever known. The least hint of corruption, even of smart practice, to say nothing of injustice, would start him on an almost automatic tirade; and the result could easily be far more serious than the immediate outburst. A crusade might be begun that he would pursue for years; some of them he kept up all his life. And when La Guardia took out after public enemies, they knew someone was after them. In such causes he was implacable, persistent, and not at all scrupulous about the weapons he used. He himself was completely fearless. There was no way to reach and stop him—and everything was, at one time or another, tried, from bribery to blackmail. He was tough.

Very early he acquired the reputation of being an angry little man. It was some time before wrongdoers learned to leave out the "little" in that appellation. Eventually he seemed to them like a giant. Week after week while he was mayor, smart-aleck journals sought to belittle him by reference to his looks. One news magazine spoke of him habitually as "New York's hen-shaped little mayor." That made it seem funnier, evidently, when his personal direction of his firemen, for instance, on freezing winter nights was described. Perhaps he was a comic figure among the busy firemen with ice and water all about. And perhaps he was in the way of the professionals. But the voters, however comic it seemed to journalists, preferred him to a stuffed shirt from the silk-stocking wards or another Tammany puppet from lower Manhattan.

His ready anger and his disposition to action showed themselves long before he ever presented himself to the New York electorate for approval. Between his Tampa experience and his first nomination there was a decade and a half of solid experience, including several incidents that were quite characteristic—for instance, when he refused what he believed to be undemocratic truckling to a queen. There was more than a hint of creativeness, too, in his invention of the preliminary examination for prospective immigrants, which infuriated the officials of the steamship companies because although it eased many a heartache it tended to reduce traffic. This interval was partly spent abroad, as will have been guessed. That was because his mother went back to her family in Budapest after his father's death, taking Fiorello with her. At nineteen he sought and obtained a clerkship in the American consulate there. Later he was sent to Trieste as an interpreter, and still later he became the American consul at Fiume.

The southeastern European ports were important funnels for the tide of emigration that was at its height in those years. Fiorello began to be harried and harassed in these jobs as he was to be all the rest of his life. There was no end to a consul's duties, and there was an infinite number of services a conscientious youngster could perform for the poor and ignorant hordes of peasants who were having their first experience, when he saw them, of steamship—and even, perhaps, of train—travel, and who had only the vaguest inflated notions of what life was to be like in the El Dorado toward which they were being drawn. There was disillusion coming to them. Fiorello yearned a bit over them and resolved that anyway the crooks who preyed on their ignorance should not have official collaboration. He did all he could to make transition easier for the movers, not always with the approval of his superiors, who were more susceptible than he to reproof from influential interests.

Incidental to this service, he acquired a sort of facility in half a dozen languages that would be very useful to him in his later years of campaigning. He even learned there, after he was twenty, the Italian that most people thought he had known from childhood. Neither in Italian, however, nor in any of the other languages, including the Yiddish, did he ever have a scholarly range. He was fluent in ordinary exchange. And this served his purpose quite as well as a broader and deeper knowledge might have done. Those who ridiculed his accent in various tongues may have hurt his pride but they did not affect his popularity.

In 1906 he decided that he must find a way out of the governmental regimentation into which he had fallen. It is not unlikely that this decision was made easier by intimations of official displeasure. Suggestions of this sort can be so delicate as to be unmeasurable and yet definite enough to constitute a warning. This kind of thing is almost a specialty of such services as he had entered on. The truth was that he was not a natural bureaucrat, and if he had stayed he might well have ended his career in a post rather less conspicuous than the one where he had begun; he would have been made to feel the disapproval of his stodgy superiors. At any rate, he simply cut loose and returned to New York.

At home, after some difficulty, he got a job as interpreter at Ellis Island and almost at once began to study law at night in the Law School of New York University. He never became very learned in the law, but then neither did Roosevelt. And it is to be doubted whether either of them had at any time serious intentions toward the profession. It was a way into politics and something to fall back on in the almost inevitable intervals of failure in any such career. This last was more important, a good deal, to the penniless young man whose father had been a bandmaster than to the young gentleman from Dutchess County who was starting in at about the same time.

These two were of an age—born in the same year, one in January, one in December—but when La Guardia was undertaking the hard grind of night school, and without any college background, Roosevelt was just entering on a clerkship with one of New York's oldest and most respectable firms, whose atmosphere was of that exclusive sort La Guardia never in all his life penetrated. Roosevelt did not earn a law degree from Columbia, although he learned enough to pass the bar examination. This lack of a degree was often thrown up to him in his later career. Nicholas Murray Butler told him he would never succeed unless he acquired it. But his neglect to do so appears to have been more from lack of interest than ability.

Anyway, Roosevelt stayed with Carter, Ledyard and Milburn for only four years. In 1910, when he saw and seized the opportunity no one else believed in and, against all the odds, became a Democratic state senator from his home district—the Twenty-sixth—La Guardia, four years behind, was passing his bar examinations. As a newly made lawyer La Guardia practiced on his own for four years, if it could be called practicing. His clients were few and poor and his fees were hard to earn and often harder to take from those who could ill afford them. His comparative idleness gave him time to haunt the Republican clubhouse and make himself useful—Republican because Tammany was Democratic and represented all that he had learned to hate in public life. And his poverty was something he was used to.

In the fall of 1914, when Roosevelt had had his first preferment and was well started as Assistant Secretary of the Navy under Woodrow Wilson and Josephus Daniels, La Guardia, rather by default, because no one else wanted it, was getting himself the Republican nomination for the Congress in a mid-Manhattan district. He campaigned so strenuously and reached so many voters that, as has been noted, he was barely defeated in that perfectly safe Tammany bailiwick. His campaigning energy marked him and made him eligible for further tries. In 1916 he ran from a Harlem district and won, although it was almost as unlikely as his other effort. This was his first political victory. It aroused his appetite for more. He took his seat just before the special session called by President Wilson in the spring of 1917, when Roosevelt had already served four years in Washington. The neophyte legislator promptly and without question voted for the declaration of war, and for the drafting of citizens as soldiers.

He had served only a few months when he was turned down for training in the gentlemen's camp at Plattsburg which it had become fashionable to attend just then for those who wanted to enlist but felt themselves to be officer material. He was, they said, too short.

But he was not too short to fly. And he had been learning the preliminaries from an acquaintance, the famous air pioneer, Bellanca. The Army Air Service took him, not knowing at first that a congressman was in their midst. Before long, and with a training that would in later years have seemed suicidally short, he was in Italy and in command of a bomber squadron at Foggia—curiously enough, the town from which his father had emigrated. Training or no training, he commanded and he flew—in the Caproni bombers which soon seemed to younger fliers hardly possible to have got off the ground or, once off, to have kept in the air.

He was fair at flying, but he got into trouble as a commander. His quarrels were not with his men but with the army bureaucracy. He repeatedly exceeded his authority for what he believed to be good cause and escaped being disciplined by a hair. Then, after Caporetto, someone in authority had the imagination to see that he would be uniquely useful as a propagandist in an Italy all but demoralized by defeat. He made hundreds of speeches during the next year and flew his bomber at the same time—a kind of high-pressure activity that suited him. It exhausted all the energy his powerful stocky body and his restless mind could furnish.

I have said enough, perhaps, about the background of his extraordinary career, to explain some of his later success. What he was before 1916, he was also afterward. If he learned some discretion, he never learned enough. He was "a natural" (in the New Yorkese he knew so well) for the Congress, for the aldermanic presidency, and for the mayoralty.

His success up to the mayoralty was phenomenal. But this for some reason is as far as politicians ever seem to get. Mayors of New York seldom move farther, as La Guardia must have known. But then he had got everything he had had by challenging the unlikely, and he saw no reason for stopping at fifty-odd. Rules do not command the respect of those who believe themselves exempt. And La Guardia felt that none of the rules applied to him.

It will not do at all to conclude from an analysis of his case that he was successful because he was "close to the people"—that is, bearing the stigmata of poverty, lack of education, and so on. It is true that he was successful; it is also true that he had a deficient schooling and earned his law degree at night. Then, too, he often betrayed an indifferent command of English and had a wayward accent. But one who is tempted to work out a cause-and-effect equation from this accidental concurrence would have to deal with the cases of Muñoz and Roosevelt. These two equally successful politicians were, in these respects, La Guardia's opposites. No one in the world was ever less like a street gamin than the aristocratic Roosevelt. And Muñoz had a background, of all things, in literature. He was an intellectual—not a scholar, but at least a hopeful artist. And he had a constituency more poverty-stricken and ignorant by far than La Guardia's.

There has been a rags-to-riches myth in America, a kind of leveler tradition, part, probably, of the whole equality misconception. The extreme form of this notion is that all men are interchangeable; that is, anyone can do any job as well as anyone else. After Jackson's day and down to Lincoln's—and even beyond—this was a quite prevalent view, one that was acknowledged by most politicians; it tended to die out as the age of large-scale enterprise with corollary specialization advanced and as higher education became widely available. Still, even in La Guardia's day there was a holdover of interchangeability nonsense, and La Guardia himself was not entirely free of it. Since he had not had a university education he was inclined to belittle those who had. He made free enough use of experts, but he abused them a good deal, and part of the calculated disparagement was the claim that they were "educated incompetents." It was something he often told them to their faces in moments of annoyance. His annoyance was apt to increase if they did not seem impressed.

La Guardia placed an extravagantly high value on the political arts. This is understandable: it was his talent, just as it was that of Roosevelt and Muñoz. With it he could, as he was apt to say, make it possible for all the experts to do their work in favorable circumstances. The implication was that no one else would have made it possible. This was true enough for some individuals, although not for all, as the case of Robert Moses, if there were no other, shows clearly enough. Moses worked in the regimes of many politicians and they all valued him. It requires planners, architects, and engineers to carry out public works, and skilled administrators to operate a municipality with even fair success. The city would not have ceased to exist if La Guardia had not won elections. This was something some of his commissioners reminded him of when they were tried too far; but they did concede, all of them, that it existed on a higher level because of him, even if there might be moments when the opposite seemed to be the fact.

The rags-to-riches pattern of the Alger heroes was being broken every day of La Guardia's life by the grand contemporary politician who, successful as La Guardia was, made his success seem almost trivial. For Roosevelt went all the way to the presidency and was re-elected three times.

Besides being almost exact contemporaries, these two had almost identical approaches and affiliations. I mean to say that they were both progressives in the rather strict American tradition and they had in their minds, however vaguely, about the same political and economic programs. According to the Alger doctrine, their degrees of success should have been reversed. And, in introspective moments, this occurred to La Guardia. In fact, I had more than one conversation about it with him during the year before Roosevelt decided—or let his decision be known—that he would run for a third term. That was a terrible year for La Guardia, one of tension which increased until it became almost unbearable. For there was no obvious successor to Roosevelt among the Democrats, and why should not La Guardia have thought of himself in that connection?

If Roosevelt was the best political operative of his time, La Guardia was certainly the next best. He was just as good a progressive— better, he sometimes thought—and he shared Roosevelt's views about foreign policy, only, as he said, more so.

On the whole, as he sized things up, La Guardia was inclined to feel in 1938 and 1939 that something of great consequence might happen to him in 1940. In thinking about this, I concluded that Roosevelt would have to run again if pressed. He was discouraged both about the New Deal, which had come to a dead end, and about the successes of the European aggressors in opposition to whom he was bitterly determined. He was not influencing American opinion as he would have liked, and the delay seemed to him potent with danger.

The only becoming way he could run again for the presidency would be in response to an aroused and demanding opinion. My bit toward that end was my debate with my old friend Ray Moley before the *Herald Tribune* Forum in October 1938. I made quite a

convincing case for the draft, as I still think, on the ground of un-
finished business. [1]

To this suggestion of mine there was a certain reaction. And there
was a very sudden one from La Guardia. He called me in the next
day and denounced me furiously. It was the highest temper I had
ever seen him display, and I had seen a number of such exhibitions.
It took him about a week to calm down, during which he raged in
diminuendo every day. I launched into a spate of words as he ran
down. I told him he was betraying a dangerous weakness which
he could not afford. He had set his heart on something so unlikely
that he ought not to have entertained it even as a vague idea. I regretted his hurt. More, I thought he might be a better President
for 1940–44 than Roosevelt, because Roosevelt had used up all his
New Deal credits and could accomplish nothing more; he might
even lose a good deal of what had been won. But it was just not
possible. He would have to have the Democratic nomination, and
how could it be got? I ran over the convention in prospect. The
politicians would be in control there. Roosevelt could force the selection of himself but he could not force anyone else's selection. If it
was not Roosevelt it would be Hull, very likely, and that possibility
was what all of us had to think about. It was, in fact, what Roosevelt
had to think about.

There was an amusing contrast between these exchanges with the
Mayor and those I had with the President when I next saw him—
which was during the following week. He had not been so pleasant
to me in years. It was apparent that the third-term suggestion was
an agreeable one and that he had been waiting for someone to make
it without being coached. In the atmosphere created by the reverberations in the press he could sense the political potentialities.
But he gave me no hint then or later of his decision. He joked
about it; he even summed up the arguments for and against; also,
he led me into another of the speculative discussions about what all
of us would do when the Republicans were in power again and we
were in exile. But he had talked that way for the whole of the year
before the 1936 election too, and it obviously meant nothing definite.

I saw the President rather oftener during the following months
than I had recently done. Naturally I watched for some hint of

[1] *Report of the Eighth Annual New York Herald Tribune Forum*, 1938, pp. 88 ff.

what he might do. I came to the wrong conclusion; partly, I think, because he kept finding arguments against another term, but partly because several times Mrs. Roosevelt referred to the possibility in a disparaging way. To begin with, she reproved me, in the gentle way she had, for bringing up the matter at the Forum. I said that if I had not done it someone else would. Yes, she said, but everyone will think you were authorized to send up a trial balloon. And they will conclude that Franklin's only hesitation is whether or not he could be elected. But if I had been brash, the President's agreeableness about it showed that he was quite willing to have the discussion begun. So I said that she might not want to endure a third term but that did not mean that the President felt the same way.

Obviously that was what was worrying her. She was working as arduously as she dared—and doing a little maneuvering too—to set her husband's mind against running again. I thought then, as I would not have thought later, that this was a powerful influence. There was also another factor that I rated as a strong one. This was the President's sense of tradition. He was known to the public as an innovator, an experimentalist, as one who believed in actions that might work or might have to be discarded; and, most spectacular of all, he had been disrespectful to the Supreme Court and had told the Congress that if they thought measures he asked for unconstitutional, that ought not to deter their passage. This kind of open-mindedness was widely misinterpreted as a lack of respect for precedent or tradition. This was a mistake. No one in the White House was ever more conscious of being the successor to great men who had gone before him and of being clothed in their habit. He also thought of himself as belonging to a naval tradition; he had wanted to go to Annapolis as a youth; he had read naval history all his life; he loved to surround himself with the collection of prints showing the ships and battles in which naval prestige was created. Also, he had been Assistant Secretary through a war. I had seen the easy but firm way in which the ceremonial of his office was administered. I thought tradition had a very strong hold on him and that this might be the real deterrent to his seeking a third term.

But, like others, I had failed to make the nice distinction I should have made between ceremonial tradition which supported his office and enhanced his effectiveness and what he would regard as limitations on it manufactured by those who had an interest in its weakening. There was no constitutional prohibition against a third term, although after reading the Republican press, as the argument went on in the first half of 1940, such a conclusion might easily have been reached by an outsider. I think now that the President very early made up his mind that the third-term barrier was no more than another myth about what Presidents ought to do or ought not to do, calculated to limit the powers of the office. There had been alliances between the special interests and congressmen for most of our history. The interests could escape regulation if divisiveness could be furthered, and this could most easily be done by weighting the power of the Congress against that of the presidency. The President represented the public interest, he was the embodiment of national union and public power; congressmen represented localities, and in those localities they attended closely to the louder voices.

It was a tremendous mistake for one to make who not only thought he knew his government from having had an unusual intimacy with it for some years but who also had had the privilege of a President's confidence. Along in the spring I began to be certain that the President was bent on retirement. This awakened in my mind more speculation about his possible successor. Much was being said and written about Farley's hopes and Hull's ambitions. I knew also that Henry Wallace thought himself eligible now, after years of preparation. But I was convinced that none of them could win against a better opponent than Landon. And this, I thought, would be so apparent that some more attractive alternative must be discovered. I ought to have seen that this weakness was precisely what made another Roosevelt term inevitable.

By 1940 I had come to think that La Guardia was presidential timber. He might even be a notable one if he could be nominated and elected. I resolved to make the suggestion, even though my making it risked the suspicion that I spoke for Roosevelt. I looked for a suitable place to speak from, and opportunely, at about that time, Look asked me if I had something on my mind to write about. I said I would like to argue La Guardia's eligibility. They agreed. But then I had an attack of caution. I made an occasion to argue the matter with La Guardia. It could hardly be described, however, as an argument. He was, that spring, campaigning as hard as anyone could. His mileage about the country was unprecedented for a New

York mayor, something the newspapers were having a good deal of
fun about. He had naturally offered himself only by implication.
But no one would have carried out that spring operation without
something serious in mind, and it was an election year.

I proposed to turn the offering by implication into a definite suggestion. Coming from me, one of his New York City commissioners,
and one known to have a certain association with Roosevelt, it was
certain to be treated seriously. Was he ready for it?

He was ready, and I wrote the articles. But they were not published, and the opportunity passed. It was too late to find another
forum by then; and, anyway, everyone but La Guardia and I seemed
to know that the President would run again. He was convinced
before I was. It was not yet time for a Progressive gathering into a
party.

17

Roosevelt had the power to, but did not, gratify the ambitions of either La Guardia or Muñoz; La Guardia's disappointments were finally to be counted as three. He might have been the President's successor, he might have been appointed Secretary of War, and he might have become a general. As to these frustrations, I am inclined to blame mostly his ticketing as undependable. That weakness for showmanship, even for the bizarre, which everyone knew him to have, had certainly clouded his reputation with those who, at that time, thought it necessary for the Democratic party to cultivate conservatism. He might at heart have been a western Progressive, but he had acted so long as the "sawed-off wop" that the stereotype was fixed. Reform was no longer on the agenda at the beginning of the forties as the war approached. The New Deal was being dismantled in a tacit trade for conservative support. The President gulped hard over each loss, but the Southerners were implacable; Dr. Win-the-War had not yet taken over from Dr. New Deal, but he was on the way to doing so.

The President had to consider that, although La Guardia was in many ways just what was needed, he did have a notorious temper. He seemed to be perpetually indignant and was always popping off without considering consequences. This reputation was largely a holdover from his irresponsible days as a congressman when he controlled the balance-of-power progressive bloc in opposition to Hooverism, but it had not been much modified by his performance as mayor; even in that responsible position he was known to be badly balanced and subject to fits of rage. That much of this was calculated, was his way of getting things done, the President no doubt knew. But there were those to tell him it was not the procedure consonant with the secretaryship of War in dangerous times. Add to this that La Guardia did not fit the pattern of coalition the President needed for the confrontation of the crisis—the Republicans did not acknowledge him—and no further explanation is really required.

Muñoz's ambitions reached their consummation when Truman was President, not while Roosevelt was in the White House. I could excuse this delay by pleading that Roosevelt did what he could to advance self-government in Puerto Rico but that the Congress was hostile and he could not use the credit he was hoarding for his war measures in a fight for the Puerto Rican cause. There was something in this, but not too much, and it was certainly not a complete explanation. For the President had had no reason, until I began to tell him a different story than he had heard before, to trust Muñoz or to further his ambitions. What he heard from Ickes was unfavorable. Ickes had taken very hard the nationalist attacks on Governor Winship and the killing by terrorists of Police Chief Riggs during Winship's administration. He suspected Muñoz of having some connection with the *nacionalistas* or, if not that, of having given them sympathy.

When I went to Puerto Rico on a mission of investigation early in 1941, having been given leave by La Guardia, Ickes was fed up, as he said, with all the unruly politicos; and most of all he was fed up with Muñoz. He had reached the hand-washing stage, he told me, and the less he heard about the island from then on the better he would like it. He had done everything, he considered, that anyone could. He had given a disproportionate attention to Puerto Rican ills; he had got rid of an objectionable Governor and had caused a good one to be sent—Winship. But Winship had been treated as badly as the impossible Gore. After Winship, Leahy had been Governor briefly. His report was that insular politics was a snake's nest. He was glad to leave. Now Guy Swope, former congressman from Pennsylvania, had succeeded. Swope was a liberal and sympathetic man, but he was having the same troubles.

A good many of the difficulties these successive governors had found themselves in had come from Muñoz, although he would contend that it was for sufficient reason. Winship and Leahy were allied with his political enemies, although Muñoz himself always spoke of Leahy as a fair-minded man who tried to see all sides. The fact was that the Governors of those days, as executives, could get nothing done except at the sufferance of the local legislature. That body controlled money, appointments, and even the Governor's household. He therefore had to accept direction from the majority; and the majority was, until 1940 an unholy coalition of far left and far right which had little or no interest in any public business. Their concentration on the benefices of politics was one that can hardly have been equaled anywhere. Governors had to conciliate them, but Muñoz harried all the authorities for patronage too. In 1940 Muñoz so nearly routed the reactionaries that only a few liberals stood between him and a legislative majority. And the necessary few could be persuaded. So Swope had an even more difficult time. He had mostly to conciliate Muñoz. But the coalition could still give lots of trouble.

Muñoz had an agenda. Ickes really sent me to see what it amounted to, although nominally I was to investigate only one segment of it—the land program. Muñoz had devised an ingenious approach, as I reported to Ickes and the President. But Ickes was far from convinced that any good could originate in another Puerto Rican politico, even if he was supposed to be a liberal. Muñoz had made life so miserable for everyone sent from Washington that, in the crucial years of the early New Deal, Gruening, Winship, and Ickes had learned to detest him. It was strange for Gruening and Ickes to be allied with the reactionary politicos. But there it was. They controlled the legislature. But now Muñoz was coming to the top and Ickes saw that he had been mistaken.

Ickes hardly knew how he had got himself into such company. He was not inclined to take the blame himself. But he was willing to allow me a wholly free hand in a situation that had completely escaped from his control and that he could not justify.

I very quickly came to consider that correction ought to be undertaken at once. I was inclined at first to consider immediate independence, or at least an announcement of eventual independence, as necessary. About this I had several talks with the President. He was against it. It was not that he thought the Puerto Rican affiliation of any advantage to the United States, except in a strategic sense, but that he felt we had a serious obligation we had not discharged. The most I could get from him was a willingness to give way to advance. It seemed to me that unless Puerto Ricans were to accept independence—which I felt certain the Congress would grant for the asking— [1] they must move toward a more agreeable status than now existed.

The attitude of President Roosevelt toward Puerto Rico was partly, then, shaped by misinformation. But partly, also, it came from the same general impulse that led him to prefer retired admirals and generals as Governors for all non-self-governing areas. I had had to join Ickes in a fervent plea in 1934 to prevent the President from returning the Virgin Islands to Navy administration; and the smaller Pacific possessions never had a civilian government during his time. The imperialist ideas in his mind were still warring with more recent ones. When he had been Assistant Secretary of the Navy he had visited Haiti and Santo Domingo on a historic occasion and had taken credit in his 1920 campaign for the vice-presidency— unjustifiably—for bringing order to those republics by way of the Marines and new constitutions. There was an admiral concealed

---

[1] An opinion confirmed by later developments, one of which was President Eisenhower's message to the United Nations in 1953, when an argument was in process concerning Puerto Rico's status, saying that independence would gladly be granted if requested. The difficulty with this statement was that the President said "when the legislature asks for it" instead of "when the people ask for it." This made an opening for the politicos of which they threatened to take immediate and embarrassing advantage, unbalancing Muñoz's carefully poised structure. It was at once apparent that unless he used stringent suppressive measures the legislators might demand so much control over federal funds for the island as to suggest their withdrawal. The Congress had consented to extremely favorable arrangements; if the Puerto Ricans demanded a control over federal expenditures not granted even to the States, there might easily have been a reaction.

This unexpected crisis, arriving suddenly because both Muñoz and the Department of State had pushed for United Nations recognition that the Commonwealth was self-governing, constituted a real threat. The small nations of the U.N. tended to confuse self-government with independence, a natural result of the long struggle for freedom from the expanding imperialisms of the world. They found it almost impossible to conceive that a non-self-governing people could choose to become affiliated with the nation which for half a century had withheld self-government.

President Eisenhower was in that limbo of education into which most Presidents retreat during their first years and from which sudden emergences are so often embarrassing. He should have said on this occasion that if the Puerto Rican people (meaning in popular referendum) asked for independence they could have it. But this was for him too fine a distinction. It was not too fine in Puerto Rico, however, and there were many professionals who now thought they saw an opening for blackmail. They could not, for their part, conceive that the United States would be willing to grant independence, a mistake that Muñoz knew the United States far too well to make.

somewhere in Roosevelt and had been, I suppose, ever since his ambition for a naval career had been thwarted by his father.

It always had to be remembered about Roosevelt, too, that these attitudes were not outright and were not always controlling. They were so little noticed most of the time that few people actually knew that he had them. Was he not the author of the Good-Neighbor Policy? The answer to this is that he came to accept it after some consideration. It is probably Sumner Welles who ought to be credited with its origin and certainly he was its chief sponsor during the Roosevelt administration. The fact is that the President had a fairly slow transition from his period of approval of naval hegemony in the Caribbean (as well as in the Pacific) to that of the full acceptance of freedom. One of the landmarks of this transition was an article written by him for *Foreign Affairs* in 1928. [2]

This was a survey of the whole range of foreign policy, but its references to the Caribbean were especially noteworthy. He went to the length, in this article, of repudiating the so-called "Roosevelt Corollary" to the Monroe Doctrine. [3]

He advocated the abandonment of "unilateral rights to interference," a phrase that implied a Pan-American organization of the states and a merging of international police powers. It stopped a good deal short, however, of suggestions for mutual aid that were to be associated with his successor's name. And actually Muñoz's ambitions for Puerto Rico had their climax in Truman's acquiescence—and, perhaps it should be said, his ignorance. It would not be fair to say that Muñoz took advantage of the President's lack of experience; nevertheless, Truman was willing to have the United States, at that time, assume the generous posture involved in the

[2] Published in July and therefore written in the spring. This would have been before his acceptance of the nomination for the governorship of New York, and before making the (second) "Happy Warrior" speech which put Al Smith into nomination at the Democratic convention in Houston. He nevertheless assumed to speak for the Democratic party. He called his article "Our Foreign Policy: A Democratic View."

[3] The reference here is to Theodore Roosevelt's doctrine that if European nations might not interfere in the Western Hemisphere it was the duty of the United States to see to it that obligations to creditor nations were duly met. It was a further duty to maintain order and to preserve peace, an obligation that ran to interference in small nations' domestic affairs on not too severe provocation.

Commonwealth status without many safeguards. This did not, and could not, have happened with Roosevelt's consent.

Looking at Puerto Rico as a problem for the United States, it is well to recall that Muñoz happened to be rising to power when a change of attitude was in process. Until the end of the war in 1945, the dominant consideration had been a strategic one. The military dispositions of the decade preceding had naturally been determined by the weapons available and the source, the objective, and the direction of possible attack. The source was Germany, the objective was the Panama Canal, and the direction was through the Caribbean island arc from Florida to Trinidad. In this arc Puerto Rico was central. Bases there were, in the strict sense, strategic and essential. Puerto Rico therefore had to be maintained as a controlled and, if possible, friendly base. As wartime Governor, this was my first responsibility. [4]

But when the African invasion was established, there was a complete change, somewhat tardily acknowledged by the military bureaucracy, but apparent at once to one with such a responsibility as mine. There was no longer any possibility of actual invasion, although the submarine blockade was still a serious problem; and the development of new weapons, together with the acceleration in airplane range and speed, made it unlikely that Puerto Rico would ever again be strategically important even if there should be another threat to the United States from the east. The significance of this was that policy could be revised. And it was then that I laid before President Roosevelt my analysis of the change and my proposals for new relationships.

In general I urged that local government should be freed from outside controls. I told the President he was quite wrong to think of the Puerto Ricans as politically immature or incapable of administering their own affairs They were, in fact, more advanced than many of the states of our Union. We ought to begin successive changes as rapidly as the Congress could be got to grant them. Specifically we ought to begin at once with the elective governorship, proceeding to a status somewhat short of full statehood—it could not be full because for a long time more economic assistance would be needed than the federal government gives to the states.

[4] This whole matter was explored in my book, *The Stricken Land*, op. cit.

We need not worry about local protection for military bases; they were no longer necessary to our defense.

While I was arguing thus with President Roosevelt, Muñoz was consolidating his political power. He had me in the governorship as a guarantee of Washington's benevolence. He controlled the American relationship which a large majority of the insular electorate believed essential. One question was how he would use the rather sudden and unexpected gift of power. The other question was whether he could make good the expectation of the electorate that progress toward autonomy would occur. He was extremely cautious about encouraging hopes. He had so little faith that anything would happen that he isolated the question of status and for years refused to discuss it. He even had the reluctance I have mentioned to serve on the committee I persuaded the President to set up for making the first recommendation to the Congress. He balked badly at my proposals and my timetable. Not only that, he made up his mind that Roosevelt would be defeated in 1944, as he had similarly made up his mind in 1940, and this confused his planning. He succeeded in alienating both Secretary Ickes and President Roosevelt, and neither of them made any energetic effort to implement the committee's recommendations about the governorship.

But President Roosevelt was re-elected. Then, within a few months, he was succeeded by the former senator from Missouri. Muñoz was undecided and confused. Our relationship, which ought to have been, I thought, close and co-operative, fell into what for me was an unwelcome strangeness. When President Roosevelt died I tried to resign but, at the new President's insistence, stayed on temporarily, meanwhile urging that my program be considered. Muñoz seemed to have little interest. But when I had left in 1946 and Jesús Piñero, one of Muñoz's political subordinates, had become interim governor, Truman showed an active interest. He saw half the problem—the need for autonomy; but he missed the other half—the continuing interest of the nation—thus reversing Roosevelt, who saw the half Truman did not see but missed the rest. He just never did think Puerto Ricans were the equal of continental Americans.

The elective governorship was approved without much interest being shown by Muñoz; he had something different in mind. And when he became Governor he was in a position to move toward his objective. Perhaps he could have moved toward it anyway. But it seems, retrospectively to have been a necessary stage in progress toward autonomy. If he did not work for it, his luck worked for him, knowing that politicians need luck as well as prescience.

18

Puerto Rico, Muñoz, and all the problems associated with the Caribbean fell rapidly toward comparative insignificance in Roosevelt's mind as the war went on toward its end. He was incredibly burdened, and it was only to be expected that as he developed a new set of objectives—those for a permanent organization of the world—he should lose sight of pretty much everything except the conditions of settlement. How could it have been otherwise? In approaching the peace, as in the management of the war, his political genius found a full and satisfactory occupation. His powers of visualization were tested to the last limit, and his talents for maneuver and manipulation were engaged in the pursuit of sublime objectives as they had never been before. He was no longer interested in winning elections, or even in winning the receding war; he was determined to establish the conditions of security. It was the same struggle that Woodrow Wilson had lost.

It has to be admitted, in view of the almost immediate splitting of the world into two ideologies and two corresponding hostile halves, that Roosevelt, too, largely wasted his effort; but it was not for the same reason that Wilson had failed. Roosevelt engineered the United Nations into being, once he had accepted the idea, as Wilson had done with the League; but the emerging organization included the United States as Wilson's had not. And if the U.N. did not become an effective instrument of peace, it did at least provide a forum for the discussion of differences, surviving crisis after crisis even when survival seemed unlikely. And I think that Roosevelt would have seen hope for the compromise of differences, however deep they might be, so long as talk went on. It is when talking stops that shooting begins. The very immoderateness of a good deal of the talk in the decade after the war was a faithful representation of clashing opinions; and since it was so representative, it was less dangerous in the open than it would have been bottled up.

It seems that Roosevelt did not at first think in terms of an immediate world organization to include all nations. His practical political sense directed his mind toward the establishment of the Big Four on a permanent basis. If their differences were reconciled they would easily prevent outbreaks of any consequence among lesser powers. His acceptance of the United Nations was a second thought, or rather a giving in to the internationalist thinking of Hull and others in the Department of State, as well as a demand from the lesser nations. Whether he was right to give in will be argued for a long time. Whether he was ever thoroughly converted, I doubt; his justification for reluctance seems to me ample in the history of post-war events.

A question that will also be argued endlessly is whether the death of Roosevelt, just as the war was coming to an end, exacerbated the post-war troubles or whether they would have sharpened anyway and he would have had to assume the leadership of the West against Russia. It is my own view that he would have found ways to reduce the antagonisms; that Russia, under his persuasion, would not have rejected the Marshall Plan and so would have been brought into co-operation in reconstruction; that the reduction of eastern Europe to satellite status might have been compromised by giving Russia guarantees against aggression, and that the Chinese revolution might have been so tamed that the United States would not have had to sever all relations with that vast nation. This, as I say, is conjecture. But it is not inaccurate to say that except for the defeat of two dictators and for the establishment of the U.N., the war was soon by way of being lost in the peace. Almost before the victors could realize what they were in for, there was a great rush to rearm both Germany and Japan against the Communist nations, thus vindicating Hitler, who had always said that the United States and Britain ought to have joined him in fighting the Soviets.

These absurdities, with their potential dangers, Roosevelt might well have avoided. It is not possible to say whether they would have been avoided if Wallace instead of Truman had succeeded Roosevelt. But it is relevant to note that Truman came from the

Senate, that he had had no experience of foreign affairs and knew very little, by his own admission, about what was going on. It took him well over a year to be educated, and that was a fatal year. It began by the use of the atom bomb, and as it ended the long undeclared war with Russia was beginning.

Even the argument against this and the contrasting possibilities show vividly the difference made in human events by political leadership—which is under consideration here. They also show the impossibility of reducing the various potentialities to measurable certainties.

The post-war period and the fatal falling out with Russia were generally agreed in the West, with some few dissenters, to have been inevitable. Nothing could have been done by Western statesmen to prevent it. This was what the statesmen and their defenders said. The few who dissented made their argument in this way: The Soviet leaders were frightened; they reacted as they did because they believed that Western hostility to communism was rapidly running toward intervention. This was especially true in the United States, where a capitalist-military group apparently had moved into control of Truman's government and was bent on an immediate preventive war. The intention was, in these American circles, to use the overwhelming strength of the United States, including the atomic bomb, of which the American monopoly had not yet been broken, to extirpate communism from the world. So the Soviet leaders believed or said they believed. And this implied the overthrow of the Russian government and military occupation until a new regime could be set up.

This Russian apprehension was extreme; the reasoning for it rested on history. After World War I the revolutionary government had been attacked and almost conquered by a Churchill-inspired coalition to which even Woodrow Wilson had been party. It also rested on contemporary analysis. The war had been entrusted to the capitalist organization in the United States which had grown incredibly rich and powerful as a result. Together with a reactionary military class, vastly expanded as a result of the war, this capitalist group felt—and its organs of opinion freely said—that two systems so antipathetic as communism and capitalism could not exist together in the world. Conflict was inevitable. It had better come while the West was strong.

The lesson in the failure of American post-war strategy is obvious. There is a realm of political decision and behavior in which only an experienced practitioner may move with success. Nations are fortunate when such a person is available in time of need; they may be ruined by its lack. More rested on this chance after 1945 than before. But experience is far from enough when the emergency is vast in scope and immediate in its demand and when finesse and good judgment are required. Literally the fate of nations rested after 1945 on the wisdom and skill of their political leaders. In the decade after Hiroshima the United States and Russia, lacking that leadership, passed through a period of jeopardy which at any moment might have turned into holocaust. It is difficult to say, as affairs were managed, quite why the culminating event, the occasion for active hostilities, did not occur. [1]

That the destiny of nations in mid-twentieth century should still be determined by the superior or inferior quality of a few men's minds is, in our highly organized world, a subject for wonder. Why was it, in matters so impregnated with consequence, that joint or co-operative decision-making had not been substituted for the incredibly risky decision-making of one or a few minds? It might be said in answer to this question that the arts of politics are backward ones, that they had not developed as rapidly as, say, the industrial arts, which were beginning to be spoken of not as arts any more but sciences. They might be backward, but they were responsible for fateful commitments, and the backwardness threatened the very safety of mankind on this earth.

It is indeed true that politics is among the last of the human activities to be reduced to systematic study. Observers and philosophers have regarded with intense interest the ordeal of political leaders, have generalized about the organization of government, and have tried to suggest ways of avoiding or softening the conflicts that have become more and more dangerous as technology has advanced. The philosophers and technicians have been very inventive. But they have not found agreement. Several radically different kinds of government still operate in the world, and they are intended to attain different objectives. But in none of them have organization and planning taken the place of individual leadership.

[1] Cf. my *Chronicle of Jeopardy* (University of Chicago, 1955).

The two most consequential nations after World War II, the United States and the Soviet Union, dominated and drew on a continent. Each was populous, productive, and expanding. Their governments stood in complete contrast theoretically, and almost as complete contrast actually. The one was a dictatorship; the other, a representative democracy. The one had a single dominant party; the other, two great and several lesser parties standing for different objectives. The one was capitalist—that is, its productive facilities were mostly privately owned and operated; the other was communist—meaning that the state owned and operated everything.

These were striking contrasts and they gave rise to an ideological quarrel that went on and on. Each side had a proselytizing zeal that tended to encroach on the other's constituency. Moreover, this tended to become actual aggression. When communism conquered eastern Europe and China it definitely limited the prerogatives and relationships of the capitalist nations. And Korea was the symbol of the limit beyond which capitalist tolerance would not stretch. After that the question written in the skies for all humanity to answer at once was this: Can a way to coexist be found? This was the supreme question of all questions ever referred to political jurisdiction. And the answer to it was not to be found by an organization equipped with any rational techniques, nor even by group counsel. The power to decide belonged to a few men, thinking things out or feeling them out for themselves. In order to escape man's dilemma in the atomic age, these few individuals had to seek peace and devise the means for making it secure. They had to do more than this—as Roosevelt came to see—they had to deposit in a neutralizing agency the potentials of war. This meant that suddenly the prerogatives of leadership, until now depended on for policy-making, had largely to be abandoned. It had to be made impossible for anyone to lead men into war. However brilliant his talents might be, whatever hold on men's minds he might be capable of getting, it must be made impossible for any leader to establish the conditions of war. He must not be able, as Mussolini and Hitler had been, to withdraw from limitations and, with his nation behind him, go berserk.

It was this formidable duty that Roosevelt set for the United Nations. The establishing of an institution to take the place of a leader was among the few self-imposed tasks of statesmanship which, if successful, would change the course of history—in this instance quite possibly save mankind from self-annihilation. It was something of the nature, in reverse, of those decisions made by groups of men on a number of occasions to abandon legislative responsibility and place it in a dictator's hands—as was done in Germany and Italy.

The process was one of strengthening and broadening the principle of leadership by institutionalizing decision-making. This was not a new conception. It suggested, in a way, a return to democracy. For democracy postulated that all should participate in decisions affecting themselves. And this had not been really the case for a very long time, either in national or international affairs. Looking back, it could be seen that, as the world had become populous and the scale of organization had grown wider, its governments had not been adapted to the change. What adaptation there had been had resulted from struggle and compromise rather than reason. There had always been two broad choices: decision-making could be institutionalized or it could be entrusted to an individual. Institutionalization meant that decisions should be arrived at by working out deliberately the consequences of alternatives and creating a program understood by all and accepted by at least a majority. To this, administrators would be required to adhere. Individual decision-making meant that one person should decide as he saw fit. He might use an apparatus of reason or he might not. He might use it for some purpose and not for others.

Such a leader would almost certainly, following Lord Acton's rule, be corrupted by power. And he would almost as necessarily become a demagogue. His decisions would in the long run not be guided by the public interest but by some symbolization of that interest infused with his own ego. What he conceived to be good for the public must, in his mind, become an absolute. It must *be* good for the public. That this was dangerous in an atomic age, Roosevelt saw in the end with complete clarity. Perhaps he saw it so clearly because he had cultivated the political arts so successfully and had become so nearly an absolute decider for his nation.

On the other hand, it was no simple matter to devolve the deciding upon an institution that would avoid the dangers of leadership and yet not become merely negative, limiting, and protective. What Roosevelt obviously had in mind to do was something of this sort.

He intended to improve the government of the United States until it should be impossible for its decisions to be suicidal ones. But more than that, he hoped meanwhile to set such limitations on sovereignty that quarrels among nations would be forced into channels of conciliation and would spend themselves in argument rather than in resorts to force.

The highest use of one man's political genius was to be stringent limitation on the future functioning of political genius. Men clever enough to reach the presidency were to be prevented from using that cleverness to imperil the nation. They might very well have the ability to place themselves in the White House without having those qualities of wisdom needed to direct a nation into peaceful and prosperous courses. There must be limitations even on them that would bind them to peace.

I ask myself how it was that a boy-child born in January in 1882 on a modest estate in the Hudson Valley had come, in sixty years, to a position of such fateful importance that he could address himself to the final dilemma of political man and apparently expect confidently to find a solution. Let us look at the exhibition of his talents at some few critical moments in his career. That examination may yield at least a clue to this success.

19

It is one of the customs of politics in the United States that a short time before a nominating convention is held or a primary is due the professionals in charge of the party's permanent machinery have several little talks. These conversations take place in easy and intimate circumstances; there is no record of them, and those who take part have almost never been known to make public what was said. Considering the number of such meetings in every year, such consistent good faith approaches the miraculous. Everything else about politics is accompanied by rivers of talk and oceans of publicity, but not these confabs of the insiders. Political philosophers are not the kind of people ever admitted to such meetings, and they know about what goes on only at a remove. It is all too likely that what they hear is a drastically expurgated account. I have never sat in one of these conclaves, of course, but I have been given accounts of many of them. I therefore have a limited knowledge of these which is at no more than one remove and has been cross-checked. As to others, my information, like that of most political observers, is strictly second-hand and perhaps doctored. Nevertheless, I have the temerity to venture a few generalizations.

In the first place, those who meet together have a complex and difficult problem. They have their own practical affairs to consider, but if these do not coincide with the public interest they must not be pursued to the point of really risking punishment by a revolting electorate—perhaps led by some adventurous malcontent; there is often a maverick who will not respect unwritten rules. The problem is to get from politics what is most wanted without stirring up trouble. The temptation is always to think that, with the use of well-known devices, trouble can be avoided even if selfish aims are pursued. This is because these devices have so often been effective as well as because what is at stake is the prospect of power and wealth—two very betraying temptations, and, because they are betraying, apt to warp the judgment. Men who are otherwise notable for caution are more likely than not to take what to the observer appears to be, judged solely from the point of view of their own interests, outrageous risks. Anyone who takes long chances will find that the averages are against him. Political bosses and their machines frequently run into embarrassing exposures, somewhat less frequently into expulsions from office, and sometimes into actual criminal punishment. If most of it seems to have been avoidable, this estimate comes from putting bosses' discretion too high and their greed and callousness too low.

Lincoln Steffens made some earnest studies of these phenomena and ended with a rather higher opinion of bosses than I have been able to reach. I do not confirm his judgment. I am inclined to believe he liked them as human beings—they are usually likable—and that this warped his judgment. Bosses differ, like all men, in all their characteristics; but I believe the average of judgment and wisdom to be much lower than Steffens put them. He was impressed by their realism, their shrewd sizing up of others' weaknesses, and their effectiveness in manipulating the evanescent forces of politics. I am more impressed by the frequency of error, always on one side, by a vulnerability that is due almost altogether to their own venality and cynicism, and by their inability to master the principles of top management so that the big enterprises of the public service can be kept running with tolerable efficiency.

Almost every time a really vigorous and determined opposition has arisen the bosses' vulnerability has proved to be such that their machine has collapsed. There is a long list of politicians who, at every level of government, have made their reputations by attacking and overthrowing a boss and his organization. They practically always succeed because the boss has been too greedy and is therefore open to attack. Steffens was inclined to stress the undoubted fact that, when all the thunder was over and the reform wave had subsided, the clearing skies disclosed bosses and machines still carrying on their old functions. I would reply that it is almost always a new boss and a rehabilitated machine. The old boss and his henchmen are lucky if they are not in jail. At the very least they will have retired to Florida or to some haven abroad. Even Frank Hague and Ed Kelly, two of the cleverest bosses of the Roosevelt era, were thus retired in good time; some others—Jimmy Walker, Sheriff Farley, Mayor Curley of Boston, and Boss Pendergast of Kansas City—were not so lucky. [1]

Some of the vulnerability suggested by these particular names was due to a peculiar human weakness that any politician of sense would suppress if he discovered it developing in himself. No boss ought to be out in the public view. It is a contradiction of function for him to become a candidate or an official. Charles Murphy and his successors, Olvany and Curry of Tammany Hall, at least knew this. They were blind enough about other matters—Curry blinder than Murphy or Olvany—but they knew better than to make public targets of themselves. So, of course, did Pendergast of Kansas City; but it was inordinate contempt for human nature that ruined him. Keeping to the bosses' role is an almost complete, but not a perfect, protection. It all depends on how outrageous his behavior has been and on how ambitious and effective the attacker may be.

What I should particularly like to call attention to, however, is that incidents, scandalous incidents involving corrupt machines are, even though they loom large on the scene of the past, really very unusual. The boss system goes on and on as a kind of low-grade infection, one that the body politic has accustomed itself to. It flares into an acute stage occasionally and has to be lanced or excised, but the excitement is usually muted and local and is soon forgotten. We are used to the system and accept its results without too much protest unless the abuses are flagrant. That the bosses allow themselves to become vulnerable at all shows their incapacity for their own jobs.

There is a hypocrisy about this that makes openings for clever and ambitious men. Democratic electorates are revolted at the suggestion that bosses manage public affairs and that political machines exist. They are susceptible of being mobilized and of voting for bosses' extermination, especially when it can be shown, as it periodically can, that the bounds of tolerability have been overstepped. All three of my exemplars rose by the use of this device. All three of them created for themselves, or functioned through, political machines

[1] Cf. Edwin O'Connor's novel, *The Last Hurrah* (Boston: Little, Brown, 1956), and Curley's own unashamed account.

and were more or less the product of the boss-machine system—because representative democracy has no other long-run and dependable device—and all three attacked it as though it could be extirpated and they were the ones to do it.

Muñoz was the beneficiary of the Iglesias-Barcelo machine, not to mention his inheritance of a matchless prestige from his father; and, although he created a new party, it was made in the image of the old. La Guardia would never have won his way to the Congress or become Mayor if he had not had a Republican organization to use and a Tammany to attack. But of all of them, as might be expected, Roosevelt made the most versatile use of the opportunities presented to him by the boss system. He was always supported by bosses, and he always attacked them. He always made deals with them, and he always betrayed them. He accepted nominations from them and help in his campaigns, and he sent their representatives into exile, put them in jail, or deprived them of office. He detested both bosses and machines; yet no one ever had larger favors from them or, as I think, caused graver consequences to the body politic from accepting their support.

It all began, so far as he was concerned, in Poughkeepsie in 1910. In that summer, at a quiet meeting of Judge John E. Mack, Mayor Sague, Thomas Lynch, and a few others, it was suggested that a young scion of the Roosevelts of Hyde Park, just up the river, might be given the nomination for one of the state legislative offices—Assembly or Senate. There was a rather complicated situation, explained in detail by various Roosevelt biographers but not relevant here, which determined, after some discussion, that the nomination should be for the Senate. After the fashion of these happenings, the subsequent convention made the nomination and Franklin Roosevelt accepted.

It is not too difficult to see why he was chosen in that small conclave of bosses; but it is, I think, instructive to consider why it must have been acceptable to the convention—a judgment ratified by subsequent election. It was because there was nothing against him. This stands out, in case after case of first-instance selection by these methods, as the *sine qua non* for a candidate. There must be nothing about him open to attack. This means a number of things. But it means most of all that he must never have said anything to offend any sizable interest, either of voters or of campaign contributors. It is better if he is not physically handicapped, has no marital difficulties, and does not drink or gamble. It is better also if he is homely but vigorous, has had a humble origin, and has accumulated some, but not too much, wealth. None of these, or any other positive attribute, however, is so important as never having said anything except to support virtue, good government, and the system of private enterprise.

Young Frank Roosevelt, as the shrewdly appraising eyes of the Poughkeepsie politicos sized him up, had some handicaps. He was jaunty, rich, well dressed, and handsome—these were not good. The wealth, of course, was only bad electorally; it was useful to an impoverished organization. So that could be forgiven. The other handicaps were all of a piece and had to be accepted if his money (or his mother's) was to be got. But Dutchess County, after all, was not unused to gentlemen. And there was also the fact that he was a Roosevelt. His father had been a good Cleveland Democrat, and any Roosevelt was vaguely identified with "Uncle Ted"—no handicap in the rural districts of New York. These were the reasons he was chosen—these and his previous precious silence on every controversial question.

20

It is possible in the Roosevelt career to identify certain crucial decisions, and perhaps for the purpose here it would be profitable to examine them briefly. It can be understood *why* they were made if not *how* they were made. The *how* will never be fully known. There may be glimpses here and there as notes or memoirs of associates come to light, but Roosevelt himself never made any—even if he understood the processes of his own mind, as few of us do; [1] and the mechanisms are unlikely ever to stand clearly revealed. But the *why* is somewhat easier, because it can be roughly assumed to have led to all that followed. By studying the result, the cause can be inferred. This is not an infallible method, but its results are, to an extent, credible. The inferences will depend on the historians' skill, understanding, and integrity; but when did any account of any era or its statesmen not depend on these?

Three of the important Roosevelt decisions were made in the early years of his political career, beginning in 1910 when Taft was in the White House. The first, of course, was that he would make the risky race for the New York State Senate on the Democratic ticket in the traditionally Republican Twenty-sixth District in the Hudson Valley. Having won this first contest because of a most unlikely combination of circumstances—in that year the great progressive-conservative schism in the Republican party was beginning—he then found himself likely to be relegated to the obscurity natural to a young and

[1] There is no Roosevelt diary, except for brief and unexciting periods. There is none, for instance, for the presidency. He made almost no records of conversations, and think of the thousands he had dealing with policy matters! And there are none that concern his thoughts. All the many tons of Roosevelt papers at Hyde Park and elsewhere lack any such direct evidence of conscious development.

probably temporary member of the legislature in Albany. The Democrats had won, but it was a Murphy victory—so Murphy thought—and the plums would go to Tammany. The young senator from Dutchess would, he decided, never be a Tammany favorite. He had either to remain obscure or to do something that would make him notorious. So, without waiting, he challenged Murphy on the United States senatorship just then falling vacant as Chauncey M. Depew passed from public life. Murphy had given orders that "Blue-eyed Billy" Sheehan was to be elected [2] because of his services to the party and to the Hall. Sheehan had been a Buffalo boss but had some time since moved to New York, had built up a prosperous law firm, had enlarged his utility clientele, and had become the recognized political representative of this whole sector of interests in New York State. As such he had made generous campaign contributions, and now that the party had won, he demanded his reward. Like many another rich man with a doubtful past, he coveted a senatorship for his old age. This was a weakness that exposed him to unnecessary risks. But Murphy should have been able to deliver without any discussion.

It was an issue made to order for a young man who had suddenly seen that the dominant machine in his state would never further his career and who had, moreover, divined, even if only vaguely and not knowing quite what it meant, that progressivism would command the majorities of the next generation. It was an opportunity to fix his name firmly in the public mind as an enemy of the bosses; the further inference that he was the inheritor of the Bryan—and even, perhaps, the La Follette—progressivism would not be too difficult, even if wholly unjustified, for the voters to make. Besides, he was a Roosevelt; and Theodore—known to him as "Uncle Ted"—had given the Roosevelt name a political value it would be too bad to waste. It was not yet a progressive name as it soon would be, but it was not exactly a conservative one either.

The Roosevelt attack took Murphy and his lieutenants—who included Al Smith and Robert Wagner, who were later to count for a good deal in Roosevelt's life—by surprise. Smith even discovered

[2] This was just at the end of the period when U.S. senators were elected by the state legislatures. The constitutional amendment providing for direct election became effective in 1913. Murphy, it should be noted, was Grand Sachem at the time.

afterward that he had given some helpful advice, all unknowing, to the potential renegade. The young man was not actually the originator and not actually the manager of the historic revolt of the twenty-one Democratic dissenters who, by refusing to attend the caucus, kept the legislature from electing a senator for nearly three months—or indeed from getting on with any business at all. Roosevelt and his colleagues did not even win what they wanted. They prevented Sheehan from being elected, but they had to settle for Judge James A. O'Gorman, who was so much a Tammanyite that he had once been Grand Sachem. But the luck that had been Uncle Ted's seemed to have transferred itself to Franklin. The public impression was that he had been the prime mover in the whole business and that he had beaten Tammany almost alone. It was an impression never given up in Roosevelt's generation. [3]

Three months after he went to Albany, a lone inexperienced upstate Democrat likely to serve a single term and then be retired to obscurity, Roosevelt had become a celebrity. A St. George had arisen to fight the evils of corruption and had slain his first dragon. But in gaining this public reputation he had incurred the enmity of the dominant state professionals. Nothing could be more certain than that they would stop him from going any farther. He would have to run again in two years. The Republicans were not likely to be so split as they had been in 1910 (as it happened, the split came to its climax in 1912 when Theodore led his Bull Moosers out of the Republican convention and himself ran as a Progressive, but that prospect was not yet evident in 1910); and even if Roosevelt won the nomination in spite of Tammany opposition, the Republicans would defeat him at election time. It was not a favorable outlook. [4]

After appraising the dismal future he could forecast for himself

---

[3] Not a little of this impression was due to the journalistic efforts of Louis McH. Howe, who conceived at this time the idea of promoting a career for Franklin in lieu of the one he himself could never achieve. Louis at this time was Albany correspondent for the New York *Herald*. Cf. Lela Stiles, *The Man behind Roosevelt* (New York: World Publishing Co., 1954); also the author's "Roosevelt and Howe," *The Antioch Review*, 1954.

[4] It did not turn out quite that way. Roosevelt not only got the nomination but was re-elected in spite of being bedridden during the entire campaign with typhoid fever. Louis Howe was by then directly enlisted in his service, and this was his second contribution to the career which was to end in the presidency—the first being his promotion of Roosevelt during the Sheehan episode.

as an anti-Tammany Democrat, Roosevelt made his third important decision, the one from which the next decade of his life was to open out. He boarded a train one day and journeyed to Trenton, where Woodrow Wilson was occupying the Governor's mansion. His visit was notice to the world—if the world had taken any notice—of his affiliation. By 1911 it was obvious that Wilson would be a strong contender for the Democratic nomination in 1912, and it followed from Roosevelt's general view of the future that if Wilson should be nominated he would win. He reasoned that the Progressives could not capture the Republican party; the most they could do was to split it; if they did this, the Democrats would win. Even Uncle Ted could not unite the Republicans and the Progressives, although it began to look as though he intended to try. If the Democrats became progressive, the future would be theirs.

This was shrewd reasoning for a young politician, better reasoning than that of Uncle Ted, who had had far more experience, and better than that of Charles F. Murphy or the other bosses, who thought they could prevent Wilson's nomination. At that time, of course, it seemed far more likely, on strict evidence, that Clark would be nominated, or, failing him, that the choice would fall to Harmon of Ohio. These were the kind of candidates who were agreeable to the professionals. But Roosevelt saw it otherwise and bet his whole future on Wilson's likely success, making the commitment complete during the next year by his public activities in Wilson's behalf. Wilson won, and so Roosevelt won. In the Wilson administration he was given the assistant secretaryship of the Navy, an office which had proved extremely useful in Uncle Ted's political progress, and with that appointment his career was transferred successfully to the national field. He was now independent of the New York bosses and identified as a successful Democratic progressive of the Wilson sort.

It is to be counted as the fourth political decision that there followed in the course of a few years a rapprochement with Tammany. It seems at first inspection almost as strange as his former bizarre attack on the Hall. In retrospect, however, it can be seen to be one of the shrewdest of the Roosevelt maneuvers. If he had not conciliated Murphy he could not have got the nomination for the vice-presidency in 1920, and he would not have become Governor of New York in 1928. Both of those were at least convenient preliminaries to the presidency. The peace with Tammany had become convenient on both sides because, in his Washington post, he had become independent. He was a novice, but evidently a serious one who had to be dealt with in one way or another. The Tammany Sachem decided not to oppose him. It has to be noted, however, that this did not happen until the young man had been given a humiliating lesson. In 1914, restless to be rising, he undertook to capture the Democratic nomination for United States senator without Tammany assistance. He offered himself in the primary in opposition to James W. Gerard, Wilson's Ambassador to Germany, who was an old-time member of the New York organization. He had no help from the Washington administration; Wilson, in fact, made it clear that he would take no sides in such local quarrels. And Roosevelt was badly beaten.

When he came to think over this experience he must have concluded that he had better compromise with Tammany. Otherwise he might never get any farther in New York. Also, he must have concluded, I should guess, that his defeat had been a good thing. Even if he had won in the primaries he could not have won the election: it turned out to be a Republican year. Anyway, he must have realized that senators seldom become Presidents, and then usually because, as compliant party hacks, they have been nudged along by bosses. Luck had been with him again in spite of an unwise anxiety to move upward too rapidly. [5]

There was a much better opportunity in 1918. By then he and Murphy had reached an accommodation; the accord with Tammany had in fact progressed so far that Murphy offered him the nomination for the governorship. He refused. His decision on that occasion, by all the rules, was wrong, and he must have regretted it almost at once. Yet if he had accepted and had been elected—as Smith actually was—he could probably not have gone on from there. No Democrat would get any farther for fourteen years—until 1932; and he could not have stayed on as Governor for seven terms. He would have been eligible for the presidential nomination in 1920 and 1924

[5] There is an extenuation, to be sure. In any political career an overlong pause is apt, for obvious reasons, to be fatal. Getting used to a leader in one spot makes that spot seem to fit him only too well. Franklin's instinct to move was sound. But the circumstances were wrong; and the timing, for which he became noted in his later career, was very poorly judged.

and, if he had been nominated, would have lost. His renomination in 1928 would have been very unlikely, and he would almost certainly have been a political has-been by 1932. On the whole, it must be concluded that he had luck again, in spite of a mistaken judgment of what his future required.

What influenced his decision most in this instance was the decision he had made to leave his civilian job and become a naval officer. For political reasons, if for no other—although the desire for active service too was very strong—this seemed indispensable. There was, for instance, the example of Uncle Ted before him. The part played in his subsequent successes by the predecessor Roosevelt's brief role as a Rough Rider in the Spanish-American War was well known. The somewhat synthetic cowboys were always turning up on political occasions, horses, chaps, spurs, lariats, campaign hats and all, to emphasize Theodore's martial record. For Franklin to have lived through the years of the war and not to have been in the armed forces must have seemed to him likely to be a serious political handicap. He had chosen his service—the Navy, naturally—and had made the preliminary arrangements, when he went to tell President Wilson what he intended. But the President had to inform him that an armistice was imminent and that he was too late. Dramatic service on the western front with the eighteen-inch naval guns mounted on railway cars—which was the duty he had selected for himself—faded into a might-have-been he would always regret.

When he discovered that he could not get into the service he was also too late to be nominated for the governorship. It had gone to Smith. All that was left was to settle down to the unglamorous job of clearing up the Navy Department's litter after the war. This went on for two years more, years that brought post-war depression, disillusion, defeat for Wilson's League of Nations, and a fatal decline in Democratic favor with the voters. This last resulted in losing control of the Congress even in 1918. The nomination for the presidency in 1920 went to Governor Cox of Ohio, who was as little involved with Wilson and the war as any Democrat could be. Because this choice seemed something of a repudiation of the President, the nomination for the vice-presidency ought to be from among the members of the official family. This made Roosevelt eligible. It is true that in that circle no one was so little in Wilson's confidence as

Roosevelt, and no one perhaps had been so little liked by the President.

Roosevelt, it must be said, had hardly been decently loyal in the pre-war neutrality period, as Wilson very well knew. He had worked openly for a bigger Navy and almost openly for joining the Allies against Germany when these were distinctly not administration policies. Yet he was a member of the group identified in the public mind with the President and so served to lessen the indignity of the convention's repudiation. At the time it seemed that Roosevelt's acceptance of the nomination might be a mistake. But this was another in the long line of decisions and events which, in retrospect, show him to have been far shrewder, usually, than his professional contemporaries, and when not shrewder, at least luckier. He cannot have expected to be elected, but he can have anticipated that a vigorous campaign would make him the most prominent member of the Democratic party. And it did.

Defeat would eliminate Cox. [6]

Among the Democrats who were prominent, only the Wilson official family remained—McAdoo, for instance. But no Wilson associate would be popular enough for nomination or election in any foreseeable future. Whatever Roosevelt's assessment of the possibilities, which has actually to be guessed at, it seems probable that he understood the situation. And he did make so striking and vigorous a vice-presidential campaign that from then on he was a marked figure among the party professionals all over the country. He had not been exactly prominent before, but he was now. The acquaintances he acquired then he kept in touch with—aided by Louis Howe, who never left his side. And so far as he could, he kept his acquaintance with the electorate.

He was retired to unofficial life after 1920—a sort of lawyer-businessman. But it was never more than semi-private. He became head of many movements and chairman of numerous committees, he was usually a delegate to state and national conventions, he spoke

[6] There was some suggestion of Cox's nomination again in 1924, but even Wilson, although sick and impotent, was opposed; and others had no loyal feeling for Cox, so nothing came of it. The compromise candidate was Davis. There was a sad break between Wilson and Tumulty, who had served him so long and faithfully, over the Cox endorsement at the convention. Tumulty thought Cox entitled to another chance.

on any and all occasions, and he industriously kept his name current as the most representative of all the Democratic leaders. Compared with Smith, for instance, he was far more widely known. Smith was a New Yorker; unlike Roosevelt, he took no pains to attain national status, something he must have regretted before autumn came in 1928. But Roosevelt never had cause for any regrets of that sort.

It was shortly after he became vice-president of the Fidelity and Deposit Company in New York that Roosevelt's siege with infantile paralysis began. He was stricken in the summer of 1921, and for all the years between then and 1928 he had to devote endless hours and days, to submit to demanding treatments, and to order his whole life in the interest of the conquest of his paralysis. He never wholly succedeed. [7] All his life his legs would be useless, but even this terrible handicap was not allowed to crush his ambitions. Soon after the acute stage of the disease had passed, he renewed his persistent correspondence, began to have numerous conferences, and in 1924 was back in the thick of things. In that year he became campaign manager for Al Smith in the attempt to get for the New York Governor the Democratic presidential nomination.

The decision to support and push Smith in this way can be seen in retrospect to have been one of the shrewdest Roosevelt ever made. Democrats would win neither in 1924 nor in 1928; by then Smith would have had his chance and his extreme weakness as a national candidate would have been thoroughly demonstrated. He would not even get the nomination in 1924; and in 1928, when he did get it, he would be so badly beaten that even the solid South would be cracked by the Republicans for the first time; five southern states would go to Hoover. For the Democratic party to nominate him

---

[7] One of the most moving phases of Roosevelt's life is this agonizing struggle to regain his mobility. He was stricken at a time when not too much was known either about the disease or about recovery from paralysis. He was a contributor to the growth of knowledge in both fields. But he suffered from experimentation which had negative results. It was found that destroyed muscular tissue cannot be rehabilitated and physical therapy turned to the building up of alternate muscles where possible and to the development of general health. Polio patients later, even when terribly crippled, were often fine physical specimens otherwise. Roosevelt himself had a magnificent upper-body development as a result of his strenuous exercises and faithfulness to a regimen he worked out for himself with the help of doctors and physiotherapists. But it was a serious matter for him that the confinements of the presidency did not allow this routine to be followed.

again would be, even in otherwise favorable circumstances, to ask for defeat. So Smith, who seemed in 1924 to stand between Roosevelt and the presidency, was by 1932 eliminated. He had been given his chance and had been unable to exploit it.

It is suggested by Roosevelt's careful biographer, Frank Freidel, that the New York governorship, attained by Roosevelt in 1928, was not a necessary preliminary to the presidential nomination in 1932. The argument is that he was already a national figure. Besides the vice-presidential campaign of 1920, his activities at the conventions of 1924 and 1928 had made him conspicuous in the party. After a whole decade the irritations with Wilson, the revulsion against foreign adventure, and the post-war malaise were long in the past, and Roosevelt's espousal of the League in 1920 was no longer counted against him. His carrying on of correspondence with numerous Democratic leaders now began to have its results. No one else was so well or so favorably known among them. It was partly as a result of this that he had been mentioned both in 1924 and 1928 as a possible candidate. Several observers had noted that either of those conventions—but especially the long-deadlocked one in 1924 when Smith and McAdoo had killed each other off and John W. Davis had been nominated as a desperate compromise—could have been stampeded for Roosevelt. It could indeed very well be argued that it was not necessary for Roosevelt to have been established in the governorship in order to be nominated in 1932. He might have been chosen anyway.

This may be the correct view to take of this decision, which, of all the decisions the future President ever made, was the most difficult. He tried his best to evade the issue. He put himself out of reach of all means of communication while the New York State convention recessed, waiting his answer. When he was finally reached he at first said no. Then, however, he said yes with obvious reluctance.

Whether there might have been another road to the White House than the one running through Albany, it is difficult to say. And in any case this must be put down as one of a number of lucky decisions, not on his schedule of fated events and made more *for* him than *by* him, which had so marked an effect on his fortunes. Mostly he made his own luck; sometimes it merely happened. This time it was

Smith and the New York Democrats who made it for him; he acceded against his better judgment.

When the call came he was at Warm Springs. It is perhaps important that Louis Howe was in New York. They had decided between them that the Democrats were unlikely to succeed anywhere in that year. The business boom was on, prosperity simply seethed, and the Republicans claimed credit for it. They had, besides, nominated a strong candidate, going outside the roster of available professionals to choose Herbert Hoover. The Democratic professionals could see little hope for Smith even if he had not had fatal personal oddities, obviously irrelevant to his qualification for office and no handicap in New York, but incongruous in the country at large. Smith, as the campaign got under way, saw what was happening to the extent that any candidate ever sees, and he had to acknowledge with desperate chagrin that he was even likely to lose New York. His own people were hesitant to have the same man for their President of whom they thoroughly approved as their governor.

It was humiliating, but he had to have Roosevelt running concurrently for the governorship; only Roosevelt, he judged, could attract enough votes in upstate New York to carry the election. It was Smith's own personal and repeated appeals to which the reluctant absentee in Warm Springs finally capitulated against his better judgment. He did not believe the ticket would win and, besides, he had been given to believe that some further pursuit of the Warm Springs regimen would restore the muscles in his legs; for that he had fought for seven long years and he was reluctant to abandon the struggle within sight of success. The only technical justification for his final weakening was that, by refusing after being so strongly appealed to, he might be accused of refusing a party call. The nomination was a sacrifice, the New York leaders made clear, which it was in the line of duty for him to make. And Louis Howe was not there to stiffen his resolution to refuse.

Once committed, of course, he made a campaign hardly less demanding than the vice-presidential attempt eight years earlier, when he had had his legs to carry him around. Judge Rosenman, in *Working with Roosevelt,* describes it in pages that are a genuine contribution to political history. Rosenman was a young Smith attaché, a Tammany apprentice, assigned to Roosevelt and expected to furnish guidance. He found himself caught in a well-directed hurricane. He felt himself lucky just to survive the rigors of those weeks of campaigning with the crippled Roosevelt. And, as everyone knows, before it was over he found himself wholly enlisted, as Louis Howe had been before him, in the furtherance of the Roosevelt career.

Roosevelt retired from the battering of adverse returns on election night, certain that he had lost along with Smith. Next day it appeared that he had survived the otherwise devastating Democratic defeat. Smith had lost New York, but Roosevelt had held it, even if by a very narrow margin. This demonstration of regard on the part of the New York electorate, confirmed two years later by the largest majority any Governor had ever had, made him more than a marked man: it made him the man who would be nominated by the Democrats for the presidency in 1932 unless someone could beat him. Smith would try; [8] other hopefuls would try too, and then they would all try together in coalition. Roosevelt's nomination, in consequence, would still seem doubtful in the middle reaches of the 1932 convention; that is, it would seem doubtful to the other politicians. Roosevelt, at the other end of the long-distance line from Chicago to Albany, calmly and cheerfully directed the compromises that effected the final victory. He was nominated; and in 1932 to be nominated by the Democrats was to be elected.

[8] The story of Smith's renunciation and his subsequent decision to challenge Roosevelt in 1932 is told by Flynn in *You're the Boss*, Rosenman in *Working with Roosevelt*, and Farley in *Behind the Ballots*, as well as by several non-participants in the proceedings. For a useful account of this campaign see Peel and Donnelly's *The 1928 Campaign* (New York: R. R. Smith, 1931); they made a similar study of the succeeding contest: *The 1932 Campaign* (New York: Farrar & Rinehart, 1935).

2 1

Pursuing the account of the Roosevelt decision-making from 1932 on might be thought to involve entering on a different order of events. Actually he was an unchanged man, exercising the same judgment in the same ways; only now he was making decisions that would maintain him in power, not ones calculated to achieve it. The party was also involved in this continuing activity. I hesitantly mention the party, because obviously it was secondary. It was an instrument for Roosevelt, the progressive, who was nominally Roosevelt, the Democrat. The party was not always a willing instrument, however; almost from the first—at least from the end of the first special session of the Seventy-third Congress (the Hundred Days)— there were signs of reluctance. There was a split, and it was a serious one.

The conservatives among the Democrats were utterly unwilling to see the party committed to the progressivism which Roosevelt believed essential to continued electoral approval, and the dissenters were very powerful in the Congress. For instance, they held the chairmanships of the committees that are so important in the congressional system. This was because the Southerners had been there throughout the Republican years and so had accumulated a seniority that had brought them to the top. But Roosevelt himself was by now determined to work out a progressive course. The differences between him and the congressional leaders were irreconcilable. The New Deal, as a consequence, never went farther than the conservatives could be coerced or persuaded into authorizing it to go. They always held a strong negative against projected change. And it took a good deal of political credit in many bargains to overcome that opposition. Often it was not enough.

The most important single domestic decision of Roosevelt's years as Governor and President was, I should say, this general commitment to progressivism. It was not reached, like most of his others, in one act or at one time. It was come to gradually and tentatively, bit by bit, until during his governorship his enlistment became irrevocable. The issue most easily identifiable as progressive, among others not so clearly that, was the issue of public as against private ownership of power facilities and the rigorous public regulation of those not publicly owned. What he said at once about this on becoming Governor was a most remarkable statement for a man who normally left his lines of retreat well open and who preferred ample escape clauses in his contracts with the people. He said:

> . . . the water power of the State should belong to all the people . . . No Commission, no, not the Legislature itself has any right to give, for any consideration whatever, a single potential kilowatt in virtual perpetuity to any person or corporation. The Legislature in this matter is but the trustee of the people . . . It is also [their] duty to see that this power, which belongs to all the people, is transformed into usable electrical energy and distributed to them at the least possible cost. It is our power; and no inordinate profits must be allowed to those who act as the people's agents in bringing this power to their homes and workshops. [1]

Even this most extreme declaration ended on a note of simple warning. It showed that Roosevelt, the progressive, was not becoming Roosevelt, the socialist. For he said, of the whole question that it was a technical one; "how much shall be undertaken by the state, how much carried out by properly regulated private enterprises, how much by some combination of the two is a practical question . . ." It was, he implied, to be decided by discovering how it could be done most efficiently. [2] New York financiers (who now controlled the state's power facilities, having just engineered a characteristic merger) might not like to hear all this talk about public service and severely regulated profits; but it was better than

[1] From the First Inaugural as Governor, Jan. 1, 1929. *Public Papers*, Vol. I, 1928–32, p. 78.

[2] Ibid., p. 78.

hearing the dread word "expropriation." What Roosevelt meant he made clearer, shortly, in a special message concerning his proposals:

> *I believe there are enough good businessmen in this State who see this problem . . . and will be glad to join with the State in this endeavor. I want to give to business this big opportunity to participate in a public service.*
>
> *If these proposals become law we shall have the opportunity of ascertaining whether or not business and finance will accept this way of developing the State's resources for its industries, its commerce, and its homes. On the one hand is the policy of public ownership and control of our power sites, dams, and power plants, with private operation of transmission lines and distributing systems, allowing a fair return on actual cash capital investment. On the other side is one of two courses—either exploitation by private interests or else public ownership and operation not only of the site, the dam, and the power, but of the transmission lines and distribution systems as well.* [3]

This was orthodox progressivism emerging in one instance. It is notable that this was put at the head of the list of issues enumerated in his first program. The others, following, were social insurance, farm relief, pensions for workers, and penal reform. Of all these, the one most consequential, in due time, would be social insurance. That would be the most important New Deal legacy to a future generation; but it would not really ripen as an issue until his presidential years. It was not something a state could undertake alone.

The key declaration, the one he chose for headlining and for identification of his kind of issue, was public power. What would come of this as to electric power, specifically, in the long run would be important even in New York State. But twenty-five years later the fight would still be going on. He would not win or settle it. Nationally the Tennessee Valley Authority would result from this same kind of declaration. But no other TVA's would emerge, nor would TVA ever become what he meant it to be. [4] His legacy on this issue would not be nearly so valuable as the Social Security System.

[3] Ibid., p. 177.

[4] Cf. Tugwell and Banfield, "Grass Roots Democracy: Myth or Reality," *Pub. Adm. Rev.*, 1950.

He must have known this. He must have known it was a fight that would go on and on and be bequeathed to the future. It is to be doubted that he ever visualized the complete public ownership of power resources. Power was to him one item of a larger program of industrial regulation, by yardstick if necessary, in the public interest.

Nevertheless, nothing so well demonstrates the Roosevelt political sagacity as the throwing out of this challenge—except the "Blue-eyed Billy" Sheehan case, which, in its strictly political context, so much resembles it. Both illustrated the occupation of a dramatic position, sure to be judged as typing the occupier, without his making any very wide or embarrassing statements on corollary issues. It was part of the method to leave much to be filled in according to the preference of the voters. This gave remarkable freedom for claims or for retreats.

Both of these were matters, also, to which the public and the press had long been sensitized, so that the keynote had only to be struck for the reverberations to resound familiarly in numerous ears. Both were sure to initiate political fisticuffs in which the initiator would be able to claim credit as a champion of the people's interests whether or not there was a favorable outcome. As a matter of fact, the outcome was not favorable—or not markedly so—in either of these cases. But it is perfectly clear that the political results were exactly what Roosevelt wanted.

Until the throwing down of this gauntlet to the power interests—and specifically to the financiers—Roosevelt had been known as a progressive largely in a general sense and by association. He was a relative of Theodore and an ex-member of Wilson's official family. But he had remained a Democrat and so had shared none of Theodore's Bull Moose adventuring in 1912, nor had he been in La Follette's crowd in 1924. That was the year he was Smith's campaign manager for the Democratic nomination and, when that failed, had supported the very conservative John W. Davis. His speeches in 1920 had suffered from the party's poverty of ideas after Wilson's leadership was exhausted. Nothing in them advanced the party or himself beyond the positions already occupied by the New Freedom. And Davis, of course, could be supported without making any progressive declarations. Smith in 1928, although as Governor he had been noted for reforms of government and for welfare legislation, had advanced no new national ideas. His position on power, if not quite so emphatic, had been about what Roosevelt's now was.

From now on Roosevelt would be a progressive—*the* progressive, the inheritor of the whole tradition—Bryan, Wilson, La Follette, Theodore Roosevelt, and all. He had defied and warned Wall Street, the money power; he needed to say no more. Actually he had no more to say, apart from the Social Security suggestion. The Democrats had not yet generated any new ideas. But what was implied in the inaugural declaration concerning power would lead in the end to the specific federal regulations of the New Deal. What the new Governor was putting forward was less a power program than a business-control program; it therefore had certain plain implications, although they were not very far developed in any declaration and very likely not in Roosevelt's mind. It was, therefore, even if still not wholly formulated—and perhaps deliberately general—extremely important as a political decision. No other ranks with it except those later ones in the foreign field, one of which led to war and the other to the United Nations.

This challenge to business may have been the most important, politically speaking, but it was by no means the only one of consequence. Several others of only lesser significance are easily distinguishable. They began to be forced on Roosevelt as the presidential race came closer. One of these was the abandonment of the truce with Tammany which had lasted since 1918. It was not too pleasant a prospect for the Governor of New York to seek the presidential nomination without the support of his own state delegation. But Roosevelt felt forced to attempt it. There were anguished protests from his close political advisers, but it could be seen afterward how necessary it was and how much more support he gained from it than he lost because of it. The investigations of Samuel Seabury into corruption in New York had disclosed a situation impossible to ignore. [5] First Sheriff Farley and then, shortly afterward, Mayor Walker were made to walk the plank with the accompaniment of helpful publicity throughout the country. Tammany, then under the leadership of John Curry, so much less a statesman than the Murphy with whom Roosevelt had dealt in the early days, was en-

---

[5] Seabury acted as counsel for the Hofstadter Legislative Investigating Committee. Roosevelt had moments when he was certain Seabury was trying deliberately to embarrass him.

raged and resentful. But Tammany's rage was Roosevelt's gain. The
hitherto lukewarm Westerners and Southerners became positively
enthusiastic as they watched the New York bosses writhe.

Another factor in the decision to abandon machine support—because the insult to Tammany carried with it the likely opposition
of the other great machines, such as Hague's in New Jersey and
the Cermak counterpart in Chicago—was the continuing rivalry of
Smith. Both Roosevelt and Smith could not have Tammany's votes,
and in a straight-out contest the Tammany support would go to
Smith. This meant, under the unit rule, that all New York's delegates
would be counted for him. So, however, would those of New Jersey,
Illinois, Massachusetts, and perhaps others where the city machines
could dictate. The Smith candidacy had proved its weakness in 1928;
but it has to be remembered that 1932 was a year when, as Louis
Howe boasted, the Democrats "could win with a Chinaman." The
nomination was the equivalent of election. Even Smith *might* have
won. He thought himself entitled to try, certainly, and was determined to have the nomination. He was not even stopped by the
knowledge that more than half of the convention's votes were
pledged to Roosevelt. It required a two-thirds majority for the
nomination, and if Roosevelt could be prevented from attaining
that number for several ballots he might be defeated as others had
in other conventions.

It was out of this hope that the stop-Roosevelt movement was
born. There were other candidates besides Smith. Even those with
remote claims pushed themselves forward to take advantage of
what was by now a plainly favorable year. Ritchie, Byrd, Baker,
and Garner were the most talked of. These—together with Ely in
Massachusetts and the big-city machines—by holding fast, could defeat Roosevelt and then at their leisure make a deal among themselves. All this was in prospect as Roosevelt undertook the final
pre-convention maneuvers. It was not too favorable an outlook. A
break had to be found somewhere. The way might be prepared for
it by immolating Tammany in the person of Walker. And the best
possibility of getting the additional votes to make up the two thirds
was in a sector where there would be no resentment—perhaps even
pleasure—in Tammany's discomfiture. That, of course, was in the
California-Texas axis controlled by Hearst, with McAdoo as his
lieutenant. McAdoo and Smith had had a historic duel to the

death—the death of both of them—in 1924, and McAdoo had not forgotten. How well Roosevelt's blandishments worked is well enough known. Garner settled for the vice-presidency, McAdoo got his revenge, Smith was humiliated, and Roosevelt got the nomination.

When it was all over, the opposing professionals must have reviewed their beginning overconfidence, their succeeding underestimation of Roosevelt, and their mistakes in strategy with some concern. The man they had regarded as an amateur had outmaneuvered all of them and done it easily. As good professionals should, they learned the lesson. The city machines never opposed him again. They made their peace; and when the South and even the midwestern farmers (who owed him so much) abandoned him, the bosses became his chief support. No one really knows whether they capitulated easily when the time came. Harry Hopkins made the deal and he left no record of the negotiations. But from 1940 on the machines had far too great leeway even for their own good. The Kefauver committee's revelations in 1950–51, which did so much to end the two decades of Democratic supremacy, were a direct result of the Hopkins deals. It was a high price to pay, but the immediate results were a third and fourth term for Roosevelt—a political feat never before equaled and never to be equaled in the future.

There were other positions taken by Roosevelt from time to time that had important political results. There were also some about which a great furor was kicked up at the time but which had no political consequences. The decision in 1933 to reverse Hoover's policy and to accept federal responsibility for welfare in several of its phases was the most important of the consequential post-election decisions. The working out of this general determination in the various early relief and public works experiments so strengthened Roosevelt's grass-roots support that nothing could ever afterward really affect it much, and this was consolidated and made permanent by the Social Security System. The electoral victory of 1936 was an astounding registration of approval for these contributions to American well-being.

A good example of apparent political dynamite which proved not to have much importance was the Court reorganization scheme undertaken very soon after the election of 1936. To see and hear what went on as this struggle progressed, one might have thought that Roosevelt had made an error so costly that he would probably never be able to recover from its effects. The loudness and savagery of the attacks were almost unprecedented. But there is no reason to believe that any political consequences persisted. Indeed it is my opinion that it was in fights like these, in which he seemed to be the center of attacks from everywhere at once, that Roosevelt confirmed and consolidated his union with the common people of the land. If those they distrusted anyway were attacking him, he must be on their side. And this included especially the press, about which the most profound distrust was evidenced in the succeeding elections, all of which went contrary to the increasingly shrill advice of the newspapers. Roosevelt may not have won his immediate objective in some of these fights—in fact, he was more often than not defeated by coalitions of opposing interests in the Congress—but they all served to strengthen rather than weaken his support among the voters. And, as I have tried to make very clear, this is the one, the ultimate, standard of the professional. Others, as political historians or theorists, may judge politicians by what they do with the power they accumulate, but the professional judges simply by the accumulation. By this strict criterion, there have been few masters of technique who can even be counted as generally in the Roosevelt class.

22

The Roosevelt decisions of the pre-presidential period were important to him and, of course, indirectly to the nation; but a number of those made in his presidential years changed the course of the nation and affected the lives of all its citizens; the consequences ran far beyond the American continent to the rest of the world. I shall not attempt to catalogue these or even to range them in order of significance. For the purpose here it will be enough to examine a few of the typical ones.

Consider, for example, the group of policy determinations clustering about the first six months of 1933, both before and after inauguration. They had to do mostly with emergence from fiscal crisis and a beginning of recovery from the depression. We are interested here in their political implications, not their success as national policies, but the two are not always separable. If the measures had, on the whole, failed entirely to bring recovery there would have been political penalties. The nation was in desperate straits, and a Roosevelt failure would very likely have caused a serious breakdown in civil discipline. It might, at worst, have amounted to revolution and, short of that, might easily have resulted in serious disorder. Actually their success, limited as it was, gave him, in 1936, a most impressive ratification by election. They were therefore political as well as economic successes. It is interesting to see how they were made.

There were at that time several theories about recovery. They are roughly recognizable as: (1) the business solution—deflation, easing up on business regulation, restoration of confidence; (2) monetary—infusing currency into the system to restore price levels and start things going and, because gold was the standard of value, to affect prices by manipulating the value of gold; (3) consumers' purchasing power—by making purchasing power available to consumers, to start factories going, thus reducing unemployment; (4) fiscal—manipulating interest rates (making money "easy") and increasing or decreasing federal spending; (5) balance—the equalizing of income among mutually supporting groups.

These were not mutually exclusive solutions. There were theorists who were inclined to have confidence in more than one—for instance, those who adhered to the "compensating budget" might also believe in relief and public works; in fact, the two might be brought together. But there was some tendency to exclusion among the experts. Those who believed in monetary measures tended to be particularly dogmatic and intolerant. Professor Warren—sponsor of the gold-buying scheme—was scornful of the agricultural adjustment program, thought relief unnecessary, and saw no need for managing the rate of interest. Irving Fisher, a well-known monetary theorist, believed in the "compensated dollar"—that is, the weighting of the unit of value so that it would buy the same amount of goods at one time as another. There were others—like Senators La Follette, Wagner, and Costigan, and La Guardia while he was still a congressman—who thought that by far the most important contribution to recovery would be a program of relief and public works. They had had a running battle with Hoover for several years and had attempted to legislate their program into existence, only to encounter his veto. But compromise had yielded something—not enough, but sufficient to make a small start.

It must be understood that the protaganists of the various approaches to recovery were clamorous in their insistence, that the public was confused, and that the situation was degenerating rapidly as the debate went on. Roosevelt as President had to make some choices and to make them at once. He had, as a result of the campaign of the summer and autumn just preceding, several more or less clear commitments. Of these, the most specifically stated was adherence to the increase of business confidence by decreasing government expenditures, reducing taxes, and securing stability of the budget. Less clearly stated, but yet generally promised, was some "farm relief," which to farmers meant higher prices for their crops. He had cautiously spoke of the limitation of supply in this connection but, knowing how touchy a subject this was, he had not said categorically that it would be required. Beyond this, he had spoken of concern for the unemployed, the poverty-stricken, the homeless—

all those in distress. But what exactly would be done for any of them was not specified. New York State, during his governorship, had had a relief agency—managed by Jesse Straus and Harry Hopkins, who were to be prominent members of his presidential family —and it might be inferred that he believed in governmental action of this sort, certainly in state action, probably in federal assistance.

The measures actually adopted during the first energetic year of his administration would fall into all the categories of the recovery theorists—even when they were inconsistent or mutually antagonistic. He did reduce government expenditures. He actually stopped —or allowed Lewis Douglas, who was Director of the Budget, to do so—such public works as Hoover had set in motion, and he reduced the salaries of government employees. Then presently, seeing that matters were getting worse rather than better, he sponsored bills for relief and public works. Also, instead of dissolving the Reconstruction Finance Corporation, he caused its capital to be enlarged and its loaning powers to be widened. It went to work at rescuing banks and business concerns in a big way. Home owners were saved from dispossession by vastly greater loans than Hoover had been willing to approve; so were the railroads and insurance companies. But also money was eased for business borrowing by reducing the rediscount rate. Inflation was resorted to by unbalancing the budget, although, with an eye on the economy commitment, a distinction was made between "ordinary" and "emergency" expenditures, and only the ordinary budget was balanced. Also, a program of currency manipulation was undertaken by gold purchases at higher and higher prices from week to week, and silver was remonetized.

If all this taken together is said to make no sense, the criticism is an economic one. In the circumstances, and gauged by the intention, such an economic conclusion is justified but irrelevant. Politically the program proved to be very effective. The further question whether it could not have been more consistent and more economically effective is quite another kind of consideration. Certainly it could have. But how could it have had better political results? Better results, as a matter of fact, would have been practically impossible. Roosevelt came out of the first four years a political hero.

This is not to say that if recovery had been complete and the economy had been stabilized Roosevelt would have lost in 1936. But such an outcome is not unthinkable, although it might perhaps

have been more likely in 1940. Some of the phenomena of that
time will illustrate what I mean. Politically it was better *to be recovering* than *to have recovered* and to have reached stability. When
recovery was so well along as to relieve the pressures of depression,
many of those who had supported Roosevelt expunged from their
minds, with amazing rapidity and completeness, the fears that had
originally led them to acquiesce in the New Deal measures. The
businessmen, for instance, were inclined to turn on Roosevelt, attacking first, of course, in classic fashion, his subordinates. The Liberty
League and the National Association of Manufacturers led the as-
sault, but the recovering farmers were not far behind. If the city
machines and organized labor had not rallied to Roosevelt, and if
the progressives had not, in a body, devoted themselves to him and
to the New Deal, he would have been defeated in 1940 and 1944.
His enormous majority in 1936 was because the cities had come
round and the conservatives had not yet wholly departed. [1] This
process of realignment might have been immensely accelerated by so
quick a recovery that business no longer needed help. And how far
it could go when real prosperity had returned was demonstrated
by the defeat of so superior a Democratic candidate as Adlai
Stevenson in 1952 and again in 1956. Recovery, it must be understood, involved very complex political manipulation and really expert timing. There was a shifting of support almost from the very
first. It went slowly at the beginning, but much more rapidly later
on, so that by 1940 the President, preparing to run for a third
term, must have been beset with political uncertainties. The defection of the conservatives was now complete, except that the South
was not likely to break away. The Southern agrarian interests were
conscious of a stake in the AAA and were basically Democrats
anyway. The midwestern farmers were lost; they were Republicans,
and no sooner had they experienced the first flow of benefits than
they began to grumble about the source of their renewed prosperity. They had learned nothing; they wanted to expand their

---

[1] Although the defections were quite numerous, led by Al Smith and including
Senators Copeland, Walsh, Burke, and even Wheeler, who had been La Follette's
running mate in 1924 (although Wheeler was motivated more by personal feelings than public ones). Besides these, most of the Southerners were against Roosevelt from the time of the Court-reform struggle, although at election time they
came round.

crops as prices rose, and if they had, and prices had gone down again, they would have blamed something else than the increase of supply. They were incorrigibly determined to have their cake and eat it too. Iowa, in fact, had not lingered in the Roosevelt camp for a decent interval. The state had shown signs of Republican leaning even in 1934.

The President was not so sure that he would be re-elected in 1940. This uncertainty was added to by Jim Farley's defection. The Hull-Garner-Farley axis had hardly bothered to conceal its machinations for the past year. In the circumstances Roosevelt took a number of precautions. He pretended not to notice Hull's disloyalty and, with one eye on the South, was affable also to Barkley and Byrnes. At the same time he insisted on Wallace for Vice-President —that was for the farmers in general and for the midwest in particular. Then, in place of Farley, he persuaded Ed Flynn of the Bronx to become chairman of the National Committee. That was for the city bosses, who, he sensed, were now to be his most reliable support. With these arrangements he defeated Willkie—but only just, and after a wearing campaign.

There had been two incidents in the second term which historians are inclined to rate as mistakes. Of one I have spoken—the Court fight. But this, it seems to me, did not count against him. Louis Howe was now dead; his judgment might have persuaded the President not to undertake the struggle. But I think not. What the Court fight did was to precipitate the defections of those who were at best lukewarm and at worst potential enemies. There was a line-up. Coming as it did very soon after the famous victory of 1936, with Roosevelt's popularity at its height, he was nevertheless defeated in the Congress. He might not have been if the Senate leader, Robinson, had not died in the midst of the battle, making it necessary for him to choose between Harrison and Barkley and, when he chose Barkley, left Harrison sore and disgruntled. But he did lose.

At this distance, however, I am inclined to think that the most important political incident of the fight was his remarkable speech to the nation concerning the issues. This seemed to me at the time a superb performance, the more so as part of the argument was directed at those who had favored constitutional amendment rather than Court reorganization as the better method of clearing the way for the changes that must come. [2] The speech might well serve as a model of fully developed presidential appeal to the people. Read aloud now, even without the Roosevelt tones of voice, its effect seems to me unmistakable:

> *Tonight, sitting at my desk in the White House, I make my first radio report to the people in my second term of office.*
>
> *I am reminded of that evening March, four years ago, when I made my first radio report to you. We were then in the midst of the great banking crisis.*
>
> *Soon after, with the authority of the Congress, we asked the nation to turn over all of its privately held gold, dollar for dollar, to the Government of the United States.*
>
> *Today's recovery proves how right that policy was.*
>
> *But when, almost two years later, it came before the Supreme Court, its constitutionality was upheld by only a five-to-four vote. In effect, four Justices ruled that the right under a private contract to extract a pound of flesh was more sacred than the main objectives of the Constitution to establish an enduring nation . . .*

He spoke then of the further measures of the New Deal to ameliorate the crisis, said that they had had to be *national* laws if they were to give balance and stability, and continued with the warning that the nation was only part way through its crisis. It was dangerous for the government not to be armed with the power to meet such an emergency as had occurred in 1929 if one should arise again. Two elections had shown that the protection was wanted —not after more years of debate, but when it had to be invoked. He went on:

> *The courts have cast doubt on the ability of the elected Congress to protect us against catastrophe . . . we are at a crisis in our ability to proceed . . . It is a quiet crisis. There are no lines of depositors outside closed banks. But to the farsighted it is far-reaching in its possibilities of injury to America. . . . I want to talk to you very simply about the need for present action in this crisis—the need to meet the unanswered challenge of one-third of a nation ill-nourished, ill-clad, ill-housed.*

[2] There were many of these, and I was one.

And he proceeded to discuss the position of the courts in a tripartite government and to explain how it was that judges were
less responsive to change and the need for adaptation than legislators or the Chief Executive. He had a plan that would make for a
greater responsiveness. He had sent it to the Congress. It would,
he said, "save the Constitution from the courts. We want a Supreme
Court which will do justice under the Constitution, not over it. . . ."

He then argued that constitutional amendment was not necessary.
Many of those who advocated it did so insincerely. They thought
the difficulties so great that no reform would result. To those who
were sincere he would say:

> We cannot rely on an amendment as the immediate or only
> answer. . . . When the time comes for action, you will find
> that many of those who pretend to support you will sabotage
> you. . . . Look at these strange bedfellows. Where before have
> you found them really at your side in fights for progress?
>
> And remember one thing more. Even if an amendment were
> passed, and even if in years to come it were to be ratified, its
> meaning would depend upon the kind of justices who would
> be sitting on the Supreme Court bench. An amendment, like
> the rest of the Constitution, is what the justices say it is. . . .

Perhaps I exaggerate the appeal this fireside chat had because I
recall it so vividly. But there was an enormous response, registered
in a huge volume of correspondence. And when the Congress rejected the legislation, it did so in a revealing orgy of self-congratula-
tion for being the defender of the Constitution from executive tam-
pering. There was a great uneasiness. And of course most of the
reforms came about within a few years almost as the President had
proposed them.

It is, however, the political impact of the struggle and defeat that
is of interest here. The President gave some indication of being
downcast over the reverse—he could hardly have felt otherwise,
considering the vast volume of criticism directed at him. The press,
almost unanimously, was bitterly and actively engaged in the battle
against him. Those who had been his reluctant collaborators until
now felt justified in desertion. He seemed to be left quite alone in
a kind of disgrace. Presently, however, a ground swell of approval

began to make itself felt. The jubilant victors could not be so certain that they had put Roosevelt in his place. Many of them, especially the Democrats, began to crawl back either into an attitude of collaboration or of equivocal neutrality.

But for once the politician was overcome by the crusader—or so the historians say. Roosevelt, stung to reprisal, undertook the purge of 1938. Again he was repulsed, and again the reactionaries were jubilant. But as Harold F. Gosnell remarked as he considered the outcome some years later:

> The attempt to discipline the conservative members of his party was not the failure it was made out to be in the press. The President indicated his preference for liberal candidates in four states. In New York and Kentucky the candidates he blessed won, and in Georgia and Maryland the candidates he had branded as conservatives won. In some games a .500 batting average is not considered bad. [3]

Besides, in the 1938 congressional elections—the "purge" was not an election but a primary attempt—the Democrats were unusually successful for a non-presidential year. The appeal was, as Gosnell says, not so much a failure as critics would have us believe.

All this was background for the difficult decisions of 1939 and 1940. No Chief Executive had ever run for a third term—not even Uncle Ted, since he had succeeded the martyred McKinley in 1901 and had been elected only once. He had made the run in 1912 as the Progressive candidate, but that was his second attempt, not his third. There could be no doubt that there was strong sentiment against third terms. Roosevelt believed this to be a sentiment fostered by those who wanted the presidential office weakened. He also believed it to have no considerable hold on people's minds. [4] Nevertheless, that he would have to wade through a thick disapproval, made vocal in a hostile press, was apparent.

Why did he decide to be a candidate again in 1940? The answer seems obvious: he had made it impossible for himself *not* to run. This is something I have spoken of before as a general characteristic

[3] *Champion Campaigner: Franklin D. Roosevelt* (New York: Macmillan, 1952), p. 172.

[4] This was the argument I made in my *Herald Tribune* Forum address in 1938.

of political leaders; here it can be seen in a specific instance. There was literally no one who was eligible. Certainly no member of the Cabinet had sufficient political appeal; and, indeed, the most any one of them had any expectation of in that year was the vice-presidential nomination. Both Wallace and Ickes felt themselves available for the second place on the ticket when it became apparent that Garner, by conspiring with Farley, had put himself out of consideration for another term. But neither really regarded it as more than a remote chance that the presidential nomination might fall to him.

The President was in a position to be safely reluctant. As I have said before, there were times when I thought he would not run again. Such people as Paul V. McNutt, who, as an ex-governor of Indiana, felt himself to be eligible, thought so too. There were several who made such campaigns as they could in the presidential silence. There were times in those two years when it might have been supposed that the contest for the nomination was one between McNutt and La Guardia. Both were extremely active. They traveled and spoke and made themselves agreeable. Both became nationally known as aspirants.

It must not be forgotten that La Guardia had watched and studied Roosevelt with the microscopic care of a potential successor throughout the New Deal period, and especially when it became apparent that Roosevelt would be unable to count on the conservative Democrats for the support of his legislative program. If not them, then he might turn to the progressives in an effort at realignment. It was for this reason, as I have already explained, that La Guardia had abandoned his Republicanism in 1936 and committed himself to Roosevelt.

La Guardia campaigned for Roosevelt that autumn as he had hitherto campaigned only for himself. Then, after the election, which had been a clear progressive victory—much more that than a Democratic one—La Guardia had a right to feel eligible for reward. This feeling was naturally deepened by his own experience in 1937 when he won his election in New York, after running as an out-and-out independent, by 450,000. When Roosevelt undertook Court reorganization, and then in 1938 the famous purge, La Guardia was justified in feeling that not a Democrat but a progressive ought to be Roosevelt's successor.

There is a passage in Jay Franklin's *La Guardia* [5] that pictures the Mayor's public position at this time:

> [*La Guardia*] . . . *had so definitely identified himself with the progressive cause in national affairs that by 1937 he rated as one of the three major political personalities of the United States—the other two being Franklin D. Roosevelt and Robert M. La Follette. The gap between Hyde Park and Varick Street had been narrowed in the course of fifty-five years until the New Deal President and the New Deal Mayor stood shoulder to shoulder, and the Wisconsin Progressive Senator stood beside them . . . The log cabin in which the elder La Follette had been born, the East Side tenement where Irene La Guardia had brought forth her first child, and the Hudson Valley mansion in which Roosevelt had been the only son—all had come together at last and symbolized a fundamental change in American affairs. . . .*
>
> *The "rendezvous with destiny" which Roosevelt foresaw was the result . . . and La Guardia's contribution to that destiny not only complemented the work of Roosevelt, La Follette, and the Western Progressives but contained elements without which Western Progressivism would have turned as sour as Senator Borah or as stale as organized charity.*
>
> *La Guardia had come to represent the most vital part of the New Deal. He represented the reality, instead of the fiction, of "the more abundant life" which Roosevelt preached but was unable to put into practice. . . .*
>
> *La Guardia had not achieved this without conscious effort. Between him and Roosevelt, as between him and the Western Progressives, there had long been a warm personal sympathy and a loose working understanding. It would not be too much to say that the man who best knew what was in Roosevelt's mind was Fiorello La Guardia, and the other way around. La Guardia*

[5] Written in 1937 and obviously a kind of hopeful campaign biography, but nevertheless indicative of progressive hopes for 1940. These hopes were very strong after the line-up on the issue of Court reorganization. It is, by the way, interesting that La Guardia shared Roosevelt's general attitude toward the courts. He often abused judges and belittled legalism. But he was among those who thought and said that the way to reform was through constitutional amendment. The quoted passage is on page 156.

knew because it was in his mind, too, and because he had studied
Roosevelt's methods as a first violinist in the Philharmonic studies
the methods of Arturo Toscanini.

This will serve for an expression of Progressive hopes and feelings
in the period just before 1940 when the question of a successor to
Roosevelt would arise. It might be remembered how Roosevelt himself had been talking in 1937. In an interview [6] in February he said:

> *I do not want to leave the country in the condition Buchanan*
> *left it to Lincoln. If I cannot, in the brief time given to me to*
> *attack its deep and disturbing problems, solve those problems,*
> *I hope at least to have moved them well on the way to solution*
> *by my successor. . . .*

There was an unmistakably elegiac note about this. And at the
same time he was saying to many people, as he had said to me when
I left the administration after the election, that he would be looking
for a new occupation in 1941. We laughed and speculated about
what it might be. I told him he too ought to go to work for Charles
Taussig—no other businessman would have either of us. "Yes," he
said, "and we can't either of us be professors after our unorthodox
behavior." So, a good many stretched ears heard what he had to say
in his radio address of March 4:

> *My great ambition on January 20, 1941, is to turn over this*
> *desk and chair in the White House to my successor, whoever*
> *he may be, with the assurance that I am at the same time*
> *turning over to him as President a nation intact, a nation at*
> *peace, a nation prosperous, a nation clear in its knowledge of*
> *what powers it has to serve its own citizens, a nation that is in a*
> *position to use those powers to the full in order to move forward*
> *steadily to meet the modern needs of humanity, a nation which*
> *has thus proved that the democratic form and methods of*
> *national government can and will succeed.*

If this sounded to La Guardia like a statement of intention, it
sounded so to others also. And if La Guardia thought the ambitions
for the nation Roosevelt had were those he had too, he was far from
alone in thinking so. From then La Guardia was a marked man, just

[6] Published in newspapers of February 27.

as Roosevelt had been from 1928, when he had entered on the New York governorship.

Something happened by 1940 to change the intention that seemed so definite in 1937. And we know well enough what it was: it was the war that broke out in Europe in 1939.

23

At some time—probably in the days of the European crisis as the war impended and then broke out—Roosevelt finally made up his mind that it was America's fight, too, and he dedicated himself—and, so far as he could, his nation—to the defeat of totalitarianism. It was a reluctant nation—a great part of it, anyway—and for the next two years he devoted his mature political talents to overcoming that reluctance and to supplying the maximum of assistance to the Allies who were opposing the dictators.

During the next two years he often found himself far ahead of majority opinion and had to withdraw temporarily; but when the nation had come a bit farther, as it always did, he pressed for still more commitments. There was the quarantine speech; there was the dagger-in-the-back speech, there was the destroyer-bases deal, there was the declaration of patrol areas in the Atlantic, and there were the rattlesnake and the arsenal-of-democracy speeches. All these were markers in his campaign of persuasion and urging. The politician was using his political arts, but not any more to further his own interests, those of his party, or those of his fellow liberals. They were dedicated to a cause.

The decision that the United States would have to join the nations fighting Hitler and Mussolini was, of all the decisions Roosevelt had ever made until then, the most selfless and high-minded. He had a deeply felt instinct that the time had come—had been long preparing—when issues of the highest consequence in the world must be decided. If they had to be decided by force the United States could not afford to have other nations carry the whole burden. It was as much an American as a European responsibility.

There is this much of truth in the numerous detractors' accounts

of the proceedings of those pre-war years. I am quite certain that
the President felt a showdown to be inevitable and, moreover, that
he felt the United States would have to be involved. This was
simple foresight available to anyone. What infuriated such high-
minded critics as Charles A. Beard—to say nothing of low-motived
others—was that he proposed to meet the crisis, when it came, head
on and without hesitation. We can see at this distance how much
better it would have been had he been able, with the nation behind
him, to warn the dictators that they had America to deal with too. It
might have modified their policies and allowed time for mutual
accommodation. It was the clamor of the isolationists, the fury of
the American fascists, which made this impossible. And the President had to resort to waiting, to opportunism, to dissimulation, even
in pursuit of the inevitable. He was not allowed to make his warning
explicit.

I think that until the month before Pearl Harbor the most talented politician of his time believed that by the use of his talents he
could avoid war. To a man like Roosevelt war was a mark of failure.
It was a resort to non-political means that are apt to gather a momentum of their own and smash through to conclusions unwanted
by anyone. War sets loose horrible and unknown forces. It should be
avoided like the plague it is by those skilled in democratic
maneuver.

That Roosevelt plotted to provoke the dictators, that he conspired
to precipitate Pearl Harbor, is nonsense. He plotted rather to check
and circumvent them. He was blamed afterward for not taking
precautions which, if he had, those people who afterward blamed
him would have pilloried him for having taken. Pearl Harbor was
as unexpected to Roosevelt as to the military commanders. What
he did think would happen, I believe, was that there would be an
attack on the Dutch East Indies, perhaps even the Philippines. But
that was MacArthur territory, and General MacArthur had the
same access to the broken Japanese codes as did Marshall, King, and
Arnold in Washington. No one says that MacArthur was remiss or
stupid or treasonable not to have been ready for December 7; they
only say it about Roosevelt. That is obviously not a historical but a
partisan judgment.

But it is equally prejudiced or naïve of the Roosevelt defenders to
contend that the President did not anticipate a crisis or even, by

1941, feel that it was an American duty to support the Allies. There is plenty of evidence that he was apprehensive about Japanese policy as far back as 1933, and about Hitler as soon as he came to power in the same year; and some of us knew that he felt by the beginning of his second term that the liberal forces in Japan had become ineffective. He often spoke to his associates about Japan's aggressions in China and about the sinister implications of Hitler's rise and his progress to complete mastery in Germany. He did not feel so strongly about Mussolini until the conquest of Abyssinia was undertaken and the League welshed on sanctions. Long before 1939 he had watched with apprehension the development of totalitarianism everywhere in the world except in western Europe, in North America, and, as he thought, in China. But it was not until 1939 that the precipitation of all his doubts and fears occurred. When France and Britain went to war, Roosevelt's heart was fully engaged as well as his mind.

If the United States was to play the part history required of the richest and most powerful nation on earth, if men of good will were to prove that they were also men of courage and conviction, Roosevelt was appointed to the leadership that would bring those resources and that courage to the rescue of those who, because of proximity, had undertaken to bear the first shocks. This, in the Roosevelt mind, was the setting for the election of 1940. The question was not whether he wanted to be elected again; I am sure that he did not want a third term and that he was deeply disinclined to break the two-term tradition. The question was whether any other leader could muster the nation's resources and bring them to the service of democracy.

It seemed to him obvious that no other leader could. Roosevelt had two possible alternatives remaining to him, it seems to me. The first was Willkie. But this was not real. No one could have predicted before it actually happened that Willkie would have got the Republican nomination; and, until he began to campaign, it was not known that he shared the Roosevelt views concerning the world struggle. Willkie would have been a real alternative only if he had stayed, as he was originally, a Democrat, if he had demonstrated any real political sagacity, and if he had ever been known as the protagonist of any cause except that of the power monopoly he represented. Roosevelt might not have felt entirely lost if he had had to hand over the presidency to Willkie after an electoral defeat, but he never had any chance to do so before campaigning began.

The other alternative was La Guardia. I feel very certain that Roosevelt considered prayerfully whether the Mayor might not succeed him in 1940. He must have concluded that La Guardia could not get the Democratic nomination. And a third-party progressive movement was not feasible. Such a departure in 1940 would merely have split the Democratic party and insured a Republican victory. The Republican party then, as later, had not only a hard core of reactionaries but also most of the xenophobic isolationists. Even to think of a Republican victory was to contemplate the defeat of the policies to which the President was now devoted.

The trouble with La Guardia was that he was so thoroughly a maverick. Roosevelt had tried before, as he would try again, to fit La Guardia into his administration. He talked with me about it first—or I to him, I forget which—when La Guardia was defeated for the Congress in the 1932 Democratic landslide. This loss in victory of one of our most valuable allies seemed ironic indeed. And all of us thought at once about his future. What occurred to the President—and he had several interludes of high glee as he pictured it—was that La Guardia could be appointed to one of the commissions in Washington which the Congress in its infinite wisdom had said should be bipartisan. It might teach them a lesson, Roosevelt thought, if to one of the Republican commissionerships he should appoint the fiery New Yorker. He found at once, however, that he would encounter confirmation trouble. The Republican resentment might very likely run to the stirring up of a real fight; and Farley, too, was violently opposed. So nothing was done, although several possibilities were explored. It was a good solution to have the ex-congressman win the mayoralty of New York and keep it. There then existed an ally in the enemy camp; one, also, who kept Tammany subdued. And every member of the New Deal fraternity in Washington supported La Guardia with all the favors and allocations available. Throughout the depression he could count on this unfailing resource. It made him independent in New York even of his Fusion colleagues—independent in the mayoralty, but not if he wanted to go farther and needed another nomination.

The alliance between the Mayor and the President was unacknowledged. Neither praised the other in any flamboyant fashion.

But when it was necessary, the implicit alliance became for the moment explicit—as when La Guardia joined with the progressives in 1936 to assure Roosevelt that if a realignment was coming he could be counted on to the limit. And in that year a realignment seemed not unlikely. The New Deal was stymied in the courts, and Landon was made to seem, by press acclamation, to be winning. Of course the dissimulation of Democratic conservatives for campaign purposes and the overwhelming Roosevelt victory showed what mastery of popular approval Roosevelt really had. The progressive gesture was lost sight of in the flood tide of that victory. Roosevelt could control the Democratic party and a realignment was not necessary. The progressives must become Democrats or reconcile themselves to outlawry.

The Roosevelt mastery was far less certain for 1940. But he could have the nomination without question. And no one else—certainly not La Guardia—could; that is, no one could who would go on to the end Roosevelt now had in view. When he had the nomination, Roosevelt's strategy was to run against Hitler more than against Willkie; and to emphasize the national character of his campaign he brought two Republicans into his Cabinet. Neither was better known than La Guardia; neither was more anti-fascist; but both were more regular. Roosevelt was suggesting that the struggle he was in was not a Democratic but a bi-partisan one and that he was an American, not a Democratic leader.

There was then the problem of the vice-presidency. This election had to be won for a great purpose, and the winning of it must not jeopardize that purpose. The vice-presidential candidate should share Roosevelt's view of American responsibility, but he ought to be of the American earth, earthy. His choice fell on Wallace for the job he would, I think, have chosen La Guardia for if he could. That Wallace was jettisoned four years later in another pre-campaign decision, at the insistence of the city bosses, ought not to obscure the benefits from choosing him for 1940. Actually it was one of Roosevelt's best political decisions as well as one of his wisest in view of his policy intentions. But, as I shall point out, this was not the reason for the choice. The benefits were incidental.

It is not always remembered now, because of what happened afterward, that Wallace was, of all the President's own associates except perhaps Ickes, the hottest for getting into the war. In this he matched La Guardia. I recall very well, early in 1940, calling to see him at the Department of Agriculture, as I sometimes did on New York City business at that time. We had long since consigned to our store of unwelcome memories the differences we had had in my last year at the department (1936) and had renewed a mutual affection which yet did not bring us together very often. We had a good deal to talk about. War was obviously coming up over the horizon. I felt rather strongly that political means ought to be used to the limit before force was resorted to. The current policies, I thought, were strengthening rather than weakening the dictators. The President, because of isolationist sentiment, could not warn them that American intervention would follow further aggression. I thought Germany had to be allowed a role in Europe of more importance than France or Britain would concede if we continued to back them. No liberal could approve the dictators, and certainly I was revolted by their behavior, but I doubted whether war would settle anything. It would only result, as it had before, in an unstable settlement that would have to be revised or would result in another war after twenty years.

Wallace was outraged. I had spoken cautiously enough, because I too had feelings that would be well enough satisfied by condign punishment for Hitler and Mussolini; but I had the reservation, which I could not overcome, that war was a simple but not a remedial resort. We might as well find the remedy now as after the agony of armed conflict. It would have to be the same in any case. But Henry would not have it. Appeasement of wrongdoers, he said, only led to further aggressions. There was no end to it. We must join the Allies. We must fight. This, I think, goes some way to account for the President's choice of Wallace for the vice-presidency. He was like-minded about the totalitarians, and that, just then, was for the President a moral issue of transcendent importance.

The President had to do everything in his power to draw together dissenting factions and to heal, now, the wide breach his pursuit of New Deal policies had opened between himself and his followers and the conservatives. Willkie polled an enormous vote. It was not mostly an isolationist vote; it was an anti-New Deal vote. Even a victorious Roosevelt could get the unity he felt the country must have only by abandoning the New Deal and appeasing the conserva-tives. It was not to be a New Deal war, as Wilson's had been a

Democratic war; it was to be an American war, and the end was to see a nation united not only in punishing the aggressors but—and here we come to his last great decision—in establishing the institutions that would make a permanent peace possible. All the world was to condemn the totalitarians and then to unite in protecting itself from another similar uprising. If his political arts could not avoid war, he would risk their use with war going on. He would try to manipulate the Moloch.

The United Nations, arising in the President's mind as the justifying end of his policy, did not arrive there suddenly. It had been there, unfolding, ever since a certain day in 1919 when, returning on the *George Washington* from Paris with the weary Wilson, he had understood for the first time how that stubborn Presbyterian felt about the League of Nations. Wilson had just fought the cynical Europeans to a finish. He had sacrificed everything—or almost everything—for consent to the setting up of his organization for peace. It was, otherwise, a dreadful treaty; but he felt that the American people ought to see, as he did, the miracle of achievement represented by the structure of the peace he had built. Actually he was returning to a disillusioned people, sick of involvement, anxious to be quit of European obligations. And he faced, although he did not yet know it, a Senate conspiracy, led by Senator Lodge, which would defeat his efforts. [1] He was bone-tired, on the verge of breaking down, but he had the zeal of the prophet in his heart and it must have been conveyed to Roosevelt as they talked.

During the first days of the homeward voyage Wilson kept to his staterooms or walked solitary on the deck, a haggard figure with cap down over his eyes and slow, lagging step. But one day he took the young Assistant Secretary to his cabin, sat at his desk with the treaty before him, and opened his mind. We know that that meeting took place, but that is all we do know, except about its results so far as young Roosevelt was concerned. The only further information about it anyone except the two principals had—and Wilson can hardly have felt much significance in his explanation to an Assistant Secretary—was what Eleanor Roosevelt recorded in her diary and what Franklin was to quote again and again in future speeches.

---

[1] Thirty-seven senators were even then agreeing not to ratify any treaty that contained the League.

This was not something said when the two were talking but something Wilson said later at a shipboard luncheon as they neared Boston:

> The United States must go in or it will break the heart of the world, for she is the only nation that all feel is disinterested and all trust. [2]

Somehow Wilson had transformed the Assistant Secretary from a not very profound young man into one with a mission in life. That purpose was to be pursued persistently, with artfulness, caution, and finally, when it could be done, as a supreme end of national policy. It would seem to have disappeared from Roosevelt's consciousness for long stretches of time. But it would reappear whenever some opportunity for furtherance offered itself; [3] and, as I have suggested, it would serve as justification for leading the nation into war, as Wilson's League had been his justification for an earlier one. Roosevelt's United Nations would be different from Wilson's League, and his Four-Power imperium which the successors of Roosevelt, Stalin, Churchill, and Chiang, could not keep together would be very different. But the intention would be the same: to organize the world for peace.

Roosevelt's last two decisions—to enter the war and to bring into being a permanent United Nations—were clearly not sudden inspirations. They were arrived at after prolonged consideration. Both had come to be less expressions of judgment or even necessity than outgrowths of attitude. Roosevelt felt that in persistently electing him to the presidency the people of the nation had chosen him for broad reasons he had made amply plain throughout the years of his leadership. It was part of him to oppose totalitarianism and just as much part of him to focus the war he had hoped to

[2] Cf. Freidel, *Franklin D. Roosevelt: The Ordeal* (Boston: Little, Brown, 1954), p. 14.

[3] For instance in 1923, when, recovering from infantile paralysis, Roosevelt drafted a plan "to preserve world peace," stimulated by the offer by Edward Bok of a prize for the best suggestion. He had already departed from the terms of the League and was feeling for a redrafted charter that would escape the old quarrels and yet be the institutional foundation for peace. The draft of this plan is printed as an appendix to Eleanor Roosevelt's *This I Remember* (New York: Harper, 1949), pp. 353–56. There is useful comment concerning it in Freidel, *op. cit.*, pp. 127–29.

avoid—against the indifference of Churchill and Stalin, as Wilson had got his League in spite of Clemenceau, Lloyd George, and Orlando—on the organization for peace. These were not political decisions. He did not take them because they would be popular. He took them in spite of their probable unpopularity. They were selfless and patriotic; they were the ultimate expression of his being. They were of a sort that matched only one or two of his earlier ones—wholly divorced from their effect on his career. I rank with them, in this respect, the controls of business represented by the Securities and Exchange Act, for instance; and, as other instances, the Social Security System and the establishment of the Tennessee Valley Authority and the Civilian Conservation Corps; also, certainly, the attempt to reform the Supreme Court. These proceeded out of an inner place, were intended for the nation's good, and were related only incidentally to the Roosevelt fortunes as a political leader.

It can now be understood, perhaps, what was meant when I said earlier of political decisions that the *why* was easier to unearth than the *how*.

The young man who entered Wilson's cabin on a February day in mid-Atlantic took a new resolution as a result of the interview. This is as nearly as we can put it. But we know that actually such lightning conversions do not happen. Roosevelt must have been growing dissatisfied bit by bit with the complacent imperialism of his youth, inherited almost without thinking from Uncle Ted. At any rate, however long the lesson had been preparing, the big-Navy executive, the admirals' darling, the young hothead who ridiculed his Navy chief—Daniels—as a pacifist and appeaser and his presidential chief—Wilson—as a literary ditherer, emerged from his private lesson convicted of sin and of superficial arrogance. When Wilson landed at Boston and the city's population rose to his challenge just as the Europeans had, something very like fervor took hold of Roosevelt, who was with him.

It does appear as though only on that day did he discover the cause of peace. It was a lasting conviction; it struck deep. When years later the old *George Washington* was to be broken up and her furnishings sold at auction, Roosevelt bought the desk and chair Wilson had used that day; and it may well have been on that desk at Hyde Park that he sketched out, more than twenty years later, the United Nations, which was his version of the League and which he, being a better politician, would bring to functioning life as Wilson had not been able to do. [4]

[4] That he did not conceive the organization to be like the one that emerged from Dumbarton Oaks does not affect the principle. He undoubtedly thought of a great-power compact with the lesser nations hardly involved; but that was not very unlike the Security Council of the Charter. But this, again, was a matter of means. The important objective was peace and its preservation.

24

There is reason enough, it seems quite plain, to conclude that it was Roosevelt's decision that the war should be turned from mere defeat of totalitarian aggression to the larger purpose of preventing its recurrence. It was his insistence, in spite of the indifference or reluctance of the other Allies, that brought about the Dumbarton Oaks drafting preliminaries and the San Francisco ratifying session. His message of greeting to this meeting was occupying his mind during the last April days at Warm Springs before the cerebral hemorrhage ended his life. Like Lincoln's, his career reached an end without the anticlimax of post-war degeneration. The exemplar for the effort of his last days—Wilson—suffered the dreadful humiliation of defeat and discredit as he sat for years paralyzed and helpless in his invalid's chair.

An interview with the invalid President, in company with Cox, the presidential nominee, just before the campaign of 1920 began, was one of the most affecting experiences of Roosevelt's life, the more so because he had not always been entirely in sympathy with his chief. It was this interview that moved both Cox and Roosevelt to accept the League as the main issue of the campaign. Wilson was a political casualty while he was still President, and when Cox and Roosevelt talked to him he was lingering in unhappy helplessness as the world went its way toward competitive nationalism and another war. This condition persisted until his death in 1924. [1]

---

[1] One of the characteristics of Roosevelt that baffles those who explore his life is that they never—or almost never—discover an exposure of his feelings. As a consequence they are at a loss to know what went on below the surface; and as a consequence of that they can never be sure of his motivation. One of the instances of this is the absence of any comment on the death of the figures who meant most to him as elders in his walk of life. Wilson died while Roosevelt was

This would almost certainly not have happened to Roosevelt if he had lived out his fourth term. In the first place, his United Nations would have come into being and have been ratified. In the second place, the fatal years when the cold war began and deepened might have had a different course. These were the years when the Soviets took over eastern Europe in lieu of the security guarantees they could not get from Truman, Byrnes, Attlee, and Bevin, and when China went the way of Russia into communism because Democracy was stifled by a competing elite. It is arguable, at least, that Roosevelt might have averted both of these catastrophes. He almost surely would have done so unless he had lost the miraculous political sensitivity of his last few years and unless his carefully cultivated rapport with Stalin had diminished. Roosevelt seemed to Stalin to be one Western representative he could trust. When he was gone there were no others, and he made his dispositions accordingly.

There is thus reinforcement for my belief that Roosevelt, from Pearl Harbor on, was a transformed figure, larger than life, purified and cleansed, and with only the world's welfare as the object of his care and strategy. This reinforcement comes from projecting the Roosevelt policies into the future, the nearly four years from whose management the stroke of fate relieved him. It was tragic, as Lincoln's removal was tragic, for the nation. Lincoln's death loosed a season of hatred, of suppression, of vengeance. The nation had hardly recovered from it after half a century. The death of Roosevelt removed the one catalyzing individual who might have stimulated and projected the tolerance and understanding without which the fatal condition for another world war at once began to take shape.

But I do not argue this probability to enlarge the already massive figure of a hero. I do it to make the point that the members of that small company of the political elite who come to almost absolute success are frequently transformed at the climax of their careers

off the Florida Keys in the houseboat *Larooco,* hoping that recovery would come from exercise in the warm water. The only notice he took of the event was an entry in the *Larooco's* log on February 5, 1924: *Yesterday when approaching the town (St. Augustine) we saw the flags at half-mast—President Wilson died Sunday morning. Our own ensign will remain at half-mast for 30 days.* He was at sea, too, in the winter of 1919, on the way to Paris, when Uncle Ted died. The only comment was made by Eleanor, who remarked that a great man had gone and that his last years must have been unhappy ones.

into practically selfless statesmen, and to suggest Roosevelt as an illustration. Their training, their experience, their victories and defeats may not make them wise; their policies may not turn out to be infallibly good; but they are released into such wisdom as they are capable of by the selflessness that comes upon them when they have no further worldly ambitions. Their judgment may still not be perfect, but it is not distorted by careerism. It makes an enormous difference in a politician's decision-making that he has been relieved of any concern for himself—except, that is, the regard of posterity. When he does not have to manage people and events any longer with a view to clearing out of his path potential rivals, when he no longer has to think of holding together a nominating coalition, when he is free to lead the people who have become his into wiser ways and happier arrangements—when all this happens, the careerist becomes the purified statesman.

I should like to make the point that it was not only true of Roosevelt that in his last days he was purged and uplifted; it is also true of others who have had political careers with comparable consummations. Certainly terminal periods with such characteristics can be identified in the lives of La Guardia and Muñoz. They are not so well marked, so easily separated out as happening at a noticeable time; and this difference has its reasons. In the case of La Guardia, he had not stopped maneuvering for his future until shortly before the end of his last term as Mayor. In the case of Muñoz, he slipped into the selflessness of climax very gradually. The separating event between Muñoz, the ambitious politician, and Muñoz, the politician using his skills solely for Puerto Rican advancement, would be found in the election of 1952. It was then that he was for the second time elected Governor; it was then that the Commonwealth Constitution became operational; it was then that the political boss merged with the chief executive of a stabilized Puerto Rico.

But because Muñoz was the active and sole boss of his machine, even when he was chief executive, he had to go on functioning almost automatically, as he had done when he was only a political boss. Habit was hard to overcome, and the institutions centering in him had hardened. He had no successor as boss any more than he had as chief executive.

He suffered more than any of the others from their common fault of having exiled those capable assistants who might have become leaders in the process of protecting himself from rivals. But then, too, he was comparatively young. Instead of having been born in 1882, as Roosevelt and La Guardia had, he had been born in 1898. Those were a long sixteen years in the circumstances of the twentieth century. Neither of his elders had to accommodate his mind to a wrenching extension into the age of nuclear energy. [2] Muñoz had to face and to preside over changes more fundamental than my other two, although they affected fewer people. And it did not matter much that his insular domain was subordinate as to its economy and therefore less than autonomous in other respects. So, for that matter, was La Guardia's. And La Guardia, too, in another decade, would have had to think of a city both threatened and incited to invention by the advance of nuclear science. Muñoz lived into the time of the world's transformation. He had to think of going on, long after the attaining of his ambition, without adequate assistance, working with the distasteful machinery of bossism, keeping himself in power simply because he was still young and he would not trust Puerto Rico's future to anyone in sight. It would have been against a politician's nature to let go before a threatening rival had been able to thrust himself forward.

I have spoken of selflessness as a characteristic of the mature politician in office. It is interesting to locate speculatively the time and the event that mark the onset of maturity, and quite often it is possible to do this with some show of evidence. But like almost everything else in politics, examination will raise doubts. In the case of Roosevelt, as in those of the others, there can be discovered, on either side of the postulated dividing line, decisions and actions that belong to the other period. Sometime before the apocalyptic advent of war when Pearl Harbor was attacked, the purging and refining had begun. The decision to accept Wallace for the vice-presidency in 1940 had, in my opinion, much in it of moral content. It proved to be a shrewd selection, but I doubt whether the President had exclusively in mind the winning of the election. What influenced him much more was something quite different. Wallace represented intelligence and moral strength of a sort matched by no other prominent Democrat, with the single exception, perhaps,

[2] Although Roosevelt had to make the first awful decision concerning it—to develop the A-bomb.

of Justice William O. Douglas. And, as is now known, Douglas was an alternative choice in Roosevelt's mind.

I will not argue this at length, but I must just say that I recall my own surprise when I learned of the decision. I had been in the West and had stopped off at Chicago to view the proceedings. They were somewhat changed from those of 1932 and 1936. The setting was the same as 1932—the hotel lobbies, the crowded apartments above, the convention hall with its milling crowds, all looked the same. But Louis Howe was dead, Jim Farley was not managing the Roosevelt forces, and the delegates were unhappy. The professionals were not running things; and for that reason Paul McNutt and Speaker William Bankhead were having quite a run. One of them would have been nominated for the vice-presidency if the delegates had had their way. But they knew it was one thing to show their preference and quite another to act on it.

Over in the Blackstone Hotel, Harry Hopkins, one-time social worker, to the old-timers that most scorned of human beings, a do-gooder, was furnished with a direct wire to the White House. To be sure, he was acting like a boss and talking like a professional, but his authority was awfully hard to accept. And at first he had no orders. Then they came. It was to be Henry Wallace. There followed just as close to a revolt among the delegates as could be managed in the circumstances, and it was only through his bound allies that Harry could enforce the edict. These allies were the big-city bosses and the labor leaders. The labor leaders were satisfied, but the bosses were aghast. Of all the possible choices, this seemed to them the worst. It was, they said, political idiocy. If Henry Wallace could add one vote to the ticket, where was it? The profane variations on this theme listened to by Harry for hours on end were almost infinite. And Harry agreed with them. He was an Iowan, too, and he knew Henry Wallace through and through. He recognized why the President wanted him and he was bound to obey orders, which he did. But he seems to have felt that it was a mistake on the President's own grounds. Had he not watched the effect on Wallace of his presidential ambition for at least seven of the eight years they had served together in Washington? If Harry believed Henry to be far from what the President thought him to be, it was characteristic of him and of his relationship to the President that he made no objection, expressed no doubts, but simply reiterated to the bosses, "The President says so. You have to do it."

If this is accepted as an early instance of rising selflessness in the President, and even as the designation of a successor, which is so antipathetic to a leader, there can be found examples of the opposite sort on the other side of the dividing line. One of them has always troubled me because it so blatantly disfigures the expected pattern. It does very well, however, for illustration here. That is the so-called Morgenthau plan for the post-war return of Germany to a pastoral state. I should not have been too surprised if this scheme had been accepted by the Roosevelt of 1913–18—the Assistant Secretary of the Navy. That young man had had views appropriate to Uncle Ted and to Uncle Ted's friend, Senator Lodge, as well as to Gussie Gardner and other old Grotonians of the time. He spoke of Germans as "Huns" and was infected with atrocity fever; he even spoke of the necessity for peace being made "at Berlin"—thus, incidentally, foreshadowing "unconditional surrender." His were the simple reactionary views of the bellicose imperialists of that time, men who had no scruples about trampling on a defeated enemy and depriving a whole people of the wherewithal to live. They approved the Versailles Treaty. They rejoiced in American power and wanted to crush all those who stood against it. The Roosevelt of that day had spoken of Daniels and Wilson as "dear, good men," but so impractical and so dangerous! They were pacifists; he was militant. They would forgive their enemies; he would exterminate them. And he thought with other warlike civilians that the armistice came too soon. [3]

But the Roosevelt who had crossed the lines of maturity, who had expressed his regrets to Daniels and made amends to Wilson in a national campaign, ought not to have entertained such vengeful thoughts in the 1940s. The Morgenthau plan can be understood as

[3] The most illuminating account of Franklin Roosevelt's attitudes and relationships in those first years in Washington is to be found in Jonathan Daniels' *The End of Innocence* (Philadelphia: Lippincott, 1954). How tolerant the older man was of the younger man's brashness and, sometimes, his downright disloyalty, is made clear in this account by Josephus Daniels' son. Jonathan was then in his teens, but he watched the events of the war with a boy's instinct for his father's welfare. He was, years later, Franklin Roosevelt's press secretary; and, like his father, he came to love the strange Hudson River aristocrat who was so different from the southern variety. It is altogether a book no Roosevelt inquirer can afford not to read.

having been born in Jewish resentment—the Jews had suffered abominably—but it was no cure for the German problem. The cure, as the President ought to have seen, was in giving scope to the German genius, not in exterminating it. The Roosevelt who saw the Russian fear of Western aggression, who stood against Churchill in all the Big Three meetings, and who begged the British to free India and to give up Hong Kong while these gestures would serve as examples—that same Roosevelt, inexplicably as I think, not only consented to but actively advocated the total destruction of German industry and the imposition of such controls as would make its reconstruction forever impossible. It does not fit. It is an irruption into the pattern of a developed statesmanship of a childish will to destroy. [4]

I should have no difficulty in finding examples of a similar sort on both sides of the dividing line of my other two. La Guardia joining with his colleagues in supporting Roosevelt in 1936 seems perhaps not to be so clear a case. Still his own immediate future would have been easier if he had kept to a safe republicanism. He had to run again in 1937, and the Republicans could hardly forgive this flagrant apostasy. He left the Republicans because at heart he was a western progressive too. The native New Yorker masquerade had been entered into for practical purposes. He looked the part, but he did not act it very well, and he felt it not at all. It was a welling up of pure patriotism that actuated him. He would have trouble ever again getting back to his long-sustained disguise.

It is true, perhaps, that La Guardia believed—as Roosevelt had always done—that the future belonged to the progressives and that, as one of them, he would be linked to rising power. But La Guardia was also a shrewd analyst when it came to his own interests. He must have known very well that the progressive conference represented a kind of inter-party group with influence in support of either party's candidates but with no claim to nomination for office by either. This was not the way to the presidency—that lay through the governorship of New York. The governorship could be had only through Republican nomination. With that in hand Roosevelt might support him covertly even against a Democrat, as he had

[4] An equally good illustration can be found in "unconditional surrender," discussed in my *Democratic Roosevelt*.

sustained his mayoralty and had favored Norris and La Follette in the West. But he could not make a Democrat of La Guardia, and the progressive venture would not change that. La Guardia knew what he was doing. It was a costly gesture, but he made it willingly. He may have thought of a Roosevelt appointment instead of further electoral victories of his own, but I doubt that. It was still too early.

In a way the self-disciplining of Muñoz is also a case in point. The *Acción Social Independentista,* which broke with the *Liberales* in 1936 and was the forerunner of the *Popular* party, was dedicated more to independence than to any other principle, and Muñoz was with the others at heart. He had the intelligence and discipline to see that his people's first need was not a change of status but a raised level of living. His fellows preferred, in the manner of hot-headed xenophobes, not to think about this. It was a solitary decision that he made to forgo independence and to concentrate on economic betterment. He gave up the same issue on which Quezon sustained himself in the Philippines, and as countless other patriot demagogues have sustained themselves in other times and places. His giving up of the status issue when he saw where it led was an act of genuine statesmanship. Perhaps he recalled his father's caution; but, anyway, the course he took was not the easy one.

The point of this, I reiterate, is that dividing lines between careerism and selfless statesmanship can be drawn but must not be taken as absolutes. There are anticipations and reversions that torment the analyst but with which he must deal. Politicians, like the rest of us, are individuals with mixed motives, the creatures of circumstance, of time, and of their own characters. As with the rest of us, there are in all of them wounds of the spirit that never heal. They have borne suffering. Also, they have had other experiences of one or another sort that must have warped their judgments and may have distorted their reactions permanently.

Indeed I should say that the man who emerges into the fierce light of political leadership would suffer more than most men from such common psychological ills. He will almost certainly be caught in dilemmas his talents are inappropriate for resolving. He will not yet have found his métier and will have struggled to meet standards beyond his capabilities. This would be worse because he would have accepted the standards by which his insufficiency could be proved. His nature would determine this. The politician of any age is an individual motivated to influence others, particularly in the direction of support for himself, and secondarily in support of the causes with which he chooses to identify himself. In appeals to others, he must be like them, be of them, even transcend them in the qualities they admire. How else can he be the leader his nature is pressing him to be?

On the way to emergence there will be times when he cannot meet the qualifications he accepts, and he must therefore have periods of profound discouragement that can have serious consequences. Many a potential leader is ruined by such an experience and never becomes what he was destined for. The rendezvous with his destiny is never kept. Others—and my three are among the others—somehow outlive or evade their depression, suppress their hurts, and eventually find that they have a talent superior to those of their then competitors, so that they come out into a kind of upper air that is easier to breathe than the stifling atmosphere of competition.

Politicians are seldom intellectuals. The exceptions in the upper levels of American public life are few. Those few are easily identifiable—the two Adamses, Jefferson, Hamilton, and Madison back in the early days; and in the later ones, John Hay, Woodrow Wilson, Henry Wallace, young Bob La Follette, and Adlai Stevenson. There are perhaps others, and there are several who are almost of the same sort—Lincoln, Cleveland, Taft, Hughes, Hoover, and perhaps even Theodore Roosevelt. But think how many there are who are unquestionably identifiable as the reverse. To go no farther back, and to take only a few, consider these: Jackson, Grant, Bryan, McKinley, Landon, and Al Smith. See, then, how easy it is to classify satisfactorily my three if the surface is penetrated only slightly. Roosevelt had the experience of Groton, Harvard, and the Columbia Law School, to be sure. But what that meant mostly was that he had spent years in an environment so unsuitable that he suffered permanent psychic injury. All his life he was compensating—unconsciously—for the deficiencies of which he was convicted—and of which he convicted himself—as he was "educated."

It is no accident that it is impossible to find in all the Roosevelt papers, or even in the memoirs of his intimates, leads to the functioning of his deciding apparatus. He became so skillful in concealing his deficiencies, and his hurts because of them, that he could never find it possible to reveal his inner life to anyone—and neither his mother nor his wife was an exception to this. Eleanor, naturally, knew she was being excluded and often guessed what she was being excluded from, but she was held well outside the forbidden citadel of her husband's spirit.

Hardly anyone writes of Roosevelt—and this is truest of those who knew him best, or perhaps I should say associated with him most closely—without saying of him that his was an exceptionally "complex" character. What this means is that even they were not allowed to understand the origins of his ideas, the depths out of which his thoughts emerged. This concealment was learned and became ingrained as the young Franklin tried with indifferent success to meet the standards of Groton, of Harvard, of the Columbia Law School, and of Carter, Ledyard and Milburn in Wall Street.

To deal with the Roosevelt history without understanding that he had suffered these frustrations and found certain compensations for them is to grope continually in the dark for explanations of his private as well as his public conduct.

I am not, I much regret, equipped with the instruments I should need to penetrate satisfactorily his motivations. But I consider that I may appropriately insist that without these instruments he cannot be understood. If those who are casually interested in his career have wondered at the superficiality of most of the accounts of his life, this is the reason. Those who write about him see how he behaved, but they have no notion of why he behaved as he did.

I said earlier that the *why* was easier to understand than the *how*, because the *why* can be inferred by examining the consequences and the *how* can be revealed only by descriptions that do not usually exist. I do not retreat from this; I now even enlarge it. The *why* can be got at only by studying the consequences *as they were intended*. And intentions open out only to those who come to the evidence properly equipped. This may not be any great comfort to political analysts, who are not usually conversant with depth psychology. But I do think that Roosevelt's mind opens only to and is understood only by those who have approached it in this way.

25

———

Genuine back-room professionals in politics have a characteristic view of the people and the affairs they manipulate. I speak of the "back-room" variety to distinguish the boss from the potential or actual candidate for office. This is not always a clear distinction, but I think the uncontaminated boss would say that he who seeks office, even if he comes out of the inner circle, suffers such a change as to destroy his identity as the pure practitioner.

There are many illustrations. Consider, for instance, such a group as Grover Cleveland, Mark Hanna, Al Smith, Bob Wagner, Frank Hague, and Ed Kelly, as contrasted with Murphy, Voorhis, Olvany, and Curry of Tammany, or their contemporaries, Jim Farley and Ed Flynn. When Smith and Wagner took office, even as legislators in their early days, and began working up the ladder, they became servants of the machine rather than its operators. They were no longer strictly on the inside. They no longer looked at what was going on from the point of view of machine success (if I may avoid definition of success); they had ambitions of their own; they had records to make, reputations to think of, a place to maintain.

If Charles F. Murphy is put in contrast with any of his protégés, or even with Franklin Roosevelt, who was on occasion glad of his assistance and who was sometimes used in turn as a convenience, it can be seen what the difference is between the one kind of professional and the other. Roosevelt owed a good deal to Murphy one way and another. If Murphy had not existed he—or someone like him—would have had to be invented. At one time he was invaluable as a symbol of wickedness which a young St. George could attack; at another he was a man with power who could grant or withhold absolutely necessary support.

So Murphy goes in and out of the Roosevelt career. Or, rather, Murphy stays put at the center of the Tammany web and Roosevelt works his way in and out as the circumstances dictate, changing his public posture to suit his own convenience. Murphy never changes either his position or his attitudes; he suffers victory or defeat with equal stoicism and pursues the purposes of the organization with that confident equanimity that is the essence of professionalism.

What I mean to do is to distinguish between two kinds of professionals: this one, who does not allow his career to be tainted with office-holding; and the other, whose office-holding *is* his career. Both are in politics for keeps; both use the same talents and the same devices; but they are, nevertheless, not to be confused. The contrast between them is one no observer can afford to neglect.

In these broad categories there are, as would be expected, several varieties that have also to be distinguished. Some of the differences will occur at once to the inquirer about the pure boss. Obviously some are venal in a sense that others are not. Some are semi-underworld characters whose function it is to batten on vice, crime, and corruption and to maintain in office those who will tolerate these civic diseases. Others are merely managers and administrators of a system that dispenses favors for votes. The favors may verge on corruption sometimes but also may frown on its rawest manifestations. This was the kind of boss who won Lincoln Steffens' heart. He was the go-between in the city between the dominant businessmen and the city officialdom. Businessmen did not want vice or crime to be tolerated, but they did not want to be overly bothered with regulations, they wanted reasonable taxes and fees, and they wanted to have no difficulty about doing what they found it convenient to do.

Whether a machine represented mostly the underworld of racketeers and criminals or whether it represented the businessmen often depended on the current administrator. This is why Tammany, for instance, or any of the other continuing municipal machines periodically fell into the lowest category, then presently, because a man of talent and responsibility rose to its head, had a period such as it experienced when Charles F. Murphy was Grand Sachem.

Roosevelt was lucky to have had Murphy at Tammany's head during the years of his rise. An Olvany or a Curry would never have had the imagination to be amused by his amateurish and ill-tempered attack in 1911 or to be willing afterward to make a working agreement with him. This was the tolerance that got Roosevelt the vice-presidential nomination and allowed him to team up with Al Smith during the years of Democratic exile. Roosevelt had a much more serious problem when in 1932 different Tammany leaders embarrassed his presidential candidacy and he had to capture the nomination without the support of his own state's delegates.

Bossism is deeply bedded in the American political system. Various suggestions for uprooting it have been made, and some have been tried. My protagonists lived through the most formidable of all American uprisings of civic virtue and its aftermath. The muck-raking episode was ended by about 1910; but 1910 was just the beginning of those reforms in democratic procedure that were hopefully calculated to end the control of the bosses. [1] The direct primary was one of these, but there were many others, the best of which applied to municipalities where the strongholds were. There was the commission structure, there was the city-manager system, and there were others. They were experiments intended to yield better government and intended to make life harder for the bosses. Of all of them, none was so much feared and proved so ineffective as the direct primary. It deserves a word.

The century's teens were years when indigenous theorists were married to the dogma of town-meeting (or grass-roots) democracy. No move was necessary to make things perfect than to arrange for all citizens to participate fully and equally. It is hardly an exaggeration to say that the whole American progressive movement, expressing itself both in economics and politics, accepted and started from this dogma. This *was* democracy; the purer it was kept the better. The conservatives and reactionaries were allowed to have a monopoly of those ideas that would make democracy more effective by using devices for selecting talents and using them, for delegating expert tasks, and for excluding incompetents from all tasks for which they were unfit. There was a strong tinge of know-nothing or leveler sentiment in the progressive mixture. My three progressives were tainted with it, and none ever really recovered from it. When their better judgment supervened because responsibility required it, they were nevertheless always slipping off into choices originating in

[1] Cf. my article, "The Sources of New Deal Reformism," *Ethics*, 1954.

what lay deeper in their minds and emotions. A concept of demos welled up pure and undefiled from schoolbooks, early teachings, hopeful beliefs—which, moreover, was continually reinforced by the stubborn unchangeableness of those to whom they looked for moral and political support.

But party conventions were made up of delegates from various localities who either were bosses or who had been selected by bosses. The people had had little or nothing to do with sending them there. The nominees chosen, therefore, were the nominees of the bosses, not of the people. The direct primary, it was argued, would return to the party's members the responsibility for choice. The convention would be abolished; instead there would be a day of voting. It was not long, as is known, before the bosses found the primaries rather more congenial than the conventions had been—after all, someone had to appear on the ballot to be voted for, so eventually the direct primary had to be put down as another in a long list of earnest attempts to realize a democracy that always seemed to escape its pursuers.

Without ever themselves really believing in what they practiced or really ever abandoning the mystique of demos, my three illustrated in their time the one alternative to bossism that had more promise than any other. That was the combining of responsible leadership with bossism. They were far from being original in practicing it. Jefferson and Jackson, not to mention other first-rank American figures, functioned in this way. And even Martin Van Buren emerged from back-room bossism to responsibility.

The genuine deep-dyed and systematic corruptions in American political life were managed by the bosses who refused responsibility and who maintained puppets in office as a front for their operations. Murphy was so much an exception as to constitute a paradox. The machine politicians who took office, even the worst of them, never maintained such conditions as Tammany fastened on New York for long periods of time. This system was shaken by the muckraker exposures, it was hurt by the succeeding reform movements, but it was put to rout only when a leader arose who could and did offer himself as an alternative boss, appealing directly to the people for support, and accepting responsibility to them for this conduct as leader and officeholder.

No competing boss in New York City was able to function with notable effectiveness so long as La Guardia was on the scene; the few challengers to Muñoz in Puerto Rico were met swiftly and effectively by his superior power; and those who developed swollen notions of their own hold on national party machinery in Roosevelt's time simply found themselves, almost before they knew what had happened to them, in exile. Jim Farley had spent his whole life rising to be the Democratic party's boss. He was elbowed to one side at the convention of 1940 by the sheerest amateur, Harry Hopkins. But Hopkins spoke in Roosevelt's name—and Roosevelt was the leader.

Leadership is the magic in effective democracy, a responsible leadership, which defines the way to go, asks approval for it, and, having got that approval, enforces the leader's will. So long as his will represents the collectivity, no one and nothing can stand against him.

26

There are always those whose careers, when they are over, refuse any kind of classification. There are many such among professional politicians. They may present difficulties because they have been one sort at one time and another at another time. Mark Hanna was for a long time McKinley's promoter, as Frank Stearns was Coolidge's, and as first George Harvey and then Colonel House were Wilson's. These men were more mentors than bosses, but they were —they had to be—very deep in practical politics too. All of these seem to have carried out their activities as a kind of serious and absorbing game. The stakes were large, the consequences of importance; those who mixed in the play had power, and this seemed to be gratifying.

These were none of them the classical back-room boss type. None of them made his living from politics. None of them was even roughly comparable to Farley or Flynn. They were businessmen who, loving power, were yet unable to—or were afraid to—grasp it for themselves. They had a vicarious satisfaction from taking part in the management of another's career.

La Guardia had no comparable friend. It is possible that if he had had a devoted promoter of the Hanna-Harvey-Stearns type he might have been maneuvered into the presidency. Without much forcing, a retrospective assessment reveals open opportunity at many junctures of which advantage might have been taken if someone of weight and devotion had been pressing hard.

There was no one like that; it is arguable that there could not have been. The nearest to it, I suppose, was Paul Windels, the Republican lawyer, who did mediate, manage, and apologize for the Mayor whenever he was allowed. And La Guardia was assisted by other capable people at one time or another—Cuneo Kieran, Stone, Blanshard, Berle, Chandler, Curran, and Morris, to mention only a few of very diverse sorts. But none of them had a happy experience, none lasted very long, and none could count on any lasting confidence.

It was this insecurity in La Guardia's service that was fatal. La Guardia as Mayor was more incapable of friendship than almost anyone I ever knew. I have said before that friendship is a difficult —almost an impossible—luxury for a leader. Sooner or later he sacrifices loyalty to a friend for some other value—usually his own ambition in combination with a conviction that it also involves a people's interest. But in La Guardia this propensity was an exaggerated one. It showed itself in many ways of which anyone trying to stay close to him and to be helpful had to be aware. There was never a real sharing of confidence; there was always suspicion, more or less acute; there were always rough manners, and sometimes there was downright ingratitude. The most devoted follower can stand only so much of this sort of thing. Presently his own defenses begin to rise, and before long he is so alienated as to be no longer more than a cautious ally.

Part of this can be seen to have its reason in the leader's masquerade. None of my three was what he seemed to be. Roosevelt emerged so slowly from immaturity and grasped so belatedly the commitments of progressive policy that he was forced to function, down to his latest grave decisions, in a confusion he could not afford to share with anyone. The disparity between the talent for political planning—to say nothing of the extraordinary luck a successful leader must have had to be a success—and downright incompetence in statesmanlike generalization is very well illustrated by Roosevelt. The gloss on it is very misleading—the charm, the adroitness, the rationalizations! But the shiny surface cannot conceal the boyish alarm, the floundering, and the justification after mistakes. Can anyone doubt this generalization after examining, say, the gold-buying policy in 1934, or the giving-up on NRA and the reinstitution of trust busting precisely on the T.R. model? Many other illustrations could be found.

But the masquerade of confident competence was necessary. If the American people had seen behind the mask, their nation might have gone to pieces from sheer collective fright several times in the

Roosevelt era. Once, in an illuminated instance, Roosevelt found a way to reassure even many of those close watchers who had penetrated the disguise. He was, Roosevelt said, acting as a "quarterback." How happy an explanation! There were four downs in which to make the necessary yardage; if one play did not succeed, three more were to follow. Americans all know football. They were disposed to watch the next play and forget the last one.

Roosevelt did not repel helpers as La Guardia did. He had no mentor. But until 1936 he had Louis Howe, and Louis was a combination of servant, critic, prophet, and wholly unscrupulous contriver. After that, and especially as the war came on, he had Harry Hopkins, who still seems to me to have had the most improbable rise to high-level politics within my knowledge. Were they friends? Not in the ordinary definition.

27

The first-rank political masters do not attain their positions through the uses of the small and agreeable techniques belonging to the craft. They get there for more consequential reasons. These have to do with grand strategy, decisions of consequence that put them at the head of movements or drifts of glacial weight and inevitability. The issues and affairs of their time, and within the area of their functioning, are grasped and used; they apprehend the wishes—perhaps latent—of their electorates. In a word, they see the beginning, or even help to set in motion, vast movements and are rolled on by them to positions of power.

This kind of discernment is an attribute of genius. But almost inevitably there will be accompaniments of lesser importance, but nevertheless characteristic, and perhaps at one time or another of instant value. They can be thought of as resembling a painting or a sculpture that is vast in conception and startling in design but is worked out with a finesse and attention to detail that are recognized by all knowledgeable observers. The man who possesses these techniques is no amateur. He is entitled to membership in the union. He is a born politician who has made a career of his talent. Such a man, if he has only the small techniques, in however highly developed a degree, will succeed; but he will not rise to unique and lonely position among the statesmen. One of Goya's lesser paintings may possibly be identified by the brush strokes, but who could mistake the masterpieces?

A leader might never arrive at supreme power without the instinct for finesse, but in itself it will not get him there; and there have been history-making leaders who were so inept as to be regarded as amateurs all their lives. Wilson was one of these; and, to go farther back, so were some of the founding fathers—Washington and Madison, for instance. On the other hand, Jefferson had an extraordinary competence in political matters, just as did Lincoln and Theodore Roosevelt.

It is my contention that, in this sense, my three should be classed as genuine professionals, the sort who love and practice their craft with success and satisfaction quite apart from their larger talents for statesmanship. Or perhaps I should say not *apart* from it—because the exquisite touch of the artist often perfected a design and so added to its grandeur—but over and above its demands. The statesmanlike qualities would be there in any case; the careful filling in of detail made all satisfyingly complete.

Let me illustrate briefly: first from the career of Muñoz, then from that of La Guardia, and last with an incident typical of the Rooseveltian method.

In the years 1953 and 1954—during Muñoz's second term as elected Governor—[1] there were two masterly demonstrations of technique, both of which involved risks concerning important matters and both of which came off with superb success. The first had to do with a general recognition of Commonwealth status, which amounted to immense enlargement of its actual restricted scope. This was because the maneuver made far more difficult any future unilateral changes by the United States Congress, which legally might make any amendment it chose at any time. The second had to do with Puerto Rico's standing as a free and willing associate of the larger union. The first deepened the American commitment, until then doubtful; the second made the tour de force of association more agreeable even to those who had theretofore been reluctant and skeptical.

After 1953 the Commonwealth arrangement was known and recognized by a very wide scattering of informed Americans; their own generosity began to seem virtuous, and the Congress which had approved it seemed more statesmanlike than Congresses usually do. The Puerto Ricans were advertised as a people who valued their new ties and who intended to respect their obligations as fellow

[1] The first term was under the amendment to the Organic (Jones) Act, which simply authorized the elective governorship; the second term was under the Commonwealth Constitution, which became effective in 1952.

citizens. The second incident involved violence of a particularly provocative sort on the part of a few intransigent insular terrorists who, in an access of frenzy, invaded the gallery of the House of Representatives and emptied several revolvers into the midst of the more than two hundred members present, wounding five before they could be suppressed. It might therefore seem a most unlikely incident to result in an outpouring of sympathy for Puerto Ricans; nevertheless, political genius turned it into a kind of triumph for Muñoz.

I need not here describe in detail either of these maneuvers. As to the first I must merely say that the Commonwealth bill having passed the Congress, a number of those who had approved it—and some others—took a longer look at it than they had hitherto done. They were more than likely surprised by the celebrations in Puerto Rico as solemn adoption ceremonies moved through their various phases; very likely, too, they were startled to hear of and see the Puerto Rican flag given place alongside the Stars and Stripes. Their second look at the act did not seem to warrant the rejoicing in Puerto Rico. The Congress had not really relinquished any of its powers. Its members began to say so.

This was extremely embarrassing to Muñoz, and he did something effective about it in an entirely unexpected place. At the moment it was convenient for the United States in the United Nations to claim that Puerto Rico should not be classified as a "non-self-governing" territory. The Trusteeship Council was notified that reports concerning Puerto Rico would no longer be submitted. There were representatives of other nations who found it equally convenient to say that Commonwealth did not make Puerto Rico "self-governing." This gave Muñoz his opportunity. He could at once commit now-doubtful congressmen, make a record for the future which it would be embarrassing to reverse, and present himself as a friend and collaborator, vis-à-vis the rest of the world, of the United States. Some of his ablest and most attractive Puerto Rican colleagues appeared at the U.N., were given status and sponsored by the United States delegates, and were allowed to make the argument before the Trusteeship Council. They were, they said, representatives of a free people with a voluntary government. If they chose to associate themselves by an overwhelming ratifying vote with their larger neighbor, that was a matter for them to decide. They rejected the implication that they did not govern themselves. What Commonwealth meant was that there were arrangements between two equals, mutually satisfactory, which both desired to maintain.

The argument would not have prevailed if Muñoz had not made an issue of it, pressed it to a conclusion, and presented the United States with a victory in the world organization. There was gratitude in Washington. He was now in a much safer position. There was no more talk about the legal doubtfulness of Commonwealth. The maneuver had been risky; it might have gone against him and been fatal to his whole scheme, but he had won his case and he could now go on to new ground.

The other incident that displayed his political genius had to do, as I have said, with nationalist terrorism. It has to be understood in connection with Muñoz's earlier affiliation with the movement for independence and his later need to dissociate himself from it—not that he was ever a terrorist or anything like it. He was, on the contrary, a genuine liberal who cared deeply for civil liberties and deplored coercion of any sort. But in the shift from separation to association as a *Popular* policy, there were former followers who had been unwilling to trust him blindly. They constituted an *independentista* party. It was not large, but it was vocal, and it furnished material for the Communist propaganda in Latin-American countries. The tenor of its verbal output was that Puerto Rico was not yet "free." Its spokesmen knew that Commonwealth had made their pleas obsolete. They knew that if there was the slightest chance of their coming to power they themselves would abhor actual independence. It would be the economic death of Puerto Rico, and they could not have survived that. They were thus hypocritical. And since they were on unsure ground their following rapidly diminished.

They did, however, form a political opposition, even if a weak one. In that sense the party was a legitimate instrument of democracy. But there existed as well a very different kind of organization, a really revolutionary one, devoted nominally to the same cause. It had had an unknown but probably fairly large membership during the provocative governorships of Reilly, Gore, Winship, and Leahy. Its roots ran far back in insular history. It was similar to the movements in the other Latin-American nations which had won freedom from Spain. It survived in Puerto Rico as a hard nucleus which was dedicated and intransigent, and its members were willing to use violence and terror and, if necessary, to die as patriots.

Puerto Rican patriotism was no longer easy to define. The United States was not standing in the way of independence. The real enemies of the terrorists were the Puerto Rican majorities who wanted to keep their ties. The obvious dissolving of the dream they once had had so clearly before them enraged the remaining minuscule group.

They had one resort, and one only, and for that complete immolation was required. They would offer themselves as sacrifices in terrorist demonstrations which would make them martyrs. They would thus win sympathy and rehabilitate their cause in Puerto Rican hearts. In pursuit of this end they carried out an attack on President Truman and on Muñoz in 1952. These were utterly senseless irruptions conceived in childish minds without even any clear objective. It was in the same pattern that in 1954 they made their way, four of them, into the House gallery and fired into the assembly below.

This attack by Puerto Ricans on American congressmen in Washington was extremely dangerous for Muñoz's carefully built structure of mutual confidence. A careless public might very well conclude that terrorism was an insular habit. More than that, an incensed Congress might take extreme measures. It was not beyond possibility that, just overnight, an independence resolution might be passed in the Congress and Puerto Rico be turned loose in a very cold world. Muñoz, after no more than a few hours' consideration, realized the danger. He probably did not see any other than protective possibilities in anything he might do. But he saw that energetic countermeasures must be taken, since the threat to his lately achieved structure was real and immediate.

He chartered a plane and, with his family and close associates, flew to Washington. Before the news was widely assimilated he was appearing on the news programs of radio and television networks, visiting the injured congressmen, presenting official apologies to the President, and generally assuring the American people, in his surprisingly hearty colloquial English, that this was an attack on the Puerto Rican people, really, and that they were stricken with shame and horror. They repudiated the injury done in their name to the very persons who had recently been so friendly and co-operative in passing the Commonwealth statute. [2]

His plea was an enormous success. When he left almost at once to return home, there remained in most minds the picture of a genuine democratic leader, himself in danger, who was determined at any risk to find for his people a better way of life than they had had before; he seemed, moreover, like just another American and not at all like a foreigner. What might have been a disaster became an occasion for a mutual drawing together that could hardly have been brought about except in a shared crisis instantly mastered. It was a personal triumph. Political finesse paid enormous profits.

It is no more difficult for anyone who had any intimate association with La Guardia to recall his instinctive certainty of touch. Frequently it was exercised in reverse, so to speak, but so sometimes was it by the others. Roosevelt knew how to indicate disfavor without commitment. His relations with such subordinates as Ickes, for instance, or, in another way, Henry Wallace, were a constant illustration of subtle blocking or just as subtle favor, never overt, never spoken, but generally understood and so completely effective.

La Guardia was subtle when he needed to be. He tried always to match Roosevelt in that regard—without success, I may say, but more because Roosevelt had the power of position and La Guardia was always the seeker than because he did not know the game quite so well. Of course he was by nature cruder and by training indurated with violence. He ruled his administrative domain, not as Roosevelt ruled his, with little pressures and little approvals, cautious givings and evasive withholdings, but with a heavy and dictatorial hand. With the leverage inherent in his powerful place Roosevelt could be easier. But in political relations, and especially those with his equals or superiors (fellow congressmen were equals, and Roosevelt was his superior), La Guardia knew his grossness and cruelty to be inappropriate. From their experiences with him they found it hard to believe what they heard from his New York associates. No one could be gentler or more reasonable than La Guardia among his progressive friends.

[2] It would be unrealistic not to acknowledge that in this maneuver he had skilled assistance. The astute law firm of Arnold, Fortas and Porter, representatives of the Puerto Rican government, and so of Muñoz, were guides and helpers. But the indispensable actor was the Governor himself.

I could go farther. It would not be very inaccurate to say that he was a different fellow altogether in Washington than he was in New York, and not only with those who looked to him for leadership. He had taken knocks in New York; he had fought there with verbal guns and stilettos in a war that sometimes seemed to have no rules, and he had won. Even his electoral appeals had had to be crude, many of them, and suited to the limited understanding of recent citizens, to the ignorance of the uneducated, and to the prejudices of the poor. He was no municipal statesman; he was a clean-up guy, out to obliterate his enemies and reward his majority with better government and increased well-being. He had no ideas about doing this except by honesty, force, and simple personal manipulation. But in Washington he was a statesman. If his record as a congressman is examined he seems less concerned with benefits for his constituents, less influenced by the desires of his backers, than almost any legislator to be found. He always stood for farm relief, for conservation measures, and for preparedness; and he was an agitator for war. To most of these his constituents were indifferent or opposed. But, like a true leader, he prevailed, carried them with him for what he believed to be the country's good.

And the delicacy, the affectionate mutual regard, and the reasonableness that marked his relationship with colleagues and friends in Washington are still talked about by those who live to remember. His reverence for La Follette the elder and for Senator Norris, his fondness for Wheeler, Costigan, the younger La Follette, Tom Amlie and the younger progressives was genuine. By the time the Democratic New Deal was prepared, La Guardia had had a sizable and well-disciplined New Deal bloc in the House, subject to his call; he had anticipated Roosevelt by years. This bloc had annoyed Hoover as much as the Democratic opposition, since most of the progressives were nominally Republican. And they were held together by La Guardia's charm, by his positive leadership, and by the group loyalty he had fostered.

And even in his own city, and with the subordinates and helpers he seemed mostly to despise, he was capable of producing, when it was most needed, a kind of winning persuasion that was irresistible. I recall one instance from 1939. It was at a time when he had been for some time particularly outrageous to his commissioners, partly because he was tired, partly because he was all too aware that unless he moved on soon he was destined to end as Mayor, and partly because his duty to the city was being neglected for his campaign all over the country to get, somehow, to Washington. He no longer wanted to be the best of all Mayors; he wanted recognition as an available national statesman. Perhaps he had a bad conscience about New York and was sensitive to the current stories about his travels and their obvious significance.

At any rate, his subordinates were very nearly at the breaking point. They were fed up with arbitrariness and ingratitude, with unfair accusations and uncertain whimsies. In the midst of this reaction there occurred the commissioners' annual dinner—with wives.

At the appropriate time, when the dishes were cleared away and La Guardia was called on to speak, he made a few gracious, rather random remarks and then, pausing and looking around the room, he said, as if in meditation: "Every commissioner a fifty-thousand-dollar man—and not a damned vote!"

There was a little pause. Then the company roared. All those present felt that no compliment they could have been paid would have been more welcome, no pay more worth while for faithful service. They were chosen people—not because of intrigue or demagoguery or party hack work, but for competence and competence alone. They forgave La Guardia in that moment for all the irritations, the unreasonable demands, the interferences, and the insults they had suffered. It was a master stroke, and La Guardia knew it. He sat down in the welter of sentiment he had evoked and allowed the ferment of his finesse to work.

What he had said was not *altogether* true. It was not true of at least half a dozen of his commissioners, who were political hacks, even if *his* political hacks; on the other hand, it *was* true of several among the thirty-odd—they had actually given up fifty-thousand-dollar jobs—and all the rest were glad to be included in so flattering a generalization. The preening of feathers around the table was almost visible, and everyone went to work next day with loyalty renewed and energies revitalized.

Roosevelt had the same sure touch. Consider, for instance, an occurrence at Casablanca. Michael Reilly was agent-in-charge of the Secret Services of the White House detail from the beginning of the war. In *Reilly of the White House* [3] he recalled something that illustrates the politician's delicate touch at its best—that use of a small opportunity that turns it to the service of a purpose.

In 1943 the French were demoralized by defeat and occupation. De Gaulle had set himself up in London as head of the Free French, but General Giraud had some sort of title to leadership of the forces outside France. This division was not made easier by De Gaulle's annoyance at not having been notified in advance of the Churchill-Roosevelt meeting in North Africa in a French colonial territory. He had been sent for after the meeting had got under way, and his dignity was injured. Giraud was present by invitation, having been brought earlier and with more éclat. What the two French leaders thought of each other was unprintable. And Roosevelt and De Gaulle had had so acrimonious a conversation that Reilly confesses to having stood by with a drawn revolver.

Still it was to the Allied interest to bring the Frenchmen together if that was possible and, even if it was not, to pretend that the rift was mending:

> *You did not have to be a Secret Service man at Casablanca to know that General Charles de Gaulle was doing a pretty fair job of sulking up in England. He did not care much for recognition of General Henri Giraud, and I've heard that he was more than slightly wounded by the fact that numbered among the millions who were surprised by our landing in North Africa was one Charles de Gaulle.*
>
> *I understand that Churchill finally persuaded De Gaulle to swallow his pet and fly to Casablanca to talk to F.D.R. . . . The General was sullen . . .*
>
> *De Gaulle and the Boss started talking French . . . I speak no French so I understood nothing except occasional words that are similar in both languages. Such as De Gaulle's continuous repetition of the words, "ma dignité" . . . The President's Dutch chin was slowly, but surely, jutting closer and closer to De Gaulle's long nose as the "ma dignités" poured out of the General's bitter mouth . . .*
>
> *The man was six foot three, the President a cripple. So Charles de Gaulle has the distinction of being the only man in the world*

---

[3] New York: Simon & Schuster, 1947. The quotation is from Chapter 15.

whose actions and my training made me conscience-bound to remove my pistol from my holster and hold it unobtrusively in my hand for half an hour. . . .

The [next] day I saw the President perform a minor diplomatic coup. Churchill and Generals de Gaulle and Giraud were sitting with the Boss for pictures. The Generals avoided looking at each other and generally showed the same fine, trustful understanding that would mark a chance meeting between a mongoose and a cobra.

The pictures all looked as though they had been posed with each of the four statesmen wearing those old-fashioned head clamps photographers used in the '90's. Sammy Schulman, the I.N.S. photographer, was in the forefront of the group of cameramen valiantly and hopelessly trying to get a decent picture. The Boss realized the problem, so he whispered something to De Gaulle and Giraud. Both Generals looked startled, as though the Boss had called them a dirty name. As the Frenchmen gazed transfixed into each other's eyes F.D.R. turned to Sammy and said, "Sammy, why don't you take a picture of the Generals together?"

Sammy knew his French politics well enough to look as flabbergasted as Sammy could ever look, but he raised his camera and pointed it at the two Generals, who were now standing side by side and looking very bleak indeed.

"No, no, Sammy, not that way," said the President. "Get a picture of them shaking hands."

Sammy looked at the Boss with a look that said plainly "You get them shaking hands."

The Boss spoke briefly to the Generals, their hands reluctantly moved together, and a historic picture was made. . . .

Theodore Roosevelt, dashing out of a pre-luncheon gathering to pluck a rose that matched the frock of a feminine guest; Lincoln breaking down the strained solemnity of wartime Cabinet meetings with a ribald story; Churchill poking fun at the unhumorous Attlee, asking his hearers not to condemn the Labor party leader for having accomplished nothing on an unofficial trip to Russia ("Even our football team came a cropper there"); Franklin Roosevelt speaking of Cordell Hull as the "father of the United Nations"—all these are instances of that talent for the precisely planted and perfectly timed small detail that contributed to the development of a whole, a whole that lay in the artist's mind, not perhaps consciously understood, but instinctively apprehended and entirely unknown to anyone else.

Working at a masterpiece is often a trying and frustrating business. Sometimes even the conception escapes for the moment; sometimes the materials are lacking or are recalcitrant and improvisation is called for; sometimes the mood fails. The thing is created in process, more by recurring persistence, flashes of illumination, and touches of color than by working to a rigid design that is always clearly seen and in control. But once it is done, anyone can understand how everything, even the small touches, the faint suggestions, the frailest maneuvers, contributed. And the masterpiece stands for all to see forever.

Like a general in the grand tradition, a supreme politician will be able to turn small adversities—or large ones—into advantages. Sometimes his ability, so mysterious—and so disconcerting to the opposition—amounts to genius. I think, for instance, of two ready examples from the Roosevelt experience. They are from the early presidency, the first term.

The Liberty League, invented by the reactionaries and joined even by Al Smith, seemed, as the campaign of 1936 approached, to gather up all the opposition to the New Deal's "spending and regimentation" and to personify American resistance to taxes and to encroachments on personal liberty. Roosevelt demolished its pretensions by wondering aloud what liberties the DuPonts, Raskob, Eugene Grace, and the New York corporation lawyers and the newspaper publishers had really lost. Another and even better illustration was the turning of the dangerous term "boondoggle" into an asset during the campaign.

There was no denying that not much constructive result was achieved by many of the "make-work" projects of the WPA. This was inevitable in the circumstances. The idea was to give the unemployed income. Only incidentally were any results in public improvements expected. But "leaf-raking" and other such jobs were in fact notorious, and the middle-income groups who worked and paid taxes were very receptive to the organized ridicule of the conservatives. When some commentator trotted out the old term "boondoggling" it was seized with avidity by every critic and enlarged into a full-scale publicity operation by the newspapers. It became a favorite theme of Landon, the Republican candidate of that year, [4] and of all the Republican orators.

Roosevelt said in the face of the rising storm: "There is a grand word going around—boondoggling. It is a pretty good word. If we can boondoggle ourselves out of the depression, that word is going to be enshrined in the hearts of the American people for years to come." The election results proved him right. He had grasped the nettle and turned it to advantage.

[4] The origin seems to have been in the testimony of a minor WPA official that certain New York projects consisted of making "leather crafts, three-ply carving, and boondoggles."

28

No leader or manipulator of masses of men is what he seems to be; his responses to stimuli are different from those of other men; none of his decisions is taken except as the continuation of a long line of previous decisions all intended to gain a general result, although the twist or the convolution of the present may seem inconsistent with what has gone before; everything he decides emerges from a complex of ambitions, pressures, necessities, and compulsions. I have said something of what this means so far as Roosevelt is concerned; I should contend that the same observations could be made of La Guardia and Muñoz if they are looked at with appropriate care.

Leaders and the events they are involved in are not to be fully understood from the study of public papers or even of such private ones as are likely to survive. These have their place. A legislative act, for instance, creates an institutional situation. But it has come into being because it was pressed for by some person or group with influence. What caused him or them to press for it may or may not be important to the inquirer. It depends on what he is looking for. If he is trying to understand the legislative process, for instance, the motives of proposers are really the energy behind the surface events he observes. If there is only an interest in the consequences of the law itself on those it may affect, however, motive may not be important. The effects will be the same no matter what the motive.

But we are here inquiring into the leadership of individuals who dominate their eras. In the area and the time of Roosevelt as President, of La Guardia as Mayor, and of Muñoz as Governor, no one—not even their enemies—doubted their potency. The exercise of extraordinary ability has consequences, and if only consequences are under analysis it is of no importance to discover the circumstances of its exercise. But if the rise to power is the object of study, then nothing about the individuals under examination is irrelevant. Consequences must be looked at, too, to see whether what was wanted was what was got, and sometimes why subsequent actions were undertaken that would modify the original ones. Hardly any institution ever came into being in a satisfactory operating state, and even if it did it soon became more or less obsolete. It will someday be modified. And it may well be altered in ways that destroy its original purpose and defeat the intention of its originator. Changes could, naturally, be in the direction of improvement, but that this is seldom the case every student of government knows. And he knows why.

Institutions usually take shape at the forcing of a leader. He may be able to prevail because he has prepared something of a mandate, specifically to change an unsatisfactory situation. Or he may feel strong enough and think the circumstances propitious enough so that he can have his way even without preparation. At any rate, he proposes. But he must almost always, except in an overriding crisis, make his proposal to an indifferent or unwilling legislature whose members have quite other purposes in mind. Each member is a leader, too, in his own area and to the degree of his abilities, and he will have taken positions that conform, more or less, with the approved attitudes prevalent in his constituency. But also he will owe some pressing debts. He will have been supported by persons, groups, or organizations in his district, and there will have been an open or tacit agreement that during his legislative tenure he will try to further the interests of those who have supported him. He is more an ambassador to the federal government than a free representative even of all his own people, to say nothing of the nation at large. In this situation alone there may have arisen grave conflicts. Those who have invested funds and influence seldom want legislative favors that are in the interest of the general constituency, or if they do, the interest will be incidental to their own. So the legislator, before he comes to Washington, is caught in a dilemma that will torment him so long as he remains. And it is likely to grow worse rather than better. When he is in Washington potential rivals back home will be furthering their own causes. And he will need more and more assistance from his own supporters. He will tend more and more to favor those who can assist him in his proliferating difficulties.

The legislator will belong to a party, however, and the party will have an organization and a leader. Much will be decided by the organization, but more will be decided by the leader pressing the party organization to approve the program on which he has been elected. The organization, being made up of professionals, will not have done much actual programming. The professional's interest is in elections. He will expect to do the electioneering work while the candidate campaigns. It is the speeches of the candidate that hold out the promises to be redeemed, and it is he who will have the responsibility. The organization, having won, is thenceforth interested in consolidating its hold on government and, by the use of patronage and the conferring of favors, in perfecting and strengthening its organization. It has little interest in anything else.

What has been approved by the electorate may be done if it is of some importance to the organization, but only when driven to it will it take coercive action, because what has been promised will be opposed by many interests who will have set up centers of reaction in the organization itself. These same interests will have listened aghast to the candidate's promises also, and they will not be slow in moving to block him off in all the ways open to them. If they cannot check him in the executive establishment, as they often can, they will redouble their efforts in the legislature; they will not give up—they have lobbyists to whom this sort of activity is all in a day's work—until the issue has lost its importance.

The legislation embodying the program, having survived the recommending and writing process in the executive, will meet ever-stiffening resistance as it progresses in the legislature. It will be introduced and then will be referred to committees. Most legislation stops right there. Only if leverage is exercised which inertia or hostility cannot overcome will the next step be taken. That is to hold hearings. At those hearings there will be an ingathering of oppositionists calculated to demonstrate the damage such legislation will do. This is the lobbyist's métier. He will demonstrate not that his employer is to be harmed but that the public interest is threatened; only in private will he remind legislators of their political debts to his principals. And unless there is really weighty representation on the other side, and unless the elected leader insists that the committee members and the House or Senate officials have party responsibilities, the committee will kill the proposal—simply not advance it to the calendar.

It is not necessary to elaborate this description. It is familiar to every earnest newspaper reader. Even when approved by the committee to which it has been referred, the legislation must be approved for action by a central committee governing the calendar. Then, if it comes to vote, the hazards multiply. This is the stage at which, if they have not succeeded in such efforts in committee, the lobbyists show their ingenuity in inventing amendments—often subtle ones, presented as improvements, which blunt the purpose or perhaps deflect it altogether, making it harmless to their employers or, best of all, even advantageous.

There must be similar action, it is to be remembered, in two Houses. The lobbyists have a half dozen opportunities for attack and for creating delays while forces are gathered and influences brought to bear. And even when passed by both Houses, there will be conference consideration. The rules say that there can be reconciliation but no substantive additions in conference. This again is a challenge to the inventive abilities of "legislative representatives," and they are often able, even at this stage, to serve their clients well. But steady effort and the use of political credit may still cause the bill to survive, to become law when it is signed by the Executive, and then to be made effective by the organization of an administrative agency.

Many such an agency, it is sad to have to report, has been staffed by saboteurs—not obvious ones, but ones upon whom, as upon the legislators, the interests affected have some hold. This can be merely a matter of sympathy. Some wit once described the federal government as "the last stronghold of private enterprise," and it was this state of affairs that was meant. By now the Chief Executive will be engaged in other struggles with the legislature, will be attending to the multitudinous affairs, domestic and foreign, which crowd in upon him, and the new agency will have such a small fraction of his attention, that what is done may be quite the reverse of what he promised when he campaigned and what he intended as the law was earnestly fought for and finally passed.

All legislation is general, more or less; what makes it specific is regulations. These are written by the administrators; and there is very wide latitude. The lobbyists' acquaintance among counsel of regulatory agencies is extensive and intimate. The insertion of a modifying clause or the deletion of one may make all the difference to some affected interest. The latter-day lobbyist has an interest in administrative law only less than his interest in legislative law. He does his best work behind the scenes; and the heat is off, the spotlight dimmed, and the curtain down when regulations are being written. There is even more privacy as they are administered.

Then there come, at later times, the "improvements." This may be when the Executive, dissatisfied with what he got in his first effort, proposes amendments; it may be when those interests that have been adversely affected try to get reconsideration. At any rate, it is a dangerous phase; all the old differences and some new ones will be aired. On the whole, the outcome is not likely to favor the public interest. If for no other reason, this would be because the leadership of the Chief Executive attenuates with every passing month. His hold on the legislators is less when their patronage demands have been satisfied, and the strength of the lobbyists increases as they discover legislators' weaknesses and bear down on them. Also, as elections approach, assistance is more desirable, even a necessity, and the lobbyist can offer it in return for favors.

My three differed in their ability to get what they wanted from this difficult process. Roosevelt got very little after the first-term honeymoon, and most of that was traded off for measures necessary to meet the oncoming international crisis. What survived was the part of his program that appealed to vast majorities in both parties—Social Security and farm relief, for instance, and the reform of Wall Street. La Guardia fought fiercely and on the whole successfully for municipal home rule and for the local laws he regarded as necessary to decent administration. Muñoz simply got everything he wanted. But comparisons are not valid. It was Roosevelt who had the opposition to overcome. La Guardia controlled the city legislature, and Muñoz had only a nominal opposition at any time during his early terms. And anyway, the situations they dealt with were too elusive for any kind of measurement. It is only open to an observer to say that, as the battles developed and were resolved, the Roosevelt reputation grew rather than diminished. There were low periods, as in 1937 when the Supreme Court reorganization fight was lost, but he was a formidable opponent. If in the end not much that he had wanted survived it was because the situations he had to deal with were impossibly difficult. An analysis of any one effort in detail almost always shows endless resource and determination. The failures from poor technique are few. But it is perhaps significant that this explanation does not have to be made of Muñoz's situations; he created them to the pattern he preferred. He could hardly lose a legislative battle to a hand-picked majority. No more could La Guardia in New York.

29

I began by suggesting that the similarities among my three politicians were striking. I may even have given the impression that they might have been interchangeable. I could not support that contention if it was surface likenesses to which I referred; the three obviously led different lives in different places, they came from various social and economic environments, they had different educations and experiences, and they did not at all look alike. Yet let us see. Were even these surface characteristics as different as they at first seem?

Consider them physically. All were hearty, full-blooded types, vital, overflowing with energy, restless, driven by urges and ambitions long before these compulsions had any focus. They were destined to struggle and to rise, and there would be full and vital pleasure in all the incidents of their careers.

I venture to summarize their similarities:

> *They were unintellectual in the scientific sense.*
> *They were strongly virile and attractive.*
> *All were extroverts, enjoying sensual pleasures—eating, drinking, exercise, entertainment.*
> *All were superb conversationalists; all knew the uses of parables.*
> *All were insensitive to others' feelings except as concerned themselves, but their awareness of others' attitudes concerning themselves was phenomenal.*
> *All seemed to have thick skins because they were abused, but this was only seeming: all were hurt and all were unforgiving; and all were anxious for approval.*
> *All were ruthless in the sense of not reciprocating loyalty; they punished friends and rewarded enemies.*

All had thick armor against probings. Not even those nearest to them knew their minds.

None held any traditions to be applicable to himself, though all were aware of them and made full use of their value to others.

They possessed talents for and used political techniques with faultless ease.

All were driven by an ambition to attain power in the political hierarchy, and all allowed it to dominate their lives.

This does not make them interchangeable. But it marks some of the characteristics of first-rank quality in the political field. And that is the point I wish to make.

30

There have been several explorations under some such heading as "The Political Theory of Franklin D. Roosevelt." [1]

There have been no such investigations of the thought of La Guardia or of Muñoz, but it can be predicted that there will be. When the returns are in, they will probably not be very satisfactory. The reasons for this are obvious. All three were practicing politicians who, during long periods of their careers, were on their way to further preferment. They were always, until very late, candidates or potential candidates. They therefore adapted their views to the tolerances of the electorate to whom they must appeal. [2]

The extent to which this adaptation required denial, interpretation, and twisting of basic beliefs is not measurable; it is, however, certainly considerable, and this is where most of the dissatisfaction for the analyzer is likely to center. He can never be certain. When he reads a speech, scans the accounts of press interviews, or examines letters, he will never be sure that what lies before him was not influenced by some immediate situation requiring equivo-

[1] Those known to me include the following: *The Political Philosophy of Franklin Delano Roosevelt* by Turner C. Cameron, Jr. (a 1940 doctoral dissertation at Princeton University), unpublished; *The Political Thought of Franklin D. Roosevelt* by Loren Baritz (a master's thesis at the University of Wisconsin, 1953), unpublished; "The Political Thought of F. D. Roosevelt: A Challenge to Scholarship," *The Review of Politics*, XI, I (January, 1949, 95). Several others are being considered or are in various stages of preparation.

[2] I must mention a most engaging and revealing account of association with La Guardia in the earlier period of his political success, written by Ernest Cuneo who was a devoted younger political secretary and assistant. It is of value to any student of politics whether or not he has an interest in La Guardia. *Life with Fiorello,* Macmillan, 1955. I have already mentioned Mathew's study of Muñoz's adventures in his quest for power.

cation. In active political life there is so much appeasement, accommodation, reconciliation, adjustment, compromise—all that kind of thing—and it is so often done for reasons impossible to uncover that defensible judgments are almost impossible. Impressions can be stated and even defended, but proof will not be forthcoming.

When, however, the practicing politician has gone through his last campaign, made his last deal, compromised for the last time, and reached retirement or death, it is possible to make a general assessment. Without depending on anyone or any one series of possible quotations from statements or writings, there nevertheless does appear something of value. This something may be so close to dominant contemporary political thought as to be almost indistinguishable from it. But close examination will reveal departures or preferences, and they may be significant—if the analyzer has been respectfully sympathetic.

Roosevelt lends himself to this kind of scrutiny because the materials are so rich. In spite of the need for being especially on guard concerning him, some generalizations can be made. He was, for instance, generally progressive, although the content of his progressivism varied according to exigency. He regarded the state with its government as an agency for enhancing the well-being of citizens. So much is clear.

But it must be said that the attribution of any conscious political theory to leaders of this sort is apt to be pretty forced. They operate within a tradition which they accept with the modifications called for by the situations in which they find themselves. So if Roosevelt was progressive, it was with a leaning toward more statism than his predecessor progressives would have approved. His feelers in the direction of collectivism, however, were so tentative that they could be and were withdrawn. There is nothing in any other Roosevelt exhibit that correlates with the Oglethorpe University speech in 1932. That seemed to lead on to a planned economy that presently no longer appeared politically acceptable. It was dropped.

La Guardia made fewer breaks outward from the framework of orthodox progressivism. But then he never really had to define a national policy. Muñoz had a far wider orientation. Also, he wrote more of his own pronouncements. But he too was not required to formulate a national policy or, very often, to consider the basic features of government. When he did he was acceptable and even eloquently democratic but without innovations. He originated the opportunity to improve representative techniques when the Commonwealth was being shaped.

It is an interesting feature of the Roosevelt and La Guardia thinking that its origins are to be looked for in the literature of the law. The elders most admired by both were men of the legal profession, and even their departures from accepted tradition were defiantly defined as legal. Both were most consciously naughty with reference to the courts.

This was natural. Both were lawyers, although neither was a distinguished one. Both were executives of the obstreperous sort who chafed at judicial restraint—which was interpreted as encroachment. One who acknowledges a body of tradition but defies it is being wicked indeed. His appeal to a higher standard is apt to have a hollow sound, and he will be somewhat handicapped by his own sense of sin.

The appeal of both Roosevelt and La Guardia was to the general interest. Both had to claim that the law was weighted in favor of special interests—that the courts interfered with an executive operating for the people as a whole. They were more than a little defiant. Roosevelt speaking of "horse-and-buggy" thinking was quoting, or almost quoting, Wilson, who was far more certain of his orientation. In a way this was an appeal from high authority to one still higher—from Brandeis to Wilson.

Holmes, who meant a great deal to Roosevelt in pre-New Deal days, would be described as a realist, I suppose, and, less certainly, as a pragmatist. It was no accident that he was a contemporary of James and Dewey. His was an original mind and, functioning with legal materials, he made a contribution as important in his field as James did in psychology or Dewey in education. His material was the kind of thing, also, that Roosevelt would have read, perhaps rather casually, in newspapers or in magazines where Supreme Court opinions would be reported. I doubt very much that Roosevelt ever read a volume or even an essay of James or Dewey. But certainly he read opinions of the Court. Also, he was a familiar in Holmes's house when his other intellectual contacts were very few. An Assistant Secretary of the Navy leads a life of action; what reflection he indulges in opens out from the problems before him. But Roosevelt had invalid years, when reading was a welcome recreation. He seems to have read history, naval history preferred, when not reading detective stories, and to have made no excursions into philosophy. But this casual knowledge of Holmes and other judges must at least have widened the range of problems he considered. And the sharp, quick logic of the Holmesian approach is in fact of the same genre as that of the Rooseveltian public papers.

It was not Holmes but Brandeis who was his intellectual guide and mentor during the gestation of the New Deal; and Brandeis was a wolf in sheep's clothing—more accurately, a doctrinaire parading as an instrumentalist. Brandeis very early drew certain conclusions from his experience which hardened into prejudices. These in time came to seem to him axiomatic. And he applied them without scruple. As a justice he occupied a position of considerable influence, even outside the Court. This influence had to be exercised discreetly— that is to say, he could not publicly give advice to a President and he could not denounce departures from the path of rectitude. But he had two means of enforcing his dogmas, and both were used on Roosevelt with devastating effect.

The first of these means was his disciples; the second was the threat of unconstitutionality. The first apostle in the Brandeis hierarchy was Frankfurter, although Morris Ernst was an earnest aspirant. Through Frankfurter, mostly, the staffing of New Deal agencies was controlled and dissenters were got rid of. And because Brandeis was, after Holmes's death, the most influential member of the Court among intellectuals and liberals—and with Roosevelt—a word from him was very nearly a command. And this was much more true after the adverse decisions on the collectivistic measures of the Hundred Days. In these Brandeis joined with reactionaries to make a majority. The Court disregarded entirely the effects of the measures and rested on principles—principles on which they agreed.

Brandeis was an atomist. He believed in small social organizations, and this applied both to business and government. Fortunately a judge never has to say precisely what he believes; he can merely reject those arrangements of which he does not approve. This is an exaggeration of the judicial process in general but not as it was practiced by Brandeis. It was a matter of indifference to him that he found himself joined with McReynolds and Van Devanter, who wanted to destroy the New Deal. He wanted to destroy it too, if for quite other reasons. He had, in fact, given warning and he was merely making good.

Roosevelt was partly intimidated and partly antagonized by the Brandeis tactics. The blandishments of Frankfurter, the alternatives offered by Corcoran and Cohen, and the threat of judicial disapproval if these were not agreed to were sufficient. The process by which it happened is unlikely ever to be revealed in any detail, but the results are plain enough.

The succumbing of Roosevelt did not mean that he became a convinced atomist. It meant that he too was a pragmatist. It was always true of him that he made up his mind about results rather than methods. The ends he had in mind in New Deal days were comprehended in the phrase "recovery and reform." The Brandeis followers offered him an alternative to collectivism in both fields. Recovery could be had by spending without collectivizing; and reform could consist in filling out the progressive agenda—reorganizing the stock market, revising the banking laws, and the like.

This can be and has been called opportunism rather than pragmatism. And perhaps it was. It might have been better to institute price controls and supervise investments and develop the codes and marketing agreements which the Court frowned on. That would have been another kind of reform. Roosevelt judged that not only Brandeis but the country as a whole was still at the trust-busting mental age. The time to collectivize had not yet come. It was obviously his judgment, furthermore, that the exercise of his leadership, the use of his talents for persuasion, and all his political contrivance would be unequal to the task of collectivization.

He retreated, as a result, to short-run objectives and to means that would achieve them and would not be disapproved by those whose support he needed.

I cite this appeasement of Roosevelt's to make the point that politicians are not men of principle and that they have only the slightest regard for theories as such. They are people with two general objectives, one of which is to maintain approval. The other is to get done what they believe to be necessary. To them governmental forms, constitutional processes, conceptions of rights and liberties are instrumental rather than fixed.

It is interesting to categorize them after the fact, to deduce from what they did what they thought, but it is not a really rewarding exercise. Roosevelt himself put the matter very well when he came to write an introduction to the first volume of his public papers. I picture him having discussed with Judge Rosenman what should be included and what omitted. I see him reading over passages pointed out to him which seemed contradictory. I hear Sam asking pleasantly for instructions. And then I hear Roosevelt dictating these sentences:

> *In these volumes those who seek inconsistencies will find them. There were inconsistencies of methods, inconsistencies caused by ceaseless efforts to find ways to solve problems for the future as well as the present. There were inconsistencies born of insufficient knowledge. There were inconsistencies springing from the seed of experimentation. But through them all, I trust that there also will be found a consistency and continuity of broad purpose.*

31

I have often imagined a conversation among my three principals—although none ever actually took place. Each of them met the others, perhaps many times, but all three, so far as I know, never met together. They all moved about the world, and my mythical meeting could have taken place at the operational seat of any one of them: in the White House in Washington, in New York's unexpectedly classic City Hall, or in Puerto Rico's four-century-old Governor's palace, La Fortaleza. The possibilities are fascinating.

If the time is imagined to be during the 1950s, Roosevelt and La Guardia would have been for some time separated from worldly concerns, except, I prefer to fancy, as observers full of reminiscent wisdom, eager to judge the technical competence of their successors and maybe just a little acid about the performance. Muñoz, although neither so experienced nor so detached as the others, not yet having finished his long governorship, would have paid his entry fee to the exclusive club with a notable string of electoral victories from 1940 on; and he would have one accomplishment to his credit that they must envy mightily, something very few other democratic leaders could brag about—that deliberately created and subsidized legislative opposition about which I spoke earlier. It was tame but actual. As a technician he would have no reason for modesty; he could be a full member.

The Puerto Rican, portly and lethargic now, except when stirred by a check to one of the caprices that more and more seemed to govern his activities, might be entertaining his distinguished, if ghostly, visitors in the Mirador atop the palace. I have imagined him as the host. The others would no longer have official quarters. Their disembodied state might make any meeting place possible, even the White House or the City Hall, but these had long since been occupied by successors. Muñoz as yet, at least, had no successor, that most detestable of all creatures to a politician. His precincts were undefiled.

It should be evident, if anything is, that all my three were adventurers in politics, successful in getting and holding onto power, capable in its use, and ferocious in its defense. All were conscious, or perhaps it should be said all knew intuitively that the purpose of the politician is to rule, not to serve. The service, if he gives it, is a concession, a benison, to which the recipient is not entitled. If he does get it, he gets it as the gracious yield of a magisterial benevolence. This should not be confused with favors or rewards to followers. These are expected; they are payment for services. But quite unaccountable graciousness is not unusual. The dispensing of good things is an agreeable relaxation.

For the central duty of power-holding, the initial capture and vigilant defense of a seat is important; and all of my three were appropriately proprietorial. You would have thought they owned the premises that two had lately graced and that one still held onto possessively. This was part of a whole at-homeness with the apparatus of power. The operational center has always been symbolic in followers' minds. The person who occupies it has, from the moment of his coming, an immensely enhanced prestige. Until he arrives he has been recognized tentatively and prospectively. When he settles in, he is visibly and solidly the embodiment of office; and if he knows how to exploit his situation he can cause it to go on enlarging until he becomes completely identified with all it represents. It becomes an accepted thing that he should be there. He may make himself for a long time nearly invulnerable to challenge because challenge seems unnatural.

He will not be quite immune. Time will be against him. Ill fortune can unseat him. Fate may be unkind. Disasters can be made to seem his fault; indeed they are very likely to. Anyone who is in a position of power is expected to stretch it indefinitely and to take the blame for any contemporary occurrence. For Presidents the fatal blows have usually been wars and depressions; but it is not at all unusual for nature's whims to be charged against a helpless administrator—drought, flood, storm, or even a severe winter involving hardship—these have to be looked out for. In their aftermath someone besides the sufferer is likely to be blamed, and the man on top is the first one to be thought of.

For Mayors there are other hazards. They are not blamed for wars or depressions, but they may be blamed for almost everything else, from juvenile delinquency to ill-swept streets, from high taxes to a failing water supply. Indeed they may be blamed because wars and depressions bear hard on their constituents.

Governors come somewhere in between. State scandals are not unknown, and Governors are expected to do something about those that occur in the cities. But a Governor has it easier in this respect than either a President or a Mayor. This may be one reason why Mayors seldom have risen to the presidency and Governors often have. Their records are apt to be better.

Besides such gross hazards, the man in office has another to guard against—or rather to think of, for there is not much he can do about it. He may prove unequal to the demands of his position. He may be inept, may rub people the wrong way, may come to be thought of as unsympathetic, or may come to seem one of those unfortunates against whom luck is running. Or he may have ill health or become senile. There have been a dozen Presidents, more or less, who seem to have been thus dogged by fate. At any rate, they lacked the gift for survival in office and were displaced after one term; [1] and there must have been hundreds of Governors and Mayors who, guided by discretion, invoked the imaginary virtue of renunciation and retired. La Guardia was one of these.

[1] Some of them made a virtue of serving only one term. There was an equalitarian period in American history, running roughly from the disappearance of the Federalists to the fading out of W. J. Bryan, when it was a political virtue to pass around the offices won by political victory. They were emoluments to be shared fairly and must not be monopolized. There was a beginning of this in Jefferson's leaving office to make way for Madison and Monroe. From Jackson's time offices were definitely spoils, and even the President whose victory had won them and whose continuance in office could hold them was not immune to the frontier conviction that any man was capable of doing any job. The strict application of the doctrine was limited to appointive offices, and it was perhaps not quite within the rules for office seekers to claim as a virtue a willingness to limit their terms to one or two. Nevertheless, they often did it. And when it was convenient —if they were not very successful in keeping public favor—they honored their contract with the electorate and retired. But some retired because they were ill or old—usually not entirely willing to go. Even Wilson, stricken with an incapacitating paralysis, wanted a third nomination. Or so it is said; and Grant certainly did.

How puissant in their calling my chosen examplars were is certainly demonstrated by their long occupancy of a paramount position. It is true that La Guardia did retire, and this may call for explanation. But he was fatally ill and died not too long afterward. His enemies said that he could not have been re-elected, which may have been true. Before his cancer killed him he displayed characteristic energy in several other activities, but it is at least arguable that his illness was upon him and that the zest for battle had for this reason failed. The other two, going on and on, finally seemed to be permanent, and their governments could hardly be conceived to be capable of functioning without them.

It will be noticed that, among the possible causes for displacement of a leader, administrative incompetence was not mentioned. This is because it is not really a decisive matter. The two Presidents most skilled in executive management were John Quincy Adams and Herbert Hoover. Neither achieved much popularity, and neither was given a second term. Adams was not even renominated. On the other hand, Jackson, Lincoln, and Grant were inefficient to a degree that would have disqualified them as chosen executives of the smallest conceivable organization. And the same would, I am sure, be true of many Governors and Mayors. Efficiency is an ill regarded—or perhaps more accurately a disregarded—virtue, likely to bring unpopularity for favors refused, for rules adhered to, for refusal to benefit individuals at public expense. And a haphazard governmental machine, not too diligent in law enforcement, a little easy with employees, and one that can be influenced and persuaded is much preferred by the politicians to one that is rigid, just, and disciplined. In time the virtues of efficiency might have counted, but by then the leader will have disappeared into a haze of sentiment. Only his humanity will be recalled, not his expensiveness. And, meanwhile, if his competence is questioned, he may divert attention by any number of devices, the favorite being the furious chastisement of some favorite devil. There is very little likelihood that inefficiency will be counted against him by many voters. His attractiveness on other grounds can easily overcome any such deficiency.

That all my three had achieved this permanence of position would color and limit any conversation among them. Their long identification as chief executives would rule out the sort of questioning and self-doubt that torment many men as they look back over their careers. Such long-sustained approval as they had commanded would have smothered any serious question concerning the worth or wisdom of their general performance. They might have doubts about detail but not about general policies.

Nor can they be imagined to have speculated much about the philosophy of government, to have dwelt, for instance, on old questions of liberty or of the rights, duties, and expectations of the individual. The form of government would not be considered. None of them could by now think of himself as part of any other system than a representative federal republic. Their talents had been suited to this kind of arrangement and their hard course in self-training had been for success within its boundaries.

None of them could possibly argue that the conceptual alternatives to representative democracy were superior to the system of which they were part. Totalitarianism either of the Nazi-Fascist or of the Communist variety had been rejected—had, indeed, become for all of them a principal foil. When all else had failed there were always Communists or Fascists to attack with loud shouts and damning accusations; big business, absentee landlords, the utility interests, Wall Street, economic royalists—none were so useful. Not many of these might be voters, but some of them were, and some could withhold campaign funds or influence local organizations of the parties. The totalitarians were mostly foreigners; few had the franchise. There were undoubtedly local sympathizers; but all my three disregarded these and committed themselves to democracy. They were justified by results. They were less committed to liberalism and to a war on reaction. But, generally speaking, that was the side they were on. They made numerous exceptions, but no real reactionary was ever safe while they were in office or running for one.

Their settled democratic commitment would preclude a questioning philosophical conversation. There was not likely to be much soul-searching. Then, too, they were extroverted men, sensual and self-satisfied. They differed in their appreciations. Muñoz was a littérateur, a poet by profession, perhaps because poetry demanded less sustained work and more inspiration. La Guardia had a taste for music at the level of Italian opera. And he fancied himself an amateur cook. The President had an urge to change the physical composition of things about him; he was always buying land and he persistently built and rebuilt houses and experimented with animals, trees, and crops. This had a fantastic extension to the projected rebuilding of much of the nation's public equipment. This, it will be seen, was not a company to interest itself in the exploration of principles. It was more likely to wonder how more could have been done than was done and to reassess the means used for gaining objectives; the objectives themselves were not likely to cause controversy. These were men who had done something to make other men more free and secure, but perhaps they might have done still more. I can imagine such a question making them uneasy, but I cannot imagine that they would ask whether they had been right to want what they had worked for.

And finally it must be kept in mind that they had substantially satisfied their ambitions. Undoubtedly La Guardia would have liked to be President if the circumstances had been different, but he would recognize now that it had been unlikely from the start and had become impossible when a party of progressives failed to materialize. His long mayoralty would seem sufficient. Muñoz was probably still worrying about a successor. But such a worry in a democratic leader is largely theoretical. He is more interested in not having one too soon than in not having a satisfactory one when he is through.

And so I think of three ample tropical chairs for three ample men arranged in a small circle on the roof of La Fortaleza. The Mirador there is open to the trade wind. On a typical evening it draws in from the sea, cooling the heated city. The gardens and the harbor are below, and across the tree tops on a rise of ground are a very old church and an equally old palace. The residence is the fabulous one first built by Ponce de Leon for his son-in-law but occupied since the American occupation by the commanding officer of the area. It was by now the most visible remaining sign of imperial might in the Caribbean, a rather empty one since Muñoz had maneuvered the Commonwealth into being and had taken over the representation of American interests as well as those of Puerto Rico.

The President was eying the Casa Blanca (as it was called locally) when the conversation began. It was obvious that neither he nor La Guardia was much pleased by Muñoz's success in appropriating American power and making Americans like it, but both would be reluctantly admiring just the same. The finesse required had been an exquisite example of the politician's art.

Muñoz, being host, would have provided generous entertainment;

there was never any skimping at La Fortaleza. Whether his visitors could any longer enjoy the food and drink as in other years, they could pretend that they did; it would hardly do for translated souls to envy those still burdened with flesh. Muñoz, a man of wry humor, was not fooled, but he was flattered to be in such company and he made no reference to the unusualness of the situation. Besides, he had very few opportunities to consort with those he considered his equals.

The trade wind, coming in gustily from the east across the Atlantic, agitated the palms. The harbor lights merged on the horizon with the street lights in Catano across the bay, and both found continuation upward in the stars of the tropical night. We may imagine the three, sitting at ease thus above the world in the Southern mildness and on a small island in the sea, to have talked far more freely than they would ever have done in life.

There was some delicacy in the relationship that had to be overcome or discounted. Neither La Guardia nor Muñoz had ever been a confidant of the President. Muñoz had actually seen him only a few times and then very formally, having been held at arm's length. La Guardia, although a contemporary and a co-worker, had been so much a political minor, but still in a position of such potential importance, that he had had to be both conciliated and used. This had been possible, difficult as it seems, because of the President's resplendent situation in a profession that was also La Guardia's but in which he occupied consistently lower terrain. The one had captured the grand prize, the other a secondary one. And their relations had been strictly regulated by the protocol of the profession. La Guardia sought, and the President yielded what would do him no harm to concede. Muñoz on one or two occasions had been given a bouquet of words, but actually the President had allowed him nothing of substance. Whether this had been due to a lingering imperial taint in the Roosevelt blood or to merely a distaste for being used in another's game, it had never been clear. But they had distrusted each other completely—if this is not tautological to say of politicians!

At any rate, there would be lingering among them some of this feeling of superiority on the one side and resentment on the other. It can be thought to be vanishing as the talk went on, as old sorenesses were eased, and as each granted the others the competence he had achieved the hard way in the fascinating mystery they all professed. But just at first there were some rather acid exchanges. La Guardia still had a painful conviction that the President might at least have made him Secretary of War instead of choosing an elderly reactionary in 1940. Muñoz thought the President might have supported his ambitions earlier instead of appearing, through his Governors, to be in league with the Puerto Rican plantocracy. The islander's lean years in the wilderness before his "movement" had begun to have wide support had left scars. The President was not exactly on the defensive, but he was willing to leave the conversational initiatives to the others until he could see how strong the resentments were.

But all had a companionable consciousness of consistent likeness throughout their careers. They had been equalitarians. If they had made a permanent change in their society it was in this direction. That had been the way humanity was going, of course, and it might be said that they had done no more than take advantage of what was bound to happen anyway—that they had drifted with a vast current even if they had paddled furiously all the while. But there had been contemporaries of theirs who had fought savagely toward some idyllic reactionary state. The three had been progressives in this sense; and whether or not they had had to be, they could all feel that they had been historically right. Some self-satisfaction was in order.

This equalitarian bias might not have been guessed from observing them. Each had definitely felt himself called to be a leader and entitled to many privileges. It followed that each had considered that he was better qualified than others to probe the future, to shape a people's course, and to decide what measures were necessary to facilitate progress toward desirable ends. This was not a light obligation, but each had accepted it as his permanent platform, and none now had the least doubt that he had been right. One of them was thinking of this as our listening in begins; he was in effect accusing the President of not having been consistent in this professed cause.

32

Muñoz: Mr. President, why did you make Puerto Rico an exception to the rule of independence for small nations? Or didn't you actually have such a rule?

Roosevelt: You are thinking about the Philippines? And that I supported Quezon's bid for separation? Well, let's be honest. You were an *independentista* who never dared say so when you ran for office. Your people never wanted it and would have rejected any serious advocate who made it an issue.

Muñoz: Did the Filipinos? Or was independence something Quezon began to make an issue of and then felt forced to follow up? And did his demand just happen to coincide with the desires of some pressure groups in the United States—producers of oils and fats who wanted to keep out palm oil, and sugar growers who wanted to reduce the imports of sugar?

Roosevelt: It's hard to separate the elements of so complex a situation. It's true that independence was the easiest solution for Quezon as well as for me. There was the pressure you speak of. It is also true that separation may not have been really wanted by the Filipinos. But I do not know that.

Muñoz: But you know, and knew then, that it was not the best course for them to follow. Independence was already obsolete and especially for small peoples. It was only good for their politicians who wanted no outside interference with their schemes and with their privileges.

Roosevelt: And why were you not that kind of a politician?

Muñoz: Since we are being honest, I will say that I discovered before it was too late just what you suggest—that even I could not persuade Puerto Ricans to regard independence as desirable—and

I had to find another way. I had to keep the American connection but to arrange things so that I should have all the freedom I should have had as President of an independent country. It is true that I have no army and can't threaten my neighbors; also, we use American money and stamps, but otherwise . . .

Roosevelt: Perhaps, now that I think it over, what made me feel differently about Puerto Rico was its relation to the Canal. But I also recall being very annoyed that Puerto Rican politicians behaved so badly—and this included you when you began to make a stir. It was your antics, I think, that convinced me Puerto Rico was not ready for independence. The Filipinos had badly behaved politicos, too, but not so badly behaved as yours. Then, too, I was annoyed by the irresponsibility of your population growth. Honestly, Puerto Ricans seemed to behave like rabbits. It was outrageous. You bred faster and faster and got poorer and poorer and sicker and sicker every year. Also, the behavior of your plantocracy was arrogant and selfish to an incredible degree. So far as I could see, they really believed in slavery and saw no connection between the prevalent poverty and their wealth.

Muñoz: But, Mr. President, I was against all that. Opposition to the plantocracy was the theme of my movement. And I must remind you that the early Governors you sent down here fell under plantocracy influence. They liked the wealthy and exclusive families. They were thorough reactionaries. Actually you had something in view for us that you would not now like to define. You may excuse it on strategic grounds—which in itself is a doubtful moral resort—but you never said so. Actually you had in mind to keep us in colonial status indefinitely. I made that impossible. I think you felt much as many of the congressional investigators did who were so fond of visiting us in the winter months. We ought to have learned English and we ought to have aspired to become a state.

Roosevelt: I won't try to answer that. Perhaps I was a little resentful. But you exaggerate. I always wanted Puerto Rico to progress, but how could it happen while those politicians were identified with your exploiters? And what you say of my Governors is not true. They worked hard, most of them, for Puerto Rican well-being. But you found it convenient to call them foreign interferers. You are right to say that I never trusted you. But that was because you were trying to put something over on me. That hurt my professional pride, I suppose. You know you tried to use the federal agencies in your island as patronage reservoirs for fattening your party. You infuriated Ernest Gruening and Harold Ickes, to say nothing of my Governors, simply by your rapacity. If they turned against you they had plenty of cause.

Muñoz: But *all* lesser political leaders tried to control federal patronage. It was done not only in Puerto Rico but in every state. Politicians all during the years of the depression were staying in office by claiming credit for federal relief and public works projects. La Guardia, here, did the same thing.

La Guardia: I could be indignant at that statement. It is true but not relevant. I was a New Dealer long before the President was. Those projects were more mine than his. I was fighting for that kind of thing when he was still sunning himself at Warm Springs and waiting for a favorable opening to re-enter politics. And I was doing all right politically too. I might say that he gave me very little help at any time. And when I needed it most he turned his back. The New Deal spending did help New York, but it was not indispensable to me personally; and even if it had been, my identification with it was legitimate.

Roosevelt: I seem to detect some resentment in you too, Fiorello. But you must realize now that it was unrealistic, if that is what is bothering you, to have thought of succeeding me. It was impossible. If you had been a Democrat . . . But if you had been a Democrat you wouldn't have been able to become Mayor, not with Tammany still in existence. No, it was fantastic. Even if I had been ready to lead a progressive coalition—a new party—you would have been a good ally but a poor partner. You were *only* a progressive, and I would have had to have millions of voters to make my majority who wouldn't have stood for you.

As things were, only a Democrat could have been elected in 1940 on our ticket, and I had no need of a successor so what need was there for you? I was heading for a showdown with Hitler. I couldn't have quit then. I thought of it, and I certainly would have if it hadn't been for the Nazi threat. But to have quit would have been to let Hitler win. Willkie was a good campaigner. You couldn't have beaten him.

La Guardia: You know very well that I was ahead of you there too. I was the best-known anti-totalitarian in the country, not except-

ing you. I could have done better than you from 1940 on in both areas
—progressive domestic policies and opposition to Hitler. I still think,
too, that you could have given it to me if you had been willing to keep
to the two-term tradition—as you should have. And I do not admit for
a minute that I could not have licked Willkie. I had just what was
needed.

Roosevelt: I seem to be unpopular with both of you. Could it be
because I belled the cat and you did not? Actually both of you had
good careers. And these recriminations are unbecoming and useless.
I can't help either of you any more—except Muñoz, perhaps, with
advice, which he will disregard anyway. No Puerto Rican politician
ever considered a continental to be his equal, much less his superior—
which I have sometimes thought to be a justifiable attitude.

We came here to talk of more important things. We had in mind
not matters of personal interest but ones of importance in our trade.
We may differ about our clashing ambitions, but we all wanted the
same thing for our governments and for our people as well as for
ourselves. For ourselves we wanted the closest possible approach to
absolute power and we wanted it to be yielded willingly by an
admiring and loyal electorate. We wanted to be loved and we wanted
to be thanked. That may have been slightly ridiculous, considering
our practicality and toughness in pursuing our own interests; but
also, if I may speak for all of us, we actually did want people to be
free, prosperous, and secure—and not only because they would
thank us for having got those desirable prizes for them. At least I
feel that I never deviated from those aims.

Muñoz: They were popular political objectives, of course, in our
time, and we wanted them to be achieved under our guidance.

Roosevelt: I said that. There's no need to bear down too hard on
the cynical note even if we are all realists here. How could we have
got something for others if we had not put ourselves in a position to
deliver it? You don't have to be a cynic to recognize that. It's how
things get done.

Muñoz: A dictator could have——

La Guardia: No, he could not. He would have recognized—as
Hitler did—that the attainment, to any degree, of such objectives
would have destroyed himself. Mr. President, you once said that a
politician's first duty was to get elected, and I guess you were right.

Nothing is possible without it, and something may be possible with it although not so much as is expected.

Roosevelt: I suggest that when we are not expressing disillusion we are being very elementary. First recrimination, then questions about the necessity of getting into office and staying there! I got there and I stayed there; so did you two, although you seem to have thought that your spheres weren't big enough.

Muñoz: Not me.

Roosevelt: Well, Fiorello was far from satisfied, and I shouldn't be surprised if you had some further ambitions that you don't speak of now. I wasn't fully satisfied either, if you must know. I was still going to be President of the World—or maybe co-President with Stalin, and Churchill, and Chiang Kai-shek. I was always driven to something further. There was a kind of momentum. I talked of retiring a good deal, but I can see now that I never meant to. And I probably headed you off, Fiorello, as I did others, without myself realizing I was doing it.

Retirement seemed attractive to me when I was especially tired—and sometimes when I was not. You know, I loved to build things and manage them, and I always thought of going back to building and running things small enough to get some satisfaction out of—a small forest in Georgia, the polio institution there, some farming experiments . . . And I would have done some writing, as you did, Fiorello, although I don't think you can be especially proud of what you did in that line. I really intended to divide my retirement between Hyde Park, with its collection of my papers, and Warm Springs, where the people and the trees both made me happy—gave me a good feeling.

But then, too, I was always conscious that Uncle Ted had behaved pretty childishly in retirement. He fumed with frustration. And none of his belated ventures were any credit to him as a politician, much less as a responsible leader. Perhaps his behavior was a warning to me—or perhaps I wanted to do better than he had at this too. I always wanted to do better the same things he had done.

Muñoz: Mr. President, you are the senior here and entitled, certainly, to your say; but you may not, in fairness, overdo it. I have some similar thoughts about leaders of our sort. May I express them?

Roosevelt: Excuse my verbosity. I thought we were to talk things out. . . .

Muñoz: We, not just you. . . . I might remark, apropos of your last suggestion about yourself, that others knew you were worried about the comparisons to be made—presumably by posterity—between yourself and T.R. I might remind you that I too had a predecessor with whom comparisons have been made. That was my father. You are probably not aware of it, but he was the leading Puerto Rican negotiator with both Spain and the United States in the days of transition, both before and after 1898, and he is still recalled with respect. It may have been his prominence that gave me my start. And I may have suffered, as you did, from a compulsion to outdo him. This is at least an interesting human trait and one politicians seem particularly likely to develop. It has nothing to do with the policies adopted by successors like ourselves—or at least not much—but it has a good deal to do with their drive to succeed.

I assume, however, that our discussion was intended to explore other sorts of wisdom from our experience. Psychology, especially the psychology of political success, strikes me as an unprofitable study for would-be emulators. They are not likely to benefit if they happen to be cast in other circumstances and to have other talents; and, since societies and their political systems are never the same in succeeding generations, circumstances will never be the same. Talents, I suppose, might, but it would be very unlikely.

Take your case. There are certainly likenesses between your development and that of T.R. I will even say that there are recognizable Roosevelt traits that show in both of you. Evidently, also, you studied him, if for no other reason than to make a better record. Perhaps some of your methodology was learned, but when I have tried to analyze it, the part that may have been acquired in this way eludes me; you seem, like the rest of us, to have improvised. I learned absolutely nothing from my father's method. He accustomed me to the atmosphere of politics and gave me the ambition to succeed, but that is all.

In your case there are phases of your career when you seem to have been patterning yourself on Jefferson; he too was devious and a master of maneuver and compromise; also, he saw that his line ought to be equalitarian. But you had moments when Sam Adams and Jackson, say, as libertarians, seemed to be your mentors; but these phases were more verbal than real. You were really a pretty thorough bureaucrat; perhaps the Navy did that for you—you had al-

most eight years of it, didn't you? Even when as President you were
giving the subordinate bureaucrats the most agony because of your
caprices, it was apparent that you counted on their industry and
competence. I think, like all Presidents, you came to have more
admiration for Washington than for any of your predecessors. He was
an admirable monolith in a horrendous wash of troubles. The waves
of controversy broke against him mercilessly, but they never changed
his character or his course. You came to seem permanent, too, a
perfect father figure. To go a step farther, Washington's longing for
retirement was one you sympathized with. I think you felt rather
close to him during the latter days of your regime.

But to go back to T.R. you won't like me to say it, but I am not so
sure he should not be given an edge in the inevitable comparison
between himself and you. In spite of his belligerence, he got what
he wanted internationally without war, and domestically your New
Deal in the end was not much advanced over his Square Deal,
for the passage of a quarter century; also, he complied with tradition
by quitting after a second term, even one that was not really a
second. He regretted it later, but he did comply. Your certainty that
the nation needed you resulted in a constitutional amendment that
will be a grave handicap to all your successors. It was pure reaction
to your hanging on too long.

Roosevelt: That's quite an indictment; it has the finish of one
thought about a good deal. I will not defend myself, however, beyond
calling attention to the success of that war you seem to feel would
have been unnecessary if I had been a better politician, and perhaps
mentioning the system of Social Security for which I claim personal
credit. Also, it is necessary to credit me with thousands of fairer
prospects in the American scene than existed before I began and,
for that matter, other thousands of better enterprises. But generally
I prefer to put it this way: every action I ever took was directed
toward making men freer, more settled, more secure, and so happier
than they had been before. I do think that I succeeded measurably
in using my political talents for these purposes. This is what I
hope to be remembered for—and so, I may say, do both of you.
You made the same professions as I. We shared the same yardstick.
Do either of you really think you reached my class?

La Guardia: Well, there is this. You didn't think out all you claim
to have accomplished. We give you credit for being a successful

politician but not for being a philosopher—a superman maybe, but not a thinker. The aspirations you mention were the accepted ones of our civilization. Moreover, we had reached the technical level that made their attainment possible.

If you had not presided over certain changes, someone else would have. They were bound to happen. Hitler and Mussolini would have used modern technology for different purposes. But they differed from us only about freedom. They aspired to prosperity and security for Germans and Italians, and those were among our highest values. It may be that their system for attaining these ends was more logical too. You seemed to think so once yourself—in the days of NRA, and other governmental experiments. Some critics said, you recall, that NRA was borrowed from the corporative state. And the war was certainly not won by free enterprise. It was won by cost-plus contracts yielding enormous profits, and otherwise by conscription of manpower. You must have felt very strange leading a nation into war to defend the principles that were immediately abandoned so that they could be defended. It sounds paradoxical still. The war got to be one to prevent the Germans—and Hitler—from taking charge of the world. The ideological results were not very great. If I understand matters, the interests in the United States that correspond with the Cartelists in Germany not only did well out of the war but remained in an immensely strengthened position after the war. They still are. And their European colleagues are now highly approved brothers. To make all perfect, the American voters have twice ratified the taking over of government by big business. That was the Eisenhower "crusade." As an educator and establisher of freedom, Mr. President, I do not give you very high marks.

Muñoz: And Stalin has not been mentioned; neither has communism. Stalin was to be one of your co-Presidents. . . .

33

As the evening progressed, the street noises reaching the Mirador from old San Juan died out. The tropical night deepened softly; the trade wind seemed to bear it in from the sea. The muted roar of waves on the shore could now be heard, and it was a little cooler. Our three, in their open-throated shirts, lounging comfortably, were the very picture of unhurried exploration.

Once or twice there had been interruptions while the refreshments were renewed. Muñoz seemed to wonder, rather, how the others disposed of theirs. His own went to the appointed place and had the usual effect. He was doing what he most liked to do—sit in good company under the stars with no danger that supplies would run low or that his companions would tire and leave him, thus averting his usual irritation with the most interesting people, who sooner or later always wanted to go to bed. His present guests had been late-stayers, too, even in life; and now it was obvious that they had no intention of being chivvied to rest. They had time enough, and apparently they had escaped from the supervision that had been so tiresome in life. This was especially true for the President. The patience and freedom of eternity were upon him. He might have wondered now why he had so much desired this very release for all men in life, when they inevitably had it coming their way after a brief delay. But he resumed.

Roosevelt: Speaking of Stalin, we tend, I am afraid, to recall too clearly our own speeches. Stalin was a politician too. It is true that he did not indulge in what he regarded as nonsense about equality or democracy. Much that we said and did he regarded as a waste of time. He was careful, however, to cultivate support. He may have cared mostly about his own people, but his was to be a proletarian state, and that is pretty inclusive; it might even have become a democracy. His conception of representation was a different one from ours. In a sense citizenship and its privileges had to be earned in the Soviet Union. I know that there was a tradition of violence that we find repugnant. But I concluded that, whatever his methods of getting there, Stalin believed he was going to the same place as ourselves.

Then there is this. I found that his idea of government was not so different from ours—that is, so far as what it ought to do is concerned. Of course he thought the individual ought to merge himself in the state. It was not for citizens to make demands but to serve; they had many duties but few rights; this is just about the reverse of our attitude. He would say that if the individual would not subordinate himself he must be forced to submit.

Yet Stalin was just as dependent on approval as I was. At Teheran and Yalta, I could see that he was negotiating—as I was—with a view to conciliating his supporters. He told me he could not intervene in the Japanese war without showing that Russia had something to gain. His Polish policy was controlled by the same considerations. This seems not to have been understood after I ceased to be available. In fact, the whole cold war in my view could have been averted if the Russian system had not been so mysterious and revolting to provincial American politicians. Plain unwillingness to believe that Stalin was a responsible politician had a lot to do with it.

La Guardia: What you needed as a successor was a man with some experience of the world, not a county politician. I could have dealt with Stalin on the same terms you did. I could have understood the requirements of a federal world organization with national states of violently different kinds. If it is true, as is sometimes said, that the final measure of a man of power rests largely on his choice of a successor, your reputation is bound to grow shakier.

Roosevelt: I gave a lot of thought to that successor problem, as a responsible leader is bound to do. I thought I had one once or twice, but I must admit that when my fourth election was approaching I had to concentrate on the election itself. The situation did not look favorable. I was told plainly that the result was in doubt, and I wanted to make the peace at the end of the war. I did what would strengthen the ticket. I took Truman. But he was much more than the county politician he had once been. He had a wide knowledge of affairs. If he failed it was for other reasons.

La Guardia: Perhaps Muñoz and I would be just as happy not to have the successor responsibility examined too closely.

Roosevelt: Stalin did not do very well in that matter either. Perhaps we have here one of the inherent disadvantages of democracy, even of the Proletarian dictatorship variety. Hereditary monarchy has a considerable advantage in knowing who is to succeed. Yet I recall many wars over succession and many regencies that were unsatisfactory. I shouldn't be surprised if on study we should conclude that the disappearance of strong monarchies from the world could be traced to the weakness of successors. Our theory has been that a democratic successor could not be *appointed.* He could be favored— as Van Buren and Taft were—but he could not actually be chosen. He must have amounted to something in democratic politics beforehand. By the way, the two I have mentioned represented poor final judgments by two competent leaders—Jackson and T.R. It may be that retiring leaders should not try to pick successors. Perhaps such a rule is as necessary, speaking historically, as the abandoning of the hereditary principle.

La Guardia: I see what you mean. The personal struggle for power is necessary to produce the tough guys needed by vast democratic governments. If they aren't talented and experienced they will soon become the victims of the professionals who are tougher than they.

Muñoz: What you two have been saying has not only to do with the successor problem but with the leadership problem itself, especially in the kind of situation presented by our generation and times.

La Guardia: All of us have reason to know how democracy chews up its men. Leaders have to outwit or defeat selfish interests intent on getting their own way all the time, and they have to make their fights count—if they choose to fight—for their own prestige, so that they can go on fighting with better and better success. My claim about myself is that I was a good fighter. About you two, I would say, Mr. President, that you were no fighter at all—a schemer, yes, but not a fighter. You ran away from a dozen fights I can think of offhand. You got a good deal done, but it might have been much more. And as for you, Muñoz, you capitulated to the interests without a murmur. If your people are better off it is because the times made them so. I don't credit you with being either a fighter *or* a schemer.

Roosevelt and Muñoz (together): Unfair! Unfair!

La Guardia: I was going to say, when I was interrupted, that the record is made now. I think I am right in interpreting it as I do. And it has some importance in the discussion of method. I will come to that in a moment, but first let me see if I can dismiss objectives as something we are fully agreed on.

First, I will leave out any mention of ways to get and keep personal power. We will grant that position has to be reached and kept if anything is to be done; also—although this is more doubtful, because there may be gross misjudgments or abuses—that whatever any of us felt we must do to attain or keep position was justified. That was our own business, and we will say that success carried its own excuses.

From there, then, I will put it this way: We wanted to promote material progress because we were moved by the misery so many people lived with. We were touched by hunger, cold, slum-living, child labor, neglected children, people living in ignorance, subject to the vicissitudes of an erratic economic system and doomed to a miserable old age. We thought all this could be measurably, perhaps spectacularly, improved by changes in public policy. Government—the state—had to be made an instrument of the will to reform. If people were not aware of the possibilities and too careless or misled to support the measures necessary, it was our duty to instruct and to lead them. Much of this effort consisted just in removing obstacles, subduing opposing interests, and creating the specific means for relieving distress. That was our job in our time. Beyond this we hoped to make the new system self-perpetuating by anchoring it in institutions people would defend because we had taught them that they must.

Roosevelt: Not a bad summary, Fiorello, but you rather neglect the spiritual side. I suppose you would say, however, and I might admit, that we assumed the spiritual values without discussing them. Hungry people are apt not to be very moral or very happy. They do not have to be wealthy to love their neighbors, to co-operate in good works, and to build a life of the spirit; but it is very hard to be a Christian if you are miserable and if your family lives in a slum.

Muñoz: It is certainly characteristic of you two that you leave out the objectives that meant most to me. Have you forgotten that when we began our careers colonialism was the worst of all injustices and that whole continents of the world lived in subjection to imperial capitalists?

Roosevelt: Who, would you say, of all contemporary leaders, did most in our time to rid the world of colonialism? You know what the answer to that is. Churchill and his crowd knew only too well. You cannot accuse me of having forgotten. But independence and international co-operation were second to a more urgent demand. Have you forgotten what had to be done in the United States —yes, and in Puerto Rico—without an instant's delay, and how irrelevant to the first necessity such considerations as colonialism were? You knew it once. You went through several elections with a ban on the discussion of status and with all the emphasis on economic improvement. We got to it as soon as we could, and to my mind you have no complaint to make.

Muñoz: As the lawyers say, I will take an exception, but let Fiorello resume.

La Guardia: As to method, then: Let me go carefully now and perhaps use some language we never allowed our ghost writers. We sank ourselves in representative democracy at every level. I began in a New York clubhouse among what I afterward called "loafers," although I now admit that they were very hard workers indeed, even if not in my interest. You, Mr. President, began as a wealthy youth who was being promoted by Poughkeepsie bosses for their own purposes and had to make your way in a hostile party. Muñoz, after a bad start as a loafer, you went back to the barrios and rose from there to the insular legislature. We all began at the bottom and learned the trade honestly.

We saw ourselves as part of the whole practical, unlovely, human, complicated, disorganized process. We swam in it; we loved it; it was our element. I should say of ourselves that we became more and more, as we went on, identified with democracy in its representative form until we achieved a kind of mystic merger with the demos itself. We felt we must have this identification and we worked slavishly and unremittingly to keep it and to widen the constituency to which it applied.

Our method was to cultivate the political garden humbly, sweatily, and without scruple. There was nothing we wouldn't do to get on, no boots we wouldn't lick, no star we wouldn't hitch our wagon to, no effort we wouldn't make. We would be demagogues; we would play-act; we would smile through our tears; we would accept humiliations; we would do what we were told. As we got along, we sloughed off as much as we could of this. But it had become part of us. We were its practitioners.

Now what I must say is that methods and objectives got mixed at a certain level. We came to stand for certain things. We were identified in spite of attempts to be equivocal and evasive and to avoid commitment. There were policies we could not repudiate and some that we embraced. We tried to believe that these were the ones certain in the long run to prevail. But sometimes, too, we hooked onto them because we thought they were necessary to any future we might have. We made a picture of ourselves. We were not only identified with people but with processes in the economic and social world. We three were either lucky or wise. We became progressives —I most certainly; you, Mr. President, a little uncertainly; and you, Muñoz, reluctantly.

The point about this is that methods and objectives merge. Politics, economics, and public moods are inseparable at the level we aspired to and which we reached.

So when we worked for better health, educational expansion, slum clearance, labor laws, social insurance, and some means for curing unemployment, we were also working for justice, freedom, and security.

Roosevelt: The Four Freedoms I spoke of were both economic and political; also, I included religion—spiritual.

La Guardia: Just a minute, I haven't finished. I want to get to the real facer—one we never solved or even approached. It was one that you danced around but never closed in on, Mr. President. It is this: The nature of the improvement process involves not more but less freedom; more security, yes, but less liberty. It brings men under the discipline of the machine and its regime. They call it automation now, but we knew it as scientific management or as serialization. It was there when we were responsible; we knew about it, but the resolution of the dilemma it was building up had not yet become imperative and we ducked it.

Roosevelt: But we were just speaking of NRA and its companion agencies.

La Guardia: Come now! You may have had fugitive thoughts about NRA as a politico-industrial organization scheme, but you let Hugh Johnson turn it into something very different. And when it went wrong from maladministration you abandoned it like a hot potato.

Roosevelt: I was under the impression that the Supreme Court killed it.

La Guardia: You know very well you were relieved to have them do it for you because it had got out of hand and you had no idea what to do with it. And did you try again? No!

But let's not argue about the past. We can at least learn from it that liberals and progressives have not yet seen their way out of this dilemma. The fact is that because of our neglect or lack of wisdom some men are now managing others in sinister ways. They are doing it by becoming owners of the machine process, by administering the prices of goods and services, and by getting control of the government itself.

The worst of this is yet to come, but anyone can see that the worst is almost here. Men must not only submit to this discipline but must like it as well. There is a new profession for which the Chinese have a name. They call it "brainwashing." We prefer the nicer name of persuasion. But public officials are already deep in it. Men must embrace their seducers.

We knew about this and we hated it, but we never learned how to control, much less to stop it. In fact, we used it. And in spite of knowing that in our hearts we were socialists, we were furtive ones. If there had been no profits in the process, it could have been controlled. Our biggest failure was to have left the people we led more prosperous, more secure, but less free. Our belief that freedom rested on a foundation of material well-being was a false one. So far the means for attaining prosperity are the very ones that stifle liberty.

Roosevelt: You are too pessimistic. True, our first efforts were feeble ones. They failed. But I have not been shaken in the belief that freedom must have an economic base. Poverty makes slaves of the best of men. Only well-being can make them free. I realize that in saying this I am only repeating a kind of cliché that goes back into the American progressive dream; I realize also that when they were faced with the necessity for accepting the institutions that would bring it into existence the progressives and liberals rebelled.

It was mostly because they would not accept it that NRA failed. If they had really been with me I could have outmaneuvered the Supreme Court. About this I do have some regrets. I now think they could have been persuaded if the attempt had not been so awkward. I was led off into the Blue Eagle campaign—that was the scheme for curing unemployment by exorcism, you remember—and since it was identified with NRA, the rest of NRA was discredited too. I still feel that the original idea was correct. But let's go on.

Suppose we were not mistaken. Suppose prosperity is the condition of well-being and that well-being is the condition of liberty. The matter becomes one of political finesse. The leader must be able to show people the connections and persuade them to accept the institutions for implementation.

I had the prestige; somehow I should have been able to make the connection. But the NRA experience was discouraging, and the progressives wanted to go back to liberal free enterprise with rules established by the Congress. I knew better, but I gave in. I knew, too, that the Germans were formidable because they had done what I had failed at—they had rationalized their industry and with it their society. Their fault was the one you point to. But they evidently had no use for liberty or democracy. To them these were not desirable objectives.

Sometimes I wonder whether the war against Germany was not a mistake. Could I have found ways to undermine Hitler, persuade the Germans to turn their efficiency to the uses of freedom, and make an ally instead of an enemy of the most advanced people on earth? My successors seem to be trying to do just that. It is now almost as though there had never been a war. But that may be because they are so frightened of communism. Or it may be because big business has taken over the whole works, there, here, and everywhere. Sometimes, as I say, I wonder . . .

34

Muñoz: That no one can enslave a prosperous people has been the premise of our careers. I will not give it up. I will not believe that we were mistaken. It is really a technical matter, and no technical matter is beyond solution. The question is: How do you lead such a people?

We really lived in primitive circumstances. Heroes were wanted, and we were heroes. I still am. But a really civilized people will not have heroes. They seem ridiculous and they are ineffective. It may be that we should think of another kind of leadership altogether. If the hero is outmoded, how about an elite?

Roosevelt and La Guardia: Shades of the Nazis (Fascists)!

Muñoz: I will not be intimidated. Maybe Hitler had something there, not original with him; there have been elites before. I seem to recall a famous one in Greece—and in Plato's *Republic*. I am thinking of one resting not on heredity as a principle, or on loyalty to the party or state, but on rigorous selection from qualifying lists. The guarantee of competence among its members would rest largely on the method of selection.

Roosevelt: We have been talking of leaders, not of administrators. Leaders make themselves. I doubt if they can be selected by examination. Still I have been hearing of the soft sell. That may be the political method of the future, but I doubt it. It rests on reason to an extent I find unrealistic. I dimly recall from my academic past that John Stuart Mill said of ordinary people that they find their preferences a satisfactory guide; in fact, he said the ordinary man has no other guide to his choices of morality, taste, or propriety. A preference can be picked up in any one of many ways, but surely leadership is an important influence. Preference can be not only for ideas but for men. Perhaps most preferences are for men—for heroes.

Muñoz: Nevertheless, the preference of civilized people might begin to run toward civilized leaders, just as for a long time it has seemed to run toward progressive ones. We have not been that sort, but we may be the last of our kind. I should think it very likely in the United States.

It may be that future generations will give us most credit for preparing the way. They will be interested to preserve neither our objectives nor our methods.

What I am thinking about is a kind of apotheosis such as the classical Communists pictured for their system. You recall? The dictatorship disappeared; the state faded as the rule of reason developed and the perfect institutions matured. Then men lived together in harmony without regulation. So we can think of ultimates—of an apotheosis of democracy. Men *might* live together in mutual regard under an agreed rule. If they should, they would have escaped the need for heroes of our sort because such crusades as we led had become unnecessary. There would be no depressions, no wars, no colonialisms. In such a world we would be obsolete. We may as well face it—we were men for our time, not for all time.

Roosevelt: Wait a minute. Can you conceive that men would easily agree on who was to have power in any circumstances, however ideal? Can you imagine them not fighting for preferred places? If not, there will have to be good and bad; there will have to be causes to campaign for and enemies to defeat.

As to ourselves, if we helped to free men from economic slavery and from the menace of German overlordship, we have a claim as valid as Washington, who taught the imperialists their first hard lesson, or Lincoln, who only freed some black men in a small area of the earth—and followed many precedents at that.

But yes, you may be right in a way. I'm afraid I reacted too violently to the suggestion of being thought of as the Paul Bunyan of politics, doing mighty impossible deeds in a world of gargantuan imaginings. I did blow up my enemies for effect and I did picture my accomplishments as very nearly divine—you remember the money-changers in the temple? The gentleman in me did not approve the politician much of the time. But even my mother, who was revolted by the company I kept, was impressed by the White House.

She would have had me get there and stay there by immaculate means, but she learned to pretend that she didn't know how it was done. And Eleanor, being a smart woman, learned very early that effects have causes and that the best effects sometimes come from unlovely causes. She often felt that my judgment was bad and that my sensibilities must be anesthetized, but she granted me the responsibility for deciding what was necessary. And she was not over-squeamish. She would defend me now, I believe, for nearly every choice I made. That is interesting, too, because no one was ever more committed to good works or less inclined to sympathy for what we used to call "the interests" than she. I always had a feeling when she was home that there was an angel under the roof. She would make a good citizen of your republic, Luis. But she allowed me some doubtful deals with the unrighteous.

Muñoz: I *was* talking about a republic, wasn't I? I must look into Plato again, although he was certainly no democrat. Majority rule with a wide suffrage would have seemed to him an invitation to demagogues.

La Guardia: Maybe he was right. If when you mention demagogues you mean us, I for one refuse to cringe. We were crossroads and street-corner artists. The arts we practiced we had as a gift and perfected by long and careful development. We needn't be ashamed.

Muñoz: But they were not necessarily joined to wisdom or to competence. Ours actually is not far from being the only occupation left that has no qualifying threshold.

La Guardia: Except the threshold of election—persuading a mass of people to trust us in one office after another.

Muñoz: But we know well enough that a million or fifty million people can be as wrong as one; perhaps more so! How did the idea spread so widely that multiplication was a guarantee of wisdom?

La Guardia: The idea was, I believe, that if a majority was mistaken they at least shared in the responsibility.

Roosevelt: Because we succeeded as majority-assemblers we ought not to rate the arts of doing it too highly. Also, we ought not to consider the results better, for that reason, than they actually are. In thinking about this I have often considered what Luis has suggested as an alternative—the setting up of some preliminary requirements for candidates. Some kind of examinations for physical and mental fitness would be possible, but of course the catch would lie in the choice of the examiners. I have concluded finally that the whole affair would be disastrous. The eliminations would include all the really creative candidates.

You see, I still feel that I was the man for my time and circumstances. And I would have been stricken from any conceivable qualifying list. So would both of you—for different reasons. Neither of you was crippled, but neither of you had any education to amount to anything, and temperamentally both of you were hopeless. You, Fiorello, were moody and capricious; you, Luis, were a playboy. No sane judges would have allowed either of you to run for anything that required judgment or industry even if you could have passed an examination on matters you would be called upon to know.

What would you think of tackling the problem of representation at the other end? It is conceivable that voters rather than candidates might be required to qualify. To conciliate the worst-prepared citizens—who will be a large number—they might be allowed one vote; the others might be allowed up to ten, depending on their qualifications. This would weight the influence on selections in favor of those with judgment. By this means people like ourselves might still be elected.

La Guardia: I can't see it any more than I can see proportional representation. The objection, again, is that the wrong—the ultrasane—people would accumulate all the weight. They would always choose negatively. The more I have thought about these mechanisms, the more I have come to value the broad and simple process of choosing by majorities from a universal adult suffrage list. Proportional representation resulted, in New York when it was tried, in the same splintering that torments France. A majority chosen by a two-party contest gives the chosen candidate and his party the responsibility. Time after time the nation, as well as lesser jurisdictions, has bowed to majority rule without question. I have come to value it very highly.

Roosevelt: Perhaps you are right. I would like to see this, as well as other suggestions, tried. You know, I had some trouble because I admitted to being experimental; I am afraid it was true. I liked to try things. But I have discovered that I only liked to try devices. About larger matters, I seemed to react even against exploring alternate possibilities. I detect a similar reluctance in both of you. For instance, in all this talk none of us has suggested the abolition of representative democracy. . . .

We should have to admit, I guess, that none of us has made any contribution to political theory, although we may have helped to test it. The most we can claim is that we did something to improve the working of our system. Each of you sponsored, if you did not invent, a new document—you, Fiorello, for New York City, and you, Luis, for Puerto Rico. I was responsible for the charter of the United Nations. None of these may have been remarkably novel, but each was the framework for a workable organization.

Muñoz: I'm afraid I must admit that my influence on the actual writing of the Commonwealth Constitution—as I call it—was largely negative, although I created the circumstances that made its writing possible. I have thought since that there were innovations I ought not to have rejected.

La Guardia: Since we are being frank, I had nothing much to do with New York's 1936 Charter. I campaigned for it after a citizens' committee had written it, but when it came to working with it I didn't even like it. It limited my freedom of action.

Muñoz: Where have we come to? Do we have to admit that all our talk about democracy was insincere and that none of us was a genuine democrat except in the pragmatic sense—that we knew how to work its machinery for our own benefit? Were our professions really the cover for an appeal to obsolete equalitarian prejudices? By the way, were we even equalitarians?

Roosevelt: Certainly we were; in the best sense, not literally. Actually, representation of any sort is an adulteration of democracy. But it is certainly the only feasible resort for any political organization larger than one that can assemble all its members in a small room. For vast nations the question is how to attenuate democracy least. I'm afraid it is true that we were more interested in keeping ourselves in power and in attaining other objectives than in keeping democracy pure. When you even begin to attenuate, the principle has been modified. The consideration that arises, as you have to go farther and farther, is: Who is benefited? Representation ought at least to represent all alike, and we know that has proved hard to insure. In fact, it never has been insured. Minorities, by the very nature of the device, are ill represented and, in some of their interests, not at all. That will be so until all men agree. So representation is not, as we picture it ideally, a device for increasing democracy at all, but rather one for getting things done with violence to the fewest desires.

I think we should admit that we not only did nothing to return democracy to its original intention but that we took advantage of the schemes that modify and distort it. We did this to get and keep power. Our plea that we used it, after we had got it, for meritorious purposes is a justification by results. Almost anything can be justified if you claim the results to be good. That was what I said about my war. It was an evil that brought good. So representation is an evil that must be measured by the good it brings. But on occasion I have denounced those who use this kind of argument. I have even called it immoral.

La Guardia: You are being so frank that now *you* exaggerate. Most of the dross was finally extracted from us, I should say, by the heats of conflict. We became pure, even if we didn't begin that way. You may say that by then our ambitions—the attainable ones—had been realized and that there was little virtue in selflessness. But it could be put another way. We had learned that only service gave satisfaction. I even quit, which gives me the edge in this company. Honesty compels me to admit that my quitting was induced by apprehension, and my arrangement for a successor was a failure. You did no better, Mr. President. Your last performances left something to be desired. You should not have run in 1944 any more than you should have in 1940.

Roosevelt: Please! Let's not go back to comparisons. You completely ignore the world arrangements that were in the making and not yet secure. Before we break up we might speak of that. May I speak first?

Muñoz: We others are hardly qualified. . . . Don't glare at me, Fiorello!

Roosevelt: What I wanted to remark is that some unfamiliar institutions will be necessary. The size, for one thing, will be unprecedented. But with the new technical facilities the bureaucracy will doubtless be frighteningly competent. Regional and ideological differences will be hard to reconcile—they always have been in the big nations—but the scale and intensity will be unprecedented. The United States was a sizable fraction of the earth, but we must now think of the whole; and we did have telephones, radio, television, and airplanes to hold it together. But we were all Americans and that meant much; our quarrels were among themselves.

We saw the presidency enlarge and evolve; we saw the Congress allow itself to become more and more obsolete. This change in relationships had become a problem even for us. How much more so it would be on a world scale.

It would be a job for first-rate leaders to set up and get going a world organization. If it became in any sense a government, it might require a multiple executive and a legislature with several under-lying layers of representation. There would have to be novel plan-ning devices. . . .

I won't enlarge on all this. But if I had lived ten more years as I had hoped I might, and if Stalin and Churchill had been my co-Presidents, we might have made a good start.

Muñoz: Gentlemen, the dawn is coming up fast. We have very little time. May I just make one more observation?

We all of us have accepted a view of the electorate as persuadable. We know that much of it is not. There are some who are committed; some who are irrational; some who are evilly intent on sabotage; some who are indifferent. But we have believed that a majority can be assembled for causes we hold out to be good. This we have be-lieved to be better than a tyrant could do. Freedom is thus justified. This has been the central difference in political theory almost since there has been any theory.

We have to ask ourselves in all honesty how this belief has to be modified by the growing tendency to bewilder the electorate by specious claims and arguments and by the monopolization of per-suasion. There is no doubt that its techniques have fallen into the control of those who mean no good to the mass of people and who believe they belong to an elite that should be kept in control if necessary by systematized trickery.

What shall we say of our faith in democracy?

La Guardia: I say it is the political leader's responsibility and I say it will be his delight to frustrate and defeat these people in the future as he has in the past. That is the essence of our art.

Roosevelt: I agree. When all is said and all the reservations made, ours is an unteachable and an unlearnable art. There will always be those with the talent. They will always make their way to the top as we did. And they will always show the way to those necessary arrangements by which people get from government what they must have: freedom and well-being.

Gentlemen, there is the sun.

...

INDEX